WEiRD OHiO

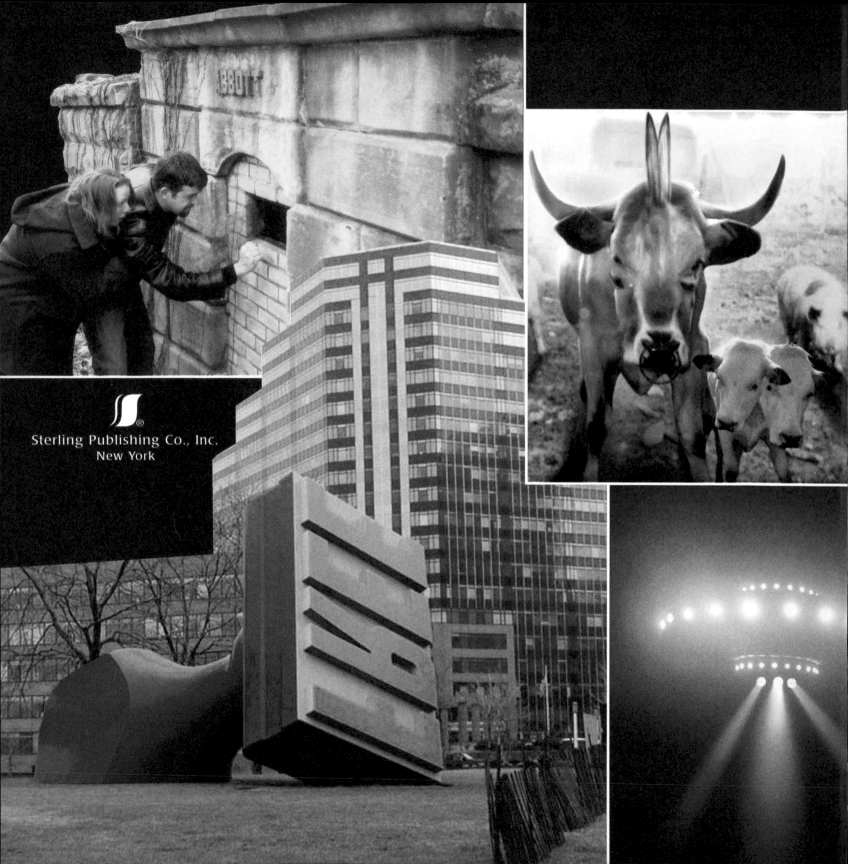

Sterling Publishing Co., Inc.
New York

WEiRD OHiO

Your Travel Guide to Ohio's Local Legends and Best Kept Secrets

by
**JAMES A. WILLIS, ANDREW HENDERSON,
and LOREN COLEMAN**

**Mark Sceurman and Mark Moran,
Executive Editors**

WEiRD OHiO

Published by Sterling Publishing Co., Inc.
387 Park Avenue South, New York, NY 10016
© 2005 Mark Sceurman and Mark Moran
Distributed in Canada by Sterling Publishing
c/o Canadian Manda Group, 165 Dufferin Street
Toronto, Ontario, Canada M6K 3H6
Distributed in Great Britain by Chrysalis Books Group PLC
The Chrysalis Building, Bramley Road, London W10 6SP, England
Distributed in Australia by Capricorn Link (Australia) Pty. Ltd.
P. O. Box 704, Windsor, NSW 2756, Australia

10 9 8 7 6 5 4 3 2 1

Manufactured in the United States of America.
All rights reserved.

Photography and illustration credits are found on page 286
and constitute an extension of this copyright page.

Sterling ISBN 1-4027-3382-8

For information about custom editions, special sales, premium and
corporate purchases, please contact Sterling Special Sales
Department at 800-805-5489 or specialsales@sterlingpub.com.

Design: Richard J. Berenson
      Berenson Design & Books, LLC, New York, NY

ONTENTS

Foreword: A Note from the Marks 6

Introduction 8

Local Legends 10

Ancient Mysteries 30

Fabled People and Places 44

Unexplained Phenomena 64

Bizarre Beasts 80

Local Heroes and Villains 100

Personalized Properties 120

Roadside Distractions 144

Roads Less Traveled 182

Haunted Places and Ghostly Tales 204

Cemetery Safari 228

Abandoned in Ohio 254

Index 278

Acknowledgments 284

Picture Credits 286

A Note from the Marks

Our *weird journey* began a long, long time ago in a far-off land called New Jersey. Once a year or so, we'd compile a homespun newsletter called *Weird N.J.*, then pass it on to our friends. The pamphlet was a collection of odd news clippings, bizarre facts, little-known historical anecdotes, and anomalous encounters from our home state. The newsletter also included the kinds of localized legends that were often whispered around a particular town but seldom heard outside the boundaries of the community where they originated.

We'd started *Weird N.J.* on the simple theory that every town in the state had at least one good tale to tell. The publication soon become a full-fledged magazine, and we made the decision to actually do our own investigating to see if we could track down where all of these seemingly unbelievable stories were coming from. Was there, we wondered, any factual basis for the fantastical local legends people were telling us about? Armed with not much more than a camera and a notepad, we set off on a mystical journey of discovery. Much to our surprise and amazement, a lot of what we'd initially presumed to be nothing more than urban legends turned out to be real—or at least to contain a grain of truth, which had sparked the lore to begin with.

After a dozen years of documenting the bizarre, we were asked to write a book about our adventures, and so *Weird N.J.: Your Travel Guide to New Jersey's Local Legends and Best Kept Secrets* was published in 2003. Soon people from all over the country began writing to us, telling us strange tales from their home state. As it turned out, what we had perceived to be something of very local interest was actually just a small part of a larger and more universal phenomenon.

When our publisher asked us what we wanted to do next, the answer was simple: "We'd like to do a book called *Weird U.S.*, in which we could document the local legends and strangest stories from all over the country," we replied. So for the next twelve months we set out in search of weirdness wherever it might be found in the fifty states. And indeed, we found plenty of it!

After *Weird U.S.* was published, we came to the conclusion that this country had more great tales than could be contained in just one book. Everywhere we looked, we found unwritten folklore, creepy cemeteries, cursed locations, and outlandish roadside oddities. With this in mind, we told our publisher we wanted

to document it ALL and do it in a series of books, each focusing on the peculiarities of a particular state.

But where would we begin this state-by-state excursion into the weirdest territory ever explored? Our first inclination was to go to the states we'd already collected the greatest volume of material about — like Ohio. During our research for *Weird U.S.*, we discovered that the Buckeye State has more than its fair share of the bizarre. Perhaps this is because Ohio might seem like the last place you'd think to look when in search of the strange! At first glance, there is little to distinguish the state as a hotbed of oddities. Its sprawling landscape of suburban neighborhoods, rural countryside, and urban blight paints a picture we were well acquainted with, being from New Jersey. But don't be fooled! As is true with our apparently normal home state, Ohio, too, is rife with weird and wonderful local legends and lore. Not only that, but there are a spate of odd and bewildering sites to behold and colorful characters to meet.

We were certain that Ohio needed a weird book all its own!

When it came to deciding which Ohio authors we wanted to collaborate with to bring *Weird Ohio* to life,

we knew just where to turn. We had become acquainted with James Willis during our research for *Weird U.S.*, to which he generously contributed some of his writing. His ongoing investigations into Ohio's paranormal goings-on made him a shoo-in for the job. Our second author, Andy Henderson, has spent years traipsing through the abandoned ruins, creepy cemeteries, and historic haunts of Ohio, collecting chilling tales and documenting strange sites for his project, forgottenohio.com. Our kind of guy. The final member of our team is renowned cryptozoologist and author Loren Coleman. Loren, though not from Ohio, has spent a great deal of time investigating reports of bizarre creatures, unexplained occurrences, and ancient riddles in the state while living in his native Illinois and later his current home, New England.

All three of these great writers possess what we like to call the "Weird Eye," and that's what is needed to search out the sorts of stories we were looking for. It requires one to see the world a different way, with a renewed sense of wonder. And once you have it, there's no going back — you'll never see things the same way again. All of a sudden, you begin to reexamine your own environs, noticing your everyday surroundings as if for the first time. And you begin to ask yourself questions like, "What the heck is that thing all about, anyway?" and "Doesn't anybody else think that's kind of weird?"

So come with us now and let Jim, Andy, and Loren take you on a tour of another side of the state you only thought you knew. With all of its dark secrets, strange stories, and offbeat sites, it is a state of mind we like to call *Weird Ohio*.

— *Mark Sceurman and Mark Moran*

Introduction

When I accepted a job offer in Ohio, I wasn't sure what to expect. I asked a friend if he knew anyone in Ohio. His response was, "No, but I think a lot of people drive through there." Not exactly a glowing review. So you can imagine my delight when I discovered that Ohio is a state that not only accepts that it's different, it has been embracing its weirdness for years.

In fact, the official weirdness started over a hundred years ago, when the time came to create a state flag. For some reason, Ohioans went down a different road and opted for a burgee (a pennantlike flag). Today, Ohio is the only state in the Union to have a burgee. Happily for *Weird Ohio,* really strange homage is a tradition that continues to this day. For instance, to honor Ohio's farming heritage, a local artist filled an entire field with giant corncobs made out of concrete.

Looking back now at my friend's comment about lots of people going through Ohio, I've come to believe that all the passing through has added to the weirdness of the state. Move on people might, but they tend to leave a bit of weirdness behind. Take, for example, gangsters like Pretty Boy Floyd and John Dillinger, who left behind bullet-ridden bodies and enough memorabilia for several roadside attractions. And let's not forget the infamous torso murderer, who left Ohio (and Eliot Ness) with a bunch of body parts and a series of unsolved murders. Of course, leave it to Ohio to turn a crime spree into a museum, complete with replicas of severed heads.

Another reason Ohio is so wonderfully weird is that people here just tend to look at things differently. Perhaps that comes from the necessity to find something exciting in the miles and miles of cornfields. Whatever the reason, consider this: If there were ever a reunion for all the people who have at one point called Ohio home, singer Scott Weiland and Stephen Spielberg just might end up sitting right next to Phyllis Diller and the ghost of Thomas Edison.

Weird Ohio has allowed me a unique opportunity to get off the highway and travel the back roads of Ohio. It is an experience I will never forget. I'm proud to call Ohio my home. I fit right in.–James A. Willis

Mark Sceurman and Mark Moran lead the pack in the study of weird places and forgotten history, so I was honored to have the opportunity to work with them on *Weird Ohio*. Their pioneering efforts in the pursuit of ghosts, abandoned towns, legendary places like midget and albino villages, and roadside oddities in New Jersey were my biggest inspiration when I began my Web site, forgottenohio.com, back in 1999. Since then, I've accumulated a collection of curiosities from my own home state and heard from thousands of people with bizarre stories to tell. I've also had the opportunity to explore most of the sites profiled in this book, from abandoned prisons in Mansfield to burned-down orphanages near Cleveland and haunted train tunnels deep in the woods of Wayne National Forest.

The more I study Ohio's strange stories and forgotten places, the more I realize it's a project I'll never finish. Each of the eighty-eight counties has its own stories, and it would take more than a lifetime to catalogue every interesting anomaly. This book offers you a great overview of the most notable weird things the Buckeye State has to offer, as well as being an excellent starting place for further explorations. I hope it inspires you to find some of these places and experience them for yourself.*–Andrew Henderson*

In Ohio, we find a unique combination of rural state, industrial state, and one that's seemingly hemmed in by water and mountains. It has a flavor about it that's midwestern, yet very eastern. And in some of the Appalachian parts of Ohio, there's even some southern mentality.

Ohioans from the ancient Mound builders to modern humans have left their mark. It is no wonder the state is now known not only as the mother of presidents but as the mother of inventors and the mother of astronauts.

We think *Weird Ohio* well conveys how profoundly curious the state is, cryptozoologically, paranormally, and mythologically. And for these reasons, it is an important gathering spot for investigators of the bizarre. In recent years, Ohio has been an extremely active area for Bigfoot reports. Maybe it's because Ohio has so many people to "see" the creatures or maybe there are more of the hairy hominids here than there are elsewhere. Maybe it has something to do with the large number of researchers who have been involved in field research in Ohio. Outside of California, we don't know of another state that has as many Bigfoot investigators. How can you not love a state like this!*–Loren Coleman*

Local Legends

Most *people love a good scary story,* especially if tinged with weirdness. In fact, entire Web sites are devoted to popularizing such myths, those tales that make the rounds both electronically and wherever humans continue to gather in the flesh. These spooky stories are like springboards for our collective unconscious and serve to fuel the dark side of our imagination. Learning that a frightening fable allegedly took place at a location you can actually visit just adds to the thrill. It's this fact that sets the legends in this chapter apart from run-of-the-mill myths.

There are certain sites throughout Ohio that have attained legendary status. Their settings might seem ordinary at first glance, but the stories that grow out of these humble landmarks are the stuff of nightmares. Sometimes it is possible to uncover the origins of the strange tales. In other instances, it's less certain how the legends came to be. Are these merely tall tales, products of overactive imaginations, or is there more to them than that?

The answer might lie in people's need to prove themselves to their peer groups and to themselves. Every culture has a rite of passage for its young adults. Some primitive tribes practice sacrificial rituals or knock the teeth out of their young. In modern times, we've pretty much done away with such traumatic practices, leaving our youth to find their own way to adulthood. Sometimes that means getting in a car and driving to the darkest place you can find to confront whatever waits there. Maybe for this reason alone, we'll always have these scary stories with us.

On the other hand, suppose the legend is not a rite of passage, but a true and actual fact? It could happen. All we can say is, check out these stories of headless horses and childish ghosts at your own risk. Many of them may be just that—stories. But if they turn out to be true, don't say you weren't warned.

Weird Times at Gore Orphanage

If Ohioans were asked to name their favorite local ghost stories, Vermilion's Gore Orphanage would certainly appear on most lists. Even though the peculiar events said to have happened there date back more than a hundred and fifty years, the orphanage is still one of the most popular Ohio destinations for those in search of the weird. The site is deserted now, with only a few bits and pieces of the foundation remaining. But it's easy enough to find—just look for the foreboding road sign directing you to Gore Orphanage Road.

Gore Orphanage was supposedly in operation sometime in the 1800s. A mysterious fire started in the building and quickly engulfed the entire structure. Lining up the usual suspects from the different versions of the tale, the likely cause of the fire was one of the following:

Old Man Gore: the owner of the orphanage, who either was attempting to collect some sort of insurance money or just didn't like children.

Disgruntled Male Employee: While he is never named, this shady character had some sort of beef with orphanage owner Mr. Gore (who in this version loves children) and decided to exact his revenge.

Unknown Crazy Man: Again, this figure is never named. All that's ever said

about him is that he lived in the woods surrounding the orphanage and hated the noise the kids made.

An Accident: The most common version of this story has one of the orphans accidentally knocking over a lantern. Regardless of how the fire started, its results were catastrophic; all of the orphans perished. In the aftermath, the authorities took away Mr. Gore's license to run an orphanage and refused to allow a new one to be constructed on the site. Nearby townspeople wanted nothing more than to quickly forget the tragedy, so they simply razed what remained of the burned-out shell of the building. After that, nature was allowed to reclaim the land. Out of sight, out of mind.

But such an event doesn't fade easily, and in this case the tragic fire somehow left a "stain" upon the area. Locals began whispering that if you ventured out to the ruins of Gore Orphanage at night, you would see the ghostly shapes of dead orphans running and playing in the woods. Or, less pleasantly, the children might appear to be on fire and would be yelling and screaming things like "Help me!" as the stench of burning flesh filled the air. Other late-night visitors reported seeing bright lights swirling and weaving through the woods, which they took to be the ghosts of the dead children. And those

who believed the fire had been set intentionally sometimes felt the spirit of the guilty party at the site in the form of a dark, shadowy shape lurking near the foundation's remains.

A final weirdness at this troubled place was the report of tiny handprints. People who had parked and left their cars near the remains would return to find children's handprints all over their vehicles. In such an isolated area, anyone coming onto the scene would be highly visible. The only explanation was that the spirits of the orphans were attempting to push the cars away from the orphanage, perhaps in a ghostly warning to stay away lest the automobile owner suffer a fate similar to theirs.

When one starts digging for the nuggets of truth in this legend, the first fact they find is that there was indeed a home for children on Gore Orphanage Road at one time. After that, though, any similarities between the truth and the legend are completely coincidental.

The actual institution didn't have the word Gore in its title. Known as the Orphanage of Light and Hope, it was started by the Reverend John Sprunger and his wife sometime around 1903. The date is a bit uncertain since the orphanage was made up of a series of buildings that the Rev. Sprunger had acquired over the years. The remains of one of these buildings, Swift Mansion, is a favorite place for curiosity seekers.

In 1817, Joseph Swift purchased over four hundred acres of dense woods and flowing streams in and around a valley in Vermilion with the intention of building a sprawling estate. Incredibly, Swift would spend more than twenty years clearing the land in preparation for his dream home. Finally, in 1840, construction began. When finished, the enormous house featured stone pillars, fifteen-foot ceilings, and more than fourteen rooms, which included servants' quarters. Swift and his family continued to live in the spacious mansion until a series of bad investments forced him to put the property up for sale.

When Nicholas and Harriet Kellogg Wilber bought the Swift Mansion in 1865, little did they know that they were opening a chapter in what would become an Ohio legend. Sadly, the main event in this chapter happened between January 13 and 19, 1893, when four of Wilber's grandchildren died in a diphtheria epidemic that swept the state; all four children were buried next to one another at nearby Maple Grove Cemetery.

Obviously, Nicholas and Harriet were distraught over the loss of their grandchildren. Rumors have circulated that in their grief the Wilbers began conducting séances inside the former Swift Mansion in an attempt to contact their departed loved ones. It would not be surprising if the séances did indeed take place: The spiritualism movement was in full force in the late 1800s, and attempts to contact those who had "crossed over" were common. Regardless, it's probably the death of the four Wilber grandchildren that provided just that little kernel of truth about children perishing on the property.

In 1895, the Wilber family sold the property to the Sutton family. Seven years later, in 1902, Sutton sold the home to the Rev. Sprunger, to be used as part of the Orphanage of Light and Hope. With that, all of the elements of the Gore Orphanage legend were in place save for one: the fire. That would take place several years after the orphanage closed down, in 1916. Abandoned and then known as the local haunted house, the once-proud Swift Mansion caught fire and burned to the ground in December 1923 . . . with no one inside.

Of course, one question still remains: If there never was a Gore Orphanage, what's up with Gore Orphanage Road? Well, that stems from a term surveyors use to describe a wedge-shaped piece of land, or gore. So while the original thoroughfare was known as Baldwin Road, locals began calling it Gore Road because of the shape of the land the road traveled through. "Orphanage" was added to the name when the Orphanage of Light and Hope began operating there.

Cries Are Traffic, Not Tragic

I feel I should set a record straight. When I was a teenager, my friends and I took an excursion to Gore Orphanage Road. Police are usually nearby to discourage this behavior, but for some reason, they weren't there that night. Armed with flashlights, we went to the ruins and DID hear what sounded like children crying. Although spooked, we followed the sound through a patch of woods and came upon a highway overpass—where every time a heavy truck passed over, it made a sound similar to moaning, and from a distance it sounds like crying. Now every time I hear the stories repeated, I have to laugh.
—*Andrea K. Smiley*

Ghostly Children Still Linger

I went to Gore Orphanage one night with some friends. We hung out for a while, and just as we thought, nothing happened. We even tried the trick where you put flour on your car to see if handprints would appear. But nothing happened.

As we were driving back out, we came to that metal bridge where you first turn onto Gore Orphanage Road. You are not going to believe this, but we saw three little children, two girls and a boy, standing on the side of the bridge. At first, I thought that it was just a bunch of teenagers, but as we got closer, you could see that they were younger. And their clothes were old-fashioned too. And just as soon as we got onto the bridge, they disappeared. We stopped the car and looked around with flashlights, but we never found anything. I just wanted to write you and tell you my story.
—*Stephanie S., Sandusky*

Little Ghostly Handprints at Gore Orphanage

I have been to the Gore Orphanage only once. It started out as a big letdown, but it turned out to be a pretty frightening night. Kids in my high school had been ranting and raving about this place for a few years before I took my trip there. I don't believe in any ghosts or stuff, so I just saw it as a big waste of gas. But my friends and I decided to make the trip to see if it was worth all the hype.

When me and my boys went there, I was a bit creeped out by the road leading up to the place. It's really dark because of the overhanging trees, and there's a messed-up looking wooden bridge you cross over. When we arrived at the site where the orphanage had once stood (which was hard to find), all four of us got out of the car and went into the woods. There were a few pillars and some bricks and stones and stuff lying around on the ground. It was definitely not an ordinary place, but I still was doubtful about it being haunted.

I did hear some strange creaking noises. My one friend was freaking out, saying it was a kid crying, and I will admit, it did sound like it could have been. I think it was the trees, though. After a while, we decided to leave. Some of the guys thought the whole trip sucked. We didn't see any little ghost kids, we didn't smell any burning flesh, and we didn't hear any doors slamming. What happened when we made our way back to the car, however, would change my tune about the Gore Orphanage forever.

As we got close to the car, my friend Jake noticed that all the windows were fogged up. He ran up ahead of us because he thought someone had been messing with his ride. It was his mom's car, and she would have been really pissed if anything happened to it. When we caught up with him, he was just standing there, dumbfounded. There wasn't another human being in sight, it was a cool night, and there was absolutely no explanation as to why the windows were fogged up. That's when my other friend Shawn pointed out the back window. There, on the misty glass, were the faint impressions of little handprints. We all freaked out instantly.

Trying to find a logical reason to explain the handprints and to calm down my friends (who were really flipping out now), I pointed out that Jake did have a little brother who is only four years old and the marks were surely made by him. Secretly, though, I was just as freaked by those little fingerprints as anyone else there.

I still can't explain how those windows got fogged up, but if those handprints had been made by Jake's little brother, how is it that nobody noticed them on the way up there that night? The whole trip freaked me out bad. I have not been back to Gore Orphanage to this day.—*Victor E.*

Gates of Hell or the Blood Bowl?

Who can resist an offer to explore the Gates of Hell? Rumors abound of just such a location in a tunnel along High Street in Columbus. The small runoff stream that it accommodates is dry most of the time, but when the waters run, they roar through the concrete bore, often as suddenly as a flash flood. The east end of the tunnel is kept obstruction-free by a wicked gate of rusted metal that extends from each side of the opening, tapering to a gap barely big enough to squeeze through. The gate occupies a huge concrete basin with steep angled sides that make it a favorite hangout of skateboarders, many of whom have thoroughly spray-painted the tunnel inside and out. The rusty obstruction, sudden rushes of water, and reputed tendency of dead bodies and other debris to wash up there inspired the skaters to give the Gates of Hell its other common name: the Blood Bowl.

There's a popular legend that claims that secret gates of hell are hidden away all over the United States. It is said that a special ritual must be performed to open each of these portals. The purpose of the gates varies, depending on which version of the legend you hear. In some, opening just one of the gates allows a passageway into hell. In others, all of the gates must be opened, unleashing "hell on this earth." There's also some disagreement as to how many of these gates exist and even about their locations. But with a catchy name like Gates of Hell, it's no surprise that the demonic gates are alleged to exist in almost every state.

The story concerning the Columbus gate, however, is different from the popular hell gate tales. For one thing, there's no backstory here, no portals to be opened or ghostly appearances. It seems that in this case it's merely a name. And truth be told, these gates of hell are nothing more than a section of a drainage culvert that runs under High Street as the water winds its way to the Olentangy River. About the only truly scary aspect of the gates is that

the tunnel passes underneath both a Tim Horton's and a White Castle.

The other name for the Gates of Hell, the Blood Bowl, does have a backstory, albeit a vague one. According to legend, the name was the result of a skateboarder (or, in some cases, someone on a bicycle) attempting to perform a trick along the slanted sides of the culvert and crashing and dying. Some versions have the individual attempting to ride through the tunnel under High Street in the dark on a dare. If someone did indeed try this, the probability that the stunt would have ended in death or, at the very least, injury is quite high. For one thing, despite the fact that the tunnel simply goes from one side of High Street to the other, the path it takes is not a straight one. Rather, halfway down the tunnel there is a ninety-degree turn, which is followed by another ninety-degree turn before it continues on its way. As if that weren't enough, the tunnel ceiling drops down sharply to only a few feet. If someone were attempting to navigate this in the dark and with water flowing through it, it's not hard to imagine a bad ending.

The Oxford Ghost

Oxford started out as a sleepy little village in the far west of the state. Once Miami University opened its doors, in 1809, though, the town started to grow by leaps and bounds, eventually becoming a city in 1971.

As with any college town (or city), Oxford could be expected to have its share of ghost stories. And it certainly does. One of them, however, has lingered so long in the annals of Oxford folklore that the place where the event supposedly occurred has become something of a tourist attraction, much to the chagrin of neighbors and Oxford police officers. In fact, the story has gotten so popular that for some it even surpasses the fame of the university itself.

Don't believe it? Ask any college student what he thinks when he hears "Oxford, Ohio." Chances are the second thing that pops into his head is Miami University. The first will be the Oxford Motorcycle Ghost.

The most popular version of this legend is set in the 1940s and involves a young couple who attended the university. Although the couple were deeply in love, the girl's parents did not approve of her boyfriend. For one thing, he didn't come from a good family. On top of that, he rode a motorcycle. Of course, the parents' disapproval only made the girl want to see her boyfriend even more. But how to do that without being found out?

After some time, a clever plan was devised. On nights when the couple was planning to meet, the boyfriend would wait with his motorcycle near the girl's house on the Oxford–Milford Road. When the girl's parents finally went to sleep, the girl would flash the house's front porch light three times. If she was unable to do that, she would walk to a spot in the middle of the road near her house and blink a flashlight three times. When the boyfriend saw the light, he would know it was time to hop on his motorcycle and pick up his girlfriend.

The boyfriend leapt onto his motorcycle and started off toward the house. Too late, he realized that the wine had severely impaired his motor skills.

One night, the girl's parents were a little late heading off to bed. The boyfriend, safely hidden in his spot along the road, grew bored and decided to occupy himself with the bottle of wine he had brought along. When the girl finally signaled that the coast was clear, the boyfriend leapt onto his motorcycle and started off toward the house. Too late, he realized that the wine had severely impaired his motor skills. As his bike reached a sharp bend in the road, he crashed headlong into a barbed-wire fence and was decapitated. Even though that tragic event took place years ago, the young man's ghost is still trying to reach his girlfriend. The girl's house has long since been torn down, but if you go to the spot where it once stood and stop and flash your headlights three times, the boy's ghost, thinking the light is his girlfriend's, will make an appearance. The first thing you will see is a ghostly white light, like that of a motorcycle headlight, which appears off in the distance ahead of your car. Slowly, the white light will continue down the road toward you, before it disappears at a sharp bend in the road—the place where the boyfriend met his untimely death.

Another popular local legend in Oxford is that at one time there was a serial rapist running rampant around campus. It should come as no surprise that eventually this legend would become entwined with the story of the motorcycle ghost. In this version, the rapist becomes the reason the boyfriend was racing so fast along the road on his motorcycle. The girlfriend, knowing there was a rapist in town, was naturally frightened, especially since she was often home alone for long periods at night. Seeing how concerned she was, the boyfriend, who lived nearby, instructed the girl that if she ever became scared, she should just flash her porch light and he would come over on his motorcycle right away.

One night, a strange car pulled into the girl's driveway. Convinced the rapist had arrived, the panicked girlfriend began frantically flashing the porch light. Seeing this, the boyfriend hopped on his motorcycle and sped off to save the day. Unfortunately, he was unable to negotiate the sharp turn and crashed, dying on impact.

In order to see the ghost in this version, you follow the same ritual of parking near the former property of the girlfriend, flash your headlights three times, and then sit back and wait.

If you're not in the mood for flashing lights, then just choose to believe the war version of the legend. In this variation, the boyfriend and girlfriend have been apart for some time due to his fighting in the war. When the young man's tour of duty is finally over, he returns to Oxford and decides to surprise his girlfriend. So he hops on his motorcycle and drives over to her house, where he finds his love in the arms of another man. Enraged and devastated, the boyfriend drives off far too fast, which results in his fatal crash at the sharp bend in the road.

If you wish to see the ghostly motorcycle headlight in this version, all you have to do is position your car before the bend on the Oxford–Milford Road and wait. Another interesting variation here is that once the headlight appears, it will drive past you. If you look in your rearview mirror, you will see the motorcycle's taillights disappearing when they reach the turn in the road.

The final version of the legend is also the most recent one. (Perhaps people who grew up on the other versions felt the story needed a more violent face-lift.) Now, when the boyfriend speeds off on his motorcycle toward his girlfriend's house he crashes headlong into a young boy riding a bicycle, killing them both instantly. As a result, when you flash your lights while sitting alongside the road, TWO different lights will appear. The first will be red and is said to be the reflector from the boy's bicycle. Shortly after the red light appears it will vanish, as a bright white light, the motorcycle headlight, crashes into it. Right after the crash, the white light will go off the road and disappear too.

Hey, two ghostly lights are better than one, right?

Witch's Tower, Evil by Any Name

Looming over the top of one of the fairways of Dayton's Community Golf Course is a giant stone tower. Perhaps due to its foreboding appearance, the structure has come to be referred to by macabre monikers like Witch's Tower and even Frankenstein's Castle. And with names like that, you just know there's got to be a ghost or two floating around.

Who built the tower is open to debate, but the popular belief is that it was constructed many years ago by a local man named John Patterson. For this reason, area residents not inclined to believe in the supernatural forgo the spooky names and simply refer to it as Patterson Tower. As for why it was constructed, that's another enigma, although most believe it was designed as some sort of observation tower.

The ghosts who are said to haunt the tower were first reported after a tragic accident that took place there in the 1960s. According to legend, a group of teenagers were enjoying themselves nearby when a violent thunderstorm suddenly rolled in. The teenagers ran for the tower, believing its solid stone would protect them. What they failed to notice was that the tower stairs were equipped with a long metal railing.

As the group quickly mounted the stairs, a sudden bolt of lightning struck a portion of the rail at the top of the tower. The rail allowed the electricity to race down the banister toward the teenagers. Two members of the group who were leaning against the handrail when the lightning struck were electrocuted and died almost instantly.

For weeks afterward, it was said, visitors could still see the charred

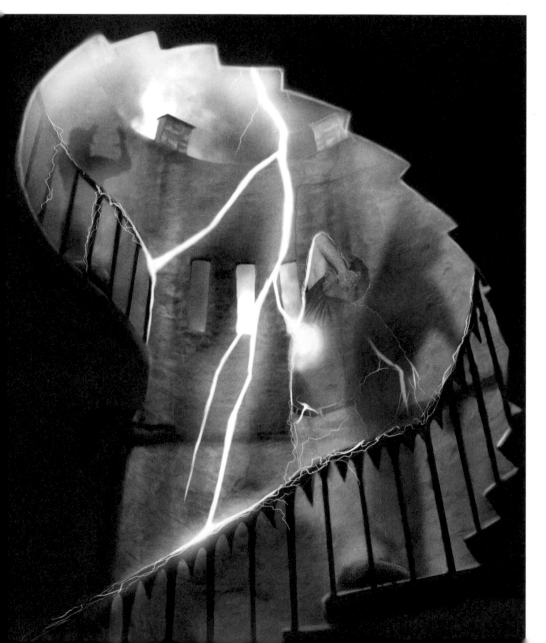

outlines of the teenagers on the tower wall. Some say that it was out of respect for the dead that officials ordered metal plates to be secured to the tower's openings, but others said it was simply to deter the curious. Either way, it didn't matter; those who wanted to catch a glimpse of the charred outlines simply pried the plates loose. Over time, though, there were fewer and fewer visitors. In fact, the tower might have faded into obscurity save for one thing: the ghosts.

The Glowing Ghosts

Legend says that on dark and stormy nights, shadowy traces of the teenage victims are seen at the tower. If there is a sudden and violent bolt of lightning, the figures will illuminate and glow as if they have just been struck by lightning, after which they once again fade into nothingness . . . until the next storm.

Today, due largely to repeated acts of vandalism, NO TRESPASSING signs have been placed around the tower. Additionally, the entranceway and lower windows have

been permanently sealed. But that has done little to dampen the popularity of the place. Indeed, in recent years new stories began circulating that a woman, dressed eerily in white, hanged herself in the tower. There is even a rumor that the real reason officials sealed off the edifice was that a young teenager decided to investigate one night and in the darkness fell to his death.

So is the tower haunted? It's hard to say. While some report uneventful visits there, others claim to have spotted darkened shapes moving about within this foreboding structure. Perhaps it is simply a case of being in the right place at the wrong time. Or maybe the spirits just quietly lie in wait for the next dark and stormy night to make their presence known.

Full-Figured Ghost Haunts Castle

I lived ten minutes away from the Castle, and I was fascinated about seeing if all the rumors were true. Unfortunately for me, I didn't return home excited, but rather the most scared I have ever been in my life.

Around seven p.m., my friend and I went up to the castle. It was still very light outside, and nothing much happened. My friend looked into the third window and saw something that looked like a shadow. I blew it off, but then I looked in the crack in the cemented-in door and saw two green eyes staring back at me. It took awhile to realize they were eyes, but when I did, I was pretty startled. I still shook it off as nothing, and we left to go kill time until dark.

Darkness came as we set out for the castle a second time later that night. It is very dark back in those woods. We started walking down Patterson, and I noticed that something light was next to me in the trees. I figured it was just a reflection of a car coming. I then looked to my right as we were approaching the castle, and that is when this full-figured, woman-looking thing dressed in white blocked my view. Pretty scared, we ran off down the road in the opposite direction. After a few seconds of running, we had to stop. "Was it real?" we asked each other. We didn't know. Twelve seconds after we stopped, we heard sticks snapping rapidly behind us. We were out of there immediately!—*Letter via e-mail*

Lady in White Doesn't Want Company

On the other side of the castle is a huge golf course. Our plan was to skip the road by going through the golf course, and from the "safety" (as we thought) of the course, we would watch the tower. We got onto the course, and oddly enough, there were weird patches of fog all over the place. We were getting close to the castle when we saw something approaching in the trees across the street. It was a white ball with a tail streaming behind it. It was going all through the trees, and at the same time, hundreds of flashes were going off around it. We looked at this for a good ten minutes in utter amazement. Then, all of a sudden, the white orb-looking thing grew into the figure of a woman right in front of our eyes! She had everything a human has except legs. She was wearing a white dress. Not only did it turn into a full-bodied figure, but it started to walk across the road toward us!

We ran and ran down the course and eventually came to a stop. We just had to go back. When we got back up to our original spot, we saw nothing. All of a sudden, we began hearing laughter. Then the woman emerged from the woods about twenty feet away from us. I have never, EVER been this scared in my life! We ran as hard as we could. The whole way out of the golf course, there was this wall of fog with a black shadow in the middle walking toward us until we got out of there.

Who knows what would have happened if we had gotten into the castle, but something was trying hard to keep us away. For anyone who is not a believer, I recommend you go there and find out the hard way that this stuff is real.—*Letter via e-mail*

Moonville Tunnel

Deep in the backwoods of Vinton County stands the Moonville Tunnel, a relic from an era long gone. The town sprang up when the Marietta and Cincinnati Railroad was built through the coal- and iron-rich woods of southeastern Ohio, in 1856. At its peak in the 1870s, Moonville boasted a population of more than one hundred—almost exclusively miners and their families. The Moonville Tunnel marked the entrance to the town.

Moonville wasn't around long, maybe thirty years or so, before modern advances made such small mining towns obsolete. By the time the 1900s rolled around, it was all but abandoned. Many of the residents are buried just west of town, in an old cemetery at the top of a steep, winding gravel road. Both the cemetery and the tunnel are about as far from civilization as it is possible to get in this state—a full hour's drive from Nelsonville or Athens, buried in the Wayne National Forest along Raccoon Creek.

Today all that remains of the town of Moonville is the small cemetery and the tunnel. Of the two, it seems that ghosts have chosen the tunnel as their territory. The only thing that's consistent about the hauntings there is that they are said to be the result of someone who was killed inside. But the Moonville Tunnel legend is actually based on historical fact. Sort of.

In one version, the victim is simply someone who ended up in the wrong place at the wrong time. Sometimes the person is a man who is somehow connected to the railroad, such as a conductor or an engineer. In other retellings of the legend, the person is someone from the town of Moonville who got caught on the tracks and was unable to avoid an oncoming train. In other instances, this person is a woman, and sometimes the woman is said to be pregnant. And if all of those variations aren't enough to make your head spin, then how about the only version that names the person who is hit by the train? He is said to be Rastus Dexter, who is described as an eight-foot-tall African American.

The newspaper article reporting the incident, in the *McArthur Democrat* of March 31, 1859, gives the real story, along with a warning about drinking too much while riding a speeding train.

A brakesman on the Marietta & Cincinnati Railroad fell from the cars near Cincinnati Furnace, on last Tuesday March 29, 1859 and was fatally injured. . . . He was taken on the train to Hamden and Doctors Wolf and Rannells sent for to perform amputation, but the prostration of the vital energies was too great to attempt it. The man is probably dead ere this. The accident resulted from a too free use of liquor.

The most complete version of the Moonville Tunnel legend is the one regarding an epidemic that swept through the town. As a result, the entire community was quarantined and trains were ordered not to stop there anymore. Low on supplies, the stranded townsfolk came up with a plan: They would send one of their own through the tunnel to the outskirts of town with a lantern. The idea was that as the train approached, the man would signal for help with his lantern. Since he would be standing outside the town's limits, the thought was that the conductor would stop the train and help.

A volunteer was selected, and it was decided that he would set out the following day. However, the next day, the man got off to a late start (because he either overslept or was hung over), and as he neared the tunnel, he heard the train approaching. Knowing the conductor would never stop for him unless he was on the other side of the tunnel, outside the town's limits, the man began sprinting through the darkness, waving his lantern wildly. Sadly, he never made it through the tunnel but was struck and killed instantly by the oncoming train. That may be why people today report seeing a ghostly lantern trailing along the track bed around the old tunnel.

stepped off the track and disappeared into the rocks nearby.

A more recent sighting, from the *Athens Messenger* in 1993, tells the story of an Ohio University student named David and his three friends, who went to Moonville to swim in Raccoon Creek. On their way back through the tunnel, they saw a light halfway down and split into two groups. Two of the boys headed toward the light, then came running back out of the tunnel, screaming, "There's no one carrying the light!" David went to check it out for himself. "He wasn't kidding," he reported. "It was just a swinging light with no one holding it!"

In the years following the disintegration of Moonville, everything disappeared but the tunnel—and the legends. After the boarding house and miners' shacks were left to wash away, the railroad took down the train platform. Trains continued to run until the late '80s, when the rails and crossties were stripped. Finally, the trestle over Raccoon Creek came down, making direct access to the tunnel available only by walking across rocks when the water is low. A ruler-straight gravel path through the forest and the ghostly pillars of the trestle supports in the creek are the only remnants of the line once known as the loneliest stretch of track between Marietta and Cincinnati.

Despite the difficulty of reaching it, the Moonville Tunnel is something of an alternative tourist attraction. Groups regularly visit, and college students from Athens stage a Halloween party there every year. Charred fire pits and beer cans are a regular sight, and the graffiti that covers the inner walls gets photographed almost as much as the distinctive openings, each with MOONVILLE written above its arch in protruding brick letters.

Today, as over a century ago, bizarre occurrences are reported on the old stretch of B&O tracks with amazing regularity. Is the lantern-waving spook just another bit of railroad folklore, or does something supernatural actually inhabit the legendary Moonville Tunnel?

One account of the ghost's habit of stopping trains appeared in the *Chillicothe Gazette* on February 17, 1895:

The ghost of Moonville, after an absence of one year, has returned and is again at its old pranks, haunting B&O S-W freight trains and their crews. It appeared Monday night in front of fast freight No. 99 west bound, just east of the cut which is one half mile the other side of Moonville at the point where Engineer Lawhead lost his life and Engineer Walters was injured. The ghost, attired in a pure white robe, carried a lantern. It had a flowing white beard, its eyes glistened like balls of fire and surrounding it was a halo of twinkling stars. When the train stopped, the ghost

Watch Out for the Phantom Behind You

In the fall of last year, a bunch of my friends and I went out to investigate the Moonville Tunnel. My dad worked on the railroad in his earlier years and was telling me about the story long before I even thought about going.

On our first few visits out to the tunnel, nothing was out of the ordinary. The next time we visited was a totally different story! We had already walked through the tunnel and were on the other side, walking down the path. Nobody wanted to walk in the back, so I, being the brave soul I am, decided to bring up the rear of the line, as long as one of my buddies walked beside me. So he and I were walking behind the rest of our friends when he jokingly told me to watch out for the guy behind me. We both just laughed, but I, of course, kept looking over my shoulder for the "guy" following me. Of course, nothing was there.

About five or six minutes later, I turned my head around to look behind me when I saw the scariest thing I've ever experienced in my entire life: There was a figure following us, only it definitely didn't look human. I didn't know if I was seeing something or not. I tried to say something to my friend, and I couldn't even talk. I simply grabbed him and turned him around. As soon as I saw the look on his face, I knew I wasn't imagining the ghostly figure. We turned and ran as fast as we could, nearly knocking everybody down in our path. When we looked back, the figure appeared to be getting closer to us. We kept running, and the next time we checked for the ghost, nothing was there.

I am certain that whatever it is in Moonville, it is still roaming the woods behind the tunnel. I haven't experienced the headless man in the tunnel, but I surely experienced something that wasn't of the norm.
—Letter via e-mail

Lantern Man Still Swinging at Moonville

All of the men in my family get together every year and go deer hunting in Moonville. We camped on the rail bed on the other side of the trestle. On the third night I was there, we were all hanging out and just goofing off. I decided I was going to go and scout for deer tracks. I got about fifteen feet from the tunnel when I saw a light swinging back and forth inside. I thought it was just one of my family members playing a trick on me, so I shined my flashlight down the tunnel, and all I saw was a light being swung by something that looked like a man, but it wasn't a real man because I could see right through him. Then he walked to the opposite side of the tunnel and just vanished.*—Anonymous*

Peekaboo

In 1984, I was working at the Zaleski CCC Camp. On the weekends, we were more or less free to do as we pleased. Well, one night a couple of guys (whom I shall refer to as RZ and RM) and I wanted to do something. We had no money, and things were looking grim. Then, one of the R's says, "Hey, let's go to the Moonville Tunnel and see the ghost!" I had no idea what they were talking about, but after a brief explanation, I was in. We packed up our backpacks, jumped in RM's Pinto, and off we went.

When we got to the tracks and parked, there were no other cars around. After a short walk in the dark (it was around midnight—I hate to be so melodramatic), we were at the front of the tunnel. We looked around, listened closely, and saw no one, heard nothing but the regular night sounds that one would associate with the woods. When we got to the tunnel, there was no one else there. We felt absolutely nothing that would lead us to believe there was someone hiding there waiting on us.

About halfway through the tunnel, RZ and RM started running. I thought maybe they were screwing with me, and I ran to catch up. At this point, I noticed they were looking over their shoulders as they ran. This was curious, because we were in a tunnel at midnight, and a few seconds earlier, all I could see was the opening at the other end. I looked back and saw a train entering the tunnel behind us. I ran like hell, but something wasn't right! We got out the other side and jumped off the tracks to the side of the tunnel. Then I realized what was wrong: no choo-choo noises.

"Did you see that?" they yelled. Yes, I had, and now I looked back down the tunnel and saw it again—a light in the mouth of the far end of the tunnel. It looked like a train light just entering a tunnel. I quickly ducked back, then peeked again—still there! Duck back again, peek again. Gone! It was just gone!

When we got the courage up to walk back through the tunnel, everything was normal. No more mysterious appearances, no more lights, no sounds of local rednecks laughing in the brush.

What did we see that night? I don't believe in ghosts, ESP, UFOs, or much of anything else, for that matter. The only reasonable explanation I can come up with is that some local high school kids happened to go to the tunnel that night with a spotlight to see if they could scare someone, and we happened along.

It would be difficult to hide while we walked past, show the light, and get away before we came back without laughing out loud. The whole thing happened in a few minutes. Still, this seems the only reasonable explanation.—*Letter via e-mail*

Cult Sacrifice at the Tunnel

I have visited the Moonville Tunnel many times and even camped overnight with friends. I've never seen the swinging lantern or any ghostlike creatures, but I have witnessed some type of cult activity.

It was the summer of 1992 the first time I saw it. A few friends of mine were going to party and showed a couple of our friends from Athens the tunnel. We walked in from Mineral, and as we came closer, I could see the tunnel had a fire built in it, so we were going to sneak up on who we figured were probably a group of teenagers. But as we were sneaking up the old tracks, we could hear chanting. We stayed hidden in the brush and watched the scariest thing I have ever seen.

There were seven men, all in what looked like hooded bathrobes—one of them was in a red robe. They kept chanting, and they opened what looked like a burlap sack and pulled either a small goat or a lamb out of it (alive; we could hear it bahing), and they cut it open down the middle while it was alive. We freaked and creeped as quietly as possible back until we could run. We decided to run to the first trestle, where we would have to cross the creek. We ran there, crossed, and went home. That was it for us.—*Letter via e-mail*

Ancient Mysteries

The *mysteries* surrounding the origin and meaning of ancient structures in faraway lands have fired the imaginations of generations of wonderers and thinkers. Books, films, and television are filled with speculation about Easter Island's giant statues, Stonehenge's stone pillars, and the pyramids of Egypt and Mesoamerica. These strange relics in exotic locations naturally lend themselves to thoughts of ancient civilizations with greater wisdom than our own or other arcane notions. But few North Americans consider the mysteries of the "ancients" near their own towns.

From the shores of the Great Lakes to those of the Ohio River, from the foothills of the Appalachians to the muddy banks of the Wabash River, vast Ohio has hosted many primordial peoples and events that have left unexplained reminders of themselves on the state's landscape. Some of these ancient phenomena are well known, but others are enigmas that have been overlooked by most investigators. It is up to the crew at *Weird Ohio* to uncover these lost wonders of the Buckeye State.

But the origin of the mound remains something of an academic controversy. Early chroniclers Ephraim Squire and Edwin Davis of Chillicothe first surveyed the site in 1846. Harvard University archaeologist Frederic Ward Putnam visited it in 1883 and again in 1885. On his second visit, Putnam was so worried that vandals and erosion would destroy the ancient work that he purchased it in the name of the university's Peabody Museum. From 1887 to 1889, he excavated the effigy and nearby conical mounds but found no human bones or artifacts within the serpent. Whatever its purpose, it was not used for burials.

The most famous drawing of the great Serpent Mound was made by the Reverend J. P. MacLean of Hamilton, Ohio. MacLean was a well-known writer on mounds and related topics. During the summer of 1884, while in the employ of the Bureau of Ethnology, he visited the Serpent Mound, taking with him a surveyor, and made a comprehensive and careful plan for the Bureau. Before him, all of the authors and commentators had published reports in which they explained the oval—the egg the serpent seems to be swallowing—as the end of the work. Putnam, who excavated the locality a year before MacLean's visit, noticed that between the oval figure and the nearby ledge was a slightly raised, circular ridge of earth, from either side of which a curved ridge extended toward the sides of the oval figure. MacLean's research and measurements demonstrated that these ridges were part of what is either a distinct figure or a very important portion of the original figure. He concluded that it bore a close resemblance to a frog, a novel idea that often has been forgotten in modern descriptions of the Serpent Mound.

MacLean, after describing three figures, put forth this query: "Does the frog represent the creative, the egg the passive, and the serpent the destructive power of nature?"

What then are readers of *Weird Ohio* to make of that frog? We are reminded of the great early-twentieth-century

intellectual Charles Fort, who wrote, "We shall pick up an existence by its frogs." Perhaps the answer lies in the frog. Frogs falling from the sky? Frogs as a sign of rebirth from the waters? Frogs becoming princes? When traveling across such weird landscapes, we must keep an open mind to the answers, and questions, found outside the oval.

In the late nineteenth century, Putnam continued his excavations of the Serpent Mound and attributed the creation of the great serpent effigy to the builders of two nearby burial mounds, which he also excavated. He felt they belonged to the culture called the Adena (800 B.C.– A.D. 100). Adena burial mounds are found near the

Serpent Mound, and since the Adena Indians were known for their earthworks, it was believed that they were the builders of the mound. (A third burial mound exists near the effigy's tail.)

Recent, twentieth-century, excavations of the Serpent Mound revealed wood charcoal that could be radio-carbon-dated. That research placed the Fort Ancient culture (A.D. 1000–1550) as the builders of the mound. The debate about who really built it continues, but who-ever its creators are, the mound has gained a reputation as a spiritual place where strange things occasionally happen. It is a New Age power center, believers say. Within the oval, a pile of stones shows evidence of a fire. This, scientists believe, indicates that it was also a signal mound.

The function or symbolic meaning of the Serpent Mound may be a mystery, but we do know that aspects of it are clearly astronomically aligned. The head is aligned with the summer solstice sunset, and the snake's coils align with the winter solstice sunrise and the equinox sunrise. Some people claim that the Indians may have built it in the wake of Halley's Comet, which appeared in 1066. Today encounters with ghosts and other spooks around the Serpent Mound are often reported, with some people even telling of experiencing psychic epiphanies near the mound.

Visitors may walk along a footpath surrounding the Serpent Mound and experience the mystery and power of this monumental effigy for themselves. They can climb a twenty-five-foot tower to get an aerial look at what may be an ancient sky calendar. A small museum contains exhibits on the effigy mound and the geology of the surrounding area. The Ohio Historical Society manages the mound. The Serpent Mound State Memorial is off state Route 73, about ten miles north of Peebles in Adams County.

Octagons and Alligators

The town of Newark literally sits on top of a former megalopolis of mound builders. While modern construction and city dwellers have destroyed much of the past glory of Newark's earthworks, hints of them are all around. Perfect circular walls enclose twenty acres of land. Nearby, a structure called the Octagon adjoins the circle, encompassing another eighteen acres. Long trackways lined with walls connect the two sites. One especially lengthy corridor runs from these two earthworks to the Licking River shore, about two and a half miles away.

Also in the vicinity of Newark are two grand examples of effigy mounds. One is called the Alligator Mound, although recently the idea that it could be the effigy of a lizard has arisen. The position the mound occupies is significant. The old placement theory is that mounds were constructed as military works, some form of fort or enclosure to protect the ancients. But with the modern examination of structures such as the Alligator Mound, we can see that they had more of a symbolic than a protective function. They were not placed at sites that were easy to protect or even necessary to secure.

The Alligator Mound is on the prominent brow of a hill about two hundred feet high, which projects out into a beautiful valley. The valley is not very wide, and directly across was a fortified camp. In the valley below it was the circular work, and a short distance below on another projecting headland was a strongly fortified hill. That it was perhaps a signal station is indicated by traces of fire.

As with other mounds in Ohio, the true meaning of

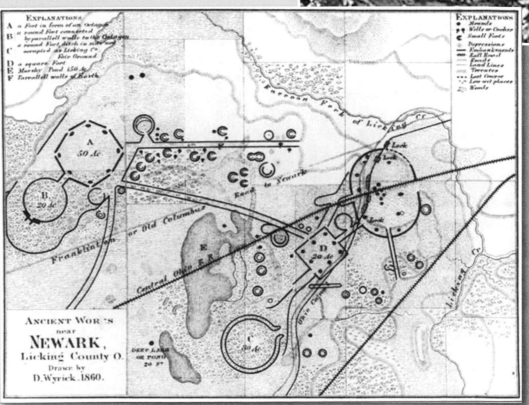

ANCIENT WORKS
near
NEWARK,
Licking County O.
Drawn by
D. Wyrick. 1860.

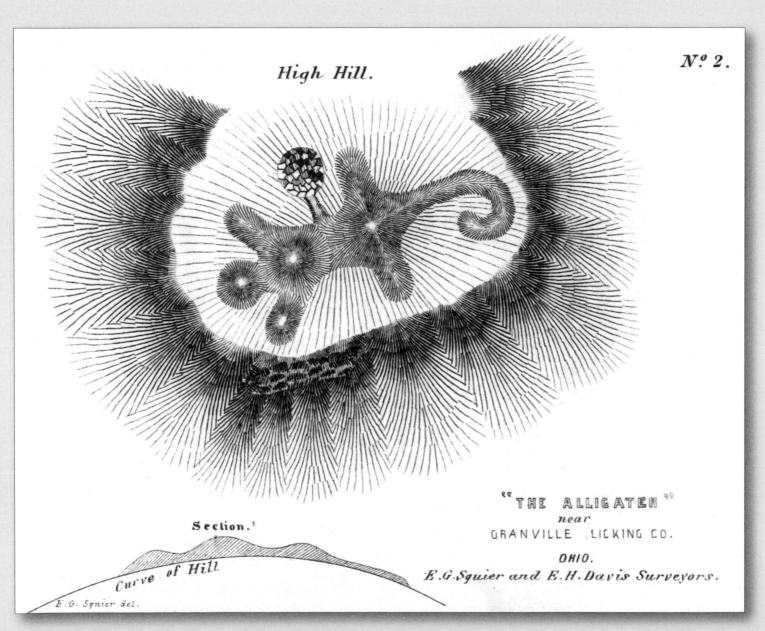

High Hill.

Nº 2.

"THE ALLIGATER"
near
GRANVILLE LICKING CO.
OHIO.
E.G.Squier and E.H.Davis Surveyors.

Section.'

Curve of Hill

E.G. Squier del.

this mound's function, and indeed of what the alligator-like animal represented, remains an open question — yet another ancient mystery in Ohio. Some believe the circle and octagon link back to ancient Europe and the "squaring of the circle," a spell brewed in a pot of alchemical mysteries, which was used to strive for perfection of the spirit and soul.

The Newark earthworks and effigy mounds are located in Licking County, southwest on Highway 79 from Newark.

City of the Dead

Mound City, outside Chillicothe, is home to one of the least known sites of the "dark side" of America: the Hopewell culture's Necropolis, or City of the Dead. It is the place where an ancient people interred the bodies of their departed.

The word Hopewell has a Ohioan origin. It is taken from an Ohio farmer, Mordecai Hopewell, who owned some of the land where mounds were dug up in 1891. The Mound City complex, which covers thirteen acres, is considered one of the best-preserved sacred Hopewell sites, dating back over 2,300 years. The magic number 23 comes up over and over again here—the location is reached today via U.S. 23, and 23 mounds exist at the site.

Much has been written of the importance of 23—the number in the *I Ching* for "breaking apart" and "coming together." The Hopewell culture appears to have placed great significance on this location, as where the "here" and the "after" would meet. The site has been called the Simulacrum of the Otherworld by occultists and is seen as haunted and mystically charged. Even the artifacts here have strong links to the afterlife. One of the most prominent is an ancient shaman's ceremonial death mask.

Those who think mounds are old news would be shocked by the discoveries being plowed from the earth near Mound City. It was here, in 2001, that a great circle—completely underground, some ninety feet across and nearly perfectly round—was found, purely by accident. Government archaeologists made the discovery using powerful magnetic sensors and scientific instruments that capture geophysical energy fluxes.

N'omi Greber, an archaeologist at the Cleveland Museum of Natural History, said the remote-sensor tools that made the find, which were developed for petroleum exploration, are opening up new vistas to archaeologists. When the huge circle popped up on computer screens analyzing data on June 29, 2001, researchers were stunned. No previous

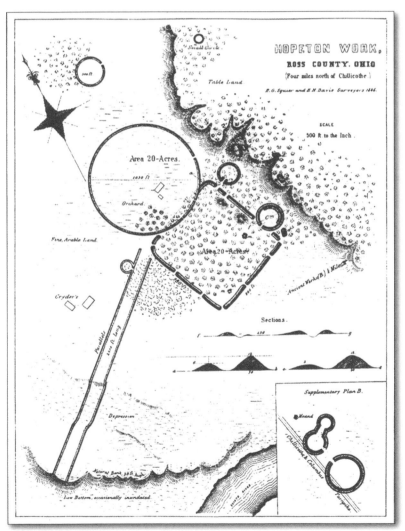

studies had prepared them for this otherworldly doughnut beneath the earth.

"We looked at historic photographs, we looked at aerial photographs, we looked at historical accounts, we asked if anybody ever had a barn or silo. Nobody has ever seen anything out there before," Jennifer Pederson, a park service researcher, told the *Cleveland Plain-Dealer.*

Archaeologists say the circle is in a region of southern Ohio that has been well combed for ancient artifacts. The area is dotted with Indian mounds, all aboveground and shown on maps. The circle was hidden beneath a three-hundred-acre tract bought by the Department of the Interior in 1997 to protect mounds that farmers were plowing to bits.

No one is certain who built the underground circle, although the Hopewell, a lost civilization that built dozens of mysterious geometric objects across Ohio before vanishing thousands of years ago, seems to be the best candidate of late. The Hopewell started building mounds and earthworks around 438 B.C., about the same time the Greeks were erecting the Parthenon in Athens. The Hopewell culture seemed to vanish around A.D. 400, not long after the Mayan temples started to be built in Mexico.

Although baffled by its purpose, government scientists say they are confident the circle is some type of man-made object. They say humans have not seen it for centuries because it was first dug out like a ditch, then covered up to keep it out of sight.

Archaeologist Greber, who has been studying Hopewell relics, told the *Cleveland Plain-Dealer* that the Ohio-based civilization is a complete mystery. "We know more about the Egyptians and the Assyrians than the people who were in our own backyard," Greber said.

"They left no writing that we know of. They just left octagons, rectangles, and circles. You try to figure out what it means and it drives you up a tree after a while. . . . Why did they do it? Why, why, why? Nobody knows."

The circle itself is on land not open to the public, but other nearby sites are. The City of the Dead at the Mound City complex is visitor friendly, with an observation deck and guided tours. The visitor's guide is very specific about what you can see in the exhibition:

The artifacts shown here all came from this mound, first excavated in 1921. Among others recovered here and now on exhibit in the visitor center are elk and bear teeth, copper ornaments, large obsidian points, and a cache of five thousand shell beads. Two copper headdresses were found, one with three pairs of copper antlers, the other representing a bear with hinged ears and legs attached with rivets. A section of the mound has been removed to show an elaborate multiple burial. All four individuals were cremated, as were the other original burials of Mound City. Among the ashes were obsidian tools, raven and toad effigy pipes, a copper headpiece in human shape, and other grave goods. There are sixteen other cremations known from this mound; a later intrusive burial on the side of the mound was discovered in 1963, when the mound was re-excavated. The effigy pipes, headdresses, and other artifacts were used in ceremonies and may also have been badges of rank or status.

Almost fifty miles south of Columbus on Highway 23, Mound City is the only section of Hopewell Culture National Historical Park currently open to visitors.

Fort Ancient

The name Fort Ancient hints at the special place this site holds in the prehistoric mysteries of Ohio. About two thousand years ago, the people of the Hopewell culture, carrying woven baskets of soil weighing thirty-five to forty pounds each, constructed eighteen thousand feet of earthen walls at Fort Ancient, near present-day Lebanon. In recognition of the enormous achievement of this massive mound-building effort and of the site's distinction as the best-preserved Hopewell hilltop enclosure in the country, Fort Ancient has been named a National Historic Landmark.

Writing in 1885, E. A. Allen noted in *The Prehistoric World: or, Vanished Races,*

FORT ANCIENT

—MUST BE SOLD, TOGETHER WITH—

284 ACRES

—OF VALUABLE—

Real Estate.

NOTICE IS HEREBY GIVEN THAT THE executors of James S. Couden, deceased, will sell at public sale at the Morrow Bank, in Morrow, Ohio, on

SATURDAY, FEBRUARY 16, 1889,

At 10 o'clock A. M., the Fort Ancient Farm, including the "Old Fort," one of the grandest archæological structures in America.

This wonderful monument of the skill and industry of a great and vanished race and the splendid farm above referred to are situated on the east bank of the Little Miami river on the Pittsburg, Cincinnati & St. Louis R. R., within ½ mile of station, 40 miles distant from Cincinnati.

This property will be sold in one entire tract or in two tracts one of 94 acres and one of 190 acres.

TERMS.

One third cash on day of sale; one-third in one year, and one third in two years. Deferred payments to bear interest from day of sale and to be secured by notes, and mortgage on premises.

A. N. COUDEN.
THEO. COUDEN.

Executors of James S. Couden, dec'd.

O'NEALL & STANLEY, Attorneys, Lebanon, O.

ja12-6t

Fort Ancient is situated on the Little Miami River, about forty miles east of Cincinnati. It was not only a fort, but was also a fortified village site, and has some features about it that are regarded as of a religious nature. The hill on which it stands is in most places very steep towards the river. A ravine starts from near the upper end on the eastern side, gradually deepening towards the south, and finally turns abruptly towards the west to the river. By this means nearly the whole work occupies the summit of a detached hill, having in most places very steep sides. To this naturally strong position fortifications were added, consisting of an embankment of earth of unusual height, which follows close around the very brow of the hill. This embankment is still in a fine state of preservation, but is now annually exposed to cultivation and the inroads of cattle, so that it will not be long before it will be greatly changed if no effort be made to preserve it. . . . We notice the wall has numerous breaks in it. Some of these are where it crosses the ravines, leading down the sides of the hill. In a few cases the embankment may still be traced to within a few feet of a rivulet. Considerable discussion has ensued as to the origin and use of these numerous gateways.

The holes in the earthen works of Ohio have been some of the most highly debated mysteries of the nineteenth century. Allen goes on to note the comments of a well-known expert on mound builders at the time: "Mr. Squier thinks that these openings were occupied by timber work in the nature of blockhouses which have long since decayed. Others, however, think that the wall was originally entire except in a few instances, and that the breaks now apparent were formed by natural causes, such as water gathering in pools, and musk-rats burrowing through the walls. . . ."

Again, in 1885, Allen writes of how the mounds within Fort Ancient superficially resemble "two serpents, their heads being the mounds, which are separated from the body by the opening which resembles a ring around the neck. Their bodies are the walls, which, as they bend in and out, and rise and fall, much resembles, [he thinks] two massive green serpents

rolling along the summit of this high hill. If any such resemblance occurs, we think it purely accidental. In relation to the wall across the isthmus, it has been thought to have been the means of defending one part of the work should an enemy gain entrance to the other. . . ."

Allen continues: "The total length of the embankment is about five miles, the area enclosed about one hundred acres. . . . Only one who has personally examined the walls can realize the amount of labor they represent for a people destitute of metallic tools, beasts of burden, and other facilities to construct it." He senses what others have, that there is "satisfactory evidence that between these walls there was a paved street . . . about two feet below the present surface, a pavement of flat stones."

Archaeologists today theorize that the walls, ranging from four to twenty-three feet in height, provided the containment parameters within which to perform ritual ceremonies or conduct commerce for the natives who lived in the region. Sections of these walls clearly were used in correlation with the positions of the sun and the moon to provide a calendar system for the ancient inhabitants.

Wisconsin's Reverend Stephen Peet, who lived from 1831 to 1914, was one of the first to subscribe to the theory that a "lost race of mound builders" existed and built sites like Fort Ancient. In his classic work *Mound Builder*, written in 1881, Peet speculated on what it would have been like to watch the events at that site:

Imagination was not slow to conjure up the scene which was once doubtless familiar to the dwellers at Fort Ancient. A train of worshipers, led by priests clad in their sacred robes, and bearing aloft the holy utensils, pass in the early morning, ere yet the mists have risen in the valley below, along the gently swelling ridge on which the ancient roadway lies. They near the mound, and a solemn stillness succeeds their chanting songs; the priests ascend the hill of sacrifice and prepare the sacred fire. Now the first beams of the rising sun shoot up athwart the ruddy sky, gilding the topmost boughs of the trees. The holy flame is kindled, a curling wreath of smoke arises to greet the coming god; the tremulous hush which was upon all nature breaks into vocal joy, and songs of gladness bursts from the throats of the waiting multitude as the glorious luminary arises in majesty and beams upon his adoring people. A promise of renewed life and happiness.

Vain promise, since even his rays cannot penetrate the utter darkness which for ages has settled over this people.

Today, the Museum at Fort Ancient offers visitors a detailed exploration of the fifteen thousand years of Native American history in the Ohio Valley, near this location. The museum's self-contained classroom and exhibits include a time line and give insights into the daily life of the site's first inhabitants. A prehistoric garden adjacent to the building offers a look at the agricultural plants and methods of these "first Ohioans."

Fort Ancient is seven miles southeast of Lebanon, in Warren County, on State Route 350.

Prehistoric Giant Beavers?

Not all ancient mysteries are bound to the human drama; some give credence to the stories, folklore, and legends of those who came before us. In 1828, British naturalist Charles Fothergill, who had immigrated to Upper Canada in 1816, went in search of the remains of the giant beaver to test his theory that Indian accounts about gargantuan beavers had a factual foundation. Native peoples had grand stories of giant animals creating valleys and flooding lands, an outrageous idea at the time. Fothergill, a publisher-painter and a member of the Legislative Assembly of Upper Canada, is to be credited, in essence, with the theory that another group of Indian tales—those of lake monsters—were actually sightings of giant beavers.

Fothergill never found his behemoth beavers. As it turned out, the first fossilized giant beaver remains were discovered in a peat swamp near Nashport, Ohio, and were described, but not named, by S. R. Hildreth in 1837. Geologist J. W. Foster called the specimen *Castoroides ohioensis* in a publication a year later. In the years since 1838, giant beaver fossil fragments, while scarce, have been found in several of the places where the Indians told of seeing the colossal creatures. *Castoroides* ranged from Florida to the Yukon and from New York State to Nebraska, although it has not been found outside of North America. Three nearly complete specimens are known, from Fairmont and Winchester in Indiana and from Minneapolis, Minnesota.

But we know the most about the giant beaver from one state: Ohio. A possible giant beaver lodge was discovered near New Knoxville in about 1912. Part of a *Castoroides* skull and the lodge itself were located in a peaty layer surrounded by loam. The lodge was said to have been almost four feet high and seven feet in diameter and made from large saplings.

The Indians' legendary animal has been revealed as remarkably real. The giant beaver was the largest rodent in North America during the Ice Age. But mysteries about this unique Ohio animal remain. Unlike the woolly mammoth and cave bear, whose images were so vividly painted on the walls of European caves from Paleolithic times, there are no paintings that depict the giant beaver's actual appearance. However, the similarity between giant beaver and modern beaver skeletons leaves no doubt to scientists like the Canadian Museum of Nature's C. R. Harington that the two animals were much alike. There was only one remarkable difference: size! The skeleton of the giant beaver displayed in Chicago's Field Museum is over seven feet long, the size of a black bear. The giant beaver weighed seven times as much as the three-foot-long modern beaver.

Another enigma remains with regard to these ancient wonders. Canadian naturalist Harington puts it this way: "Giant beavers evidently died out near the close of the last glaciation, about ten thousand years ago. Because they coexisted with early humans in North America, it seems unusual that there is no evidence that people hunted them. Surely a *Castoroides* pelt would have made an excellent coat or sleeping robe!" Someday we may actually find such a prehistoric relic, which will go far toward answering many lingering questions.

Fabled People and Places

Throughout history, adventurous explorers have sought to find mythic lands and mysterious peoples. Here at *Weird Ohio*, we too are on a quest to discover fabled locales and elusive populations. As medieval knights searched for the Holy Grail or the Spanish conquistadors sought El Dorado, we endeavor to find places with names like Knockemstiff, Rogue's Hollow, and Top O' the World. We travel the rural back roads and wooded trails of the state seeking legendary bands of bulbous-headed mutants and isolated enclaves of little people.

We search for these curious lands or people for we have faith that there is more to our wondrous state than just prefab strip malls and postapocalyptic industrial landscapes.

As we travel, we keep an open mind, knowing that these fabled people and places may be like Brigadoon and must be believed to be seen and not the other way around. For we want to believe in them, even though we know that these things we seek may exist only in our own collective imagination.

Knockemstiff

Yes, it really is called Knockemstiff. Or was; no one can quite agree just when and precisely where the oddest of all oddly named Ohio towns lived and, sadly, died. The maps that still show its location give us a general idea: It was somewhere along Ross County's Black Run, probably along Minney Hill or Windy Ridge Road. Beyond that, there's nothing much more conclusive. It was probably on one of the viciously pitched and twisting dirt roads that wind through the countryside southwest of Chillicothe. There used to be a general store, but it's gone; there used to be a bar, but it closed. There never was a Knockemstiff post office. It's enough to make you wonder if the name was just some cartographer's joke.

But the people who live in this part of Huntington Township know Knockemstiff. Every so often, a reporter gets curious and comes by to interview them about their "town" and its bizarre name. They usually tell one of a handful of stories. One says it was named after a big brawl at the local tavern, which was a fixture for many decades as well as the last remaining business in the area. Another tells of a woman who asked a preacher how she could get her cheating husband to stay home. "Knockemstiff," the preacher replied.

Besides the naming of the town, there are numerous other Knockemstiff mysteries, like Devil's Leap. Located behind the old McComis property, these cliffs are haunted by the ghost of a suicide who was said to have leapt from the top because he was tormented by the voice of the devil in his head. Supposedly you can hear him scream all the way down.

The creepiest story out of Knockemstiff is that of the permanently foggy dip in the road known as Foggymoore. One night, a lady and her daughter were driving home and happened upon a man lying in the road on his side with one hand propping up his head, casually smoking a cigarette. Instead of getting up and moving, the guy simply floated away, still in the lying-down position.

Then there is a specter of a beautiful girl named Lindy Sue, who is said to wander the hollows of Knockemstiff. Apparently, she was parked in a buggy with her boyfriend, Clem Slatterson, on a bridge over Paint Creek one night. Later that evening, dogs all over the area started howling uncontrollably. Lindy's body was later discovered on the bridge, strangled. The horse was found a couple of days later by a search party, dead of fright, the buggy smashed. Clem was nowhere to be found. Lindy's ghost haunts the area to this day, but Clem has never been heard from.

Our own trip to Knockemstiff took us past large country homes with lots of property, as well as broken-down trailers and plywood shacks. The dirt roads are almost impassable in the rain, but it's worth the trip just to say you've been to a place called Knockemstiff.

Top Supernatural Entertainment

Your journey to the Top O' the World starts alongside a
dark, winding road. As you park your car and begin the walk up
the darkened dirt path, you find yourself double-checking every few
feet to make sure nothing's following you. Then you start to rewind in
your head one of the legends associated with the area: A young family man
falls from a horse and receives a massive head injury. Perhaps due in part to his
injuries, the man goes insane one night and kills his entire family with an ax while
they sleep. He then goes out to the barn and kills all his horses, including the one that
had injured him. When he was done, the man hanged himself inside the barn. Is it any
wonder this whole area is said to be filled with ghosts?

At the top of the hill, in the Summit County Metro Park, you catch your first glimpse of the barn. You
listen intently for the sound of ghostly horses or screams from a man in anguish. Nothing. Scanning the
woods, you search for movement. But nothing is stirring—at least not yet.

You've heard the stories, so you know exactly where to position yourself in order to see the ghost of the ax-wielding father begin his nightly journey from the house to the barn. About fifteen minutes into your nocturnal surveillance, you nervously light a cigarette. Forty-five minutes and three cigarettes later, you decide to call it quits. Tonight, nothing supernatural is happening.

Back at your car, you wonder whatever made you think you were really going to see anything tonight; you're getting too old to be chasing ghosts. And then you hear it: a long, drawn-out neigh from a horse . . . coming from somewhere behind you. You spin around just in time to hear the sound dissipate over the top of the hill that blocks the old barn from your view. The sound gone, several seconds pass before you realize that you're still holding your breath. You let it out with a loud hissing sound and immediately begin rationalizing. What you just heard must have a natural explanation. But you can't think of one. Stepping into your car, you're reminded of just how wonderful the sound of a car engine turning over can sound. Within seconds, your tires are spraying gravel as you make your way back to civilization . . . with nary a look back in the rearview mirror.

Though the property now called Top O' the World had several owners in the past, it wasn't until it was purchased by Rhea H. and E. Reginald Adam that it acquired its picturesque name. One glance around the property and you know where the name came from. From every angle, the valleys and ravines below give the feeling that you are on top of the world, staring down.

In 1967, the Adam family donated the 162-acre parcel of land, including the house and the barn, to

the Metro Parks system. The entire property was then added to an existing hiking trail, opening up what was once private property to large numbers of curiosity seekers. It wasn't long before the ghost stories started making their rounds. In 2003, concerned over the condition of the house as well as the repeated vandalism and break-ins, park officials had the house demolished. Thank goodness they decided to leave the barn standing!

There is a popular legend in Cuyahoga County, a variation on the man-thrown-from-a-horse story, that says there once was a very rich farmer who lived in the area with his wife and their seven children. The man was so well off that he was able to erect seven barns, one in honor of each of his children, throughout the Cuyahoga Valley. Of course, this is much too romantic a tale to make a good ghost story, so one night the husband went insane and slaughtered his wife and seven children with an ax. He then proceeded to bury their bodies in the first six barns. When he was finished burying the last body, he went out to the seventh barn, the one at Top O' the World, and committed suicide by hanging himself from the rafters. It is the tortured spirit of this farmer that is sometimes spotted as a darkened shape moving through the woods surrounding the barn and sometimes even inside the barn itself.

Seen It ALL at Top O' the World

Since I was sixteen, me and my brother and all our friends have gone up to Top O' the World, most commonly at night. I have seen a man in black in the high grassy area, been chased out by him, been chased out by a guy in black on horseback, been chased out by what I can only describe as half man, half wolf. I've seen spirits of dead children playing in the area around the parking lot and in the parking lot itself. One in particular that got close enough to me was a young girl, maybe about five or six, in a blue printed dress playing with a ball. The other child was a slightly older boy dressed in overalls.

One night, our friend Debby's car was tossed from the road. I was in our friend Chris's van watching as something large and black plowed into the side and lifted it, then watched as something on the other side threw the car back onto the road. Later as we returned to our friend's house, we inspected the large dent on the side, and there is NO WAY it could have been a tree or rock that had done it.

In one incident, me and my friend Matt found a way into the house, and we went into one of the upstairs bedrooms. There was a small doorway leading to a crawl space. As we looked into it, I could feel something watching us from both inside and from the doorway at the same time. It was at that time that a real quick temperature drop happened in the room, and we decided it was time to get out. As we were leaving through the window, I had this horrible feeling that something was on its way up from the basement, and it definitely did NOT want us inside right then.

The whole Highland Square/Walhaven/Valley area seems to have its spirits, some good, some bad. Some are ones that you just really don't want to get involved with. —*RV Wray*

On a Quest for Midget Town

There is a Midget Town around Cincinnati, but it's not like people think. In the early '60s, an eccentric farmer who owned property on the outskirts of the Rumpke (the local waste-management company) landfill decided to go into business running hayrides on his property. He constructed a miniature frontier village, complete with tiny little houses. He also obtained, or else he constructed, tiny red trucks to pull the wagons for the hayrides. Furthermore, his own home, which sits right there among the tiny frontier village, is built into a hillside and appears to be partially underground. The whole operation sits practically on top of the road it's on. It's the middle of the boondocks. The absolute last thing you would expect is to suddenly be driving through a freaking carnival with tiny little houses. It's easy to imagine how someone driving through very late at night might be made completely hysterical if they came upon it.

Despite major vandalism problems due to teens seeking evil midgets, the ranch is still in operation, and they apparently do pretty well renting wagons for festivals and fairs. This could be one explanation for the tales of Midget Town. Or maybe, just maybe, there really is a town full of evil midgets hiding on the outskirts of Cincinnati. Maybe what I found is just their cover story.—*Leon*

Midget Town, Ohio—A River Runs Through It

We have a Midget Town here in Cincinnati. It is near an old fairground, along a road that runs next to the tributary for the Great Miami River. Only midgets live there. They will shoot rock salt and throw rocks at you if you come down there and are over four feet tall. I have never been shot at, but I can tell you the place is definitely not right.—*The Mack Daddy Soprano*

Rock-Throwing Residents in Midget Town, Cincinnati

Essentially, it's part of an old fairground or something similar. It's a miniature town and looks like it was built for kids to play in or something. It's along an old road that follows a tributary that runs into the Great Miami River. The midgets are most likely little figments of people's imagination. I've been down that road many times with no sign of anything. Of course, they could all just come out of the houses after I round the bend.—*Anonymous*

The Vanishing Villagers

I remember as a kid hearing about a ghost town supposedly around Cincinnati, where everyday at like 7 PM or something, everyone disappears. Swings are left swinging, merry-go-rounds still spinning. All of the homes have curtains drawn and no lights on. —*Anonymous*

The Real Skinny on Munchkinland

So where is Tiny Town? Does it even exist? Did a couple of retired circus midgets actually live out here years ago and unwittingly foster these bizarre legends?

Actually, as it turns out, there is a Tiny Town. The "real" one is apparently located not far from Buffalo Ridge, behind the Rumpke dump. And the legend, like so many others, is based on willful misinterpretation and embellishment. The *Cincinnati Post* gives the lowdown on the real story:

From the *Cincinnati Post,* January 10, 1999
By David Wecker

How Anna Ritter's Little Story Got Out of Hand

Anna Gay Ritter heard one time that a good way to ruin a person's business is to make a joke out of it. At any rate, she's not sure how all the stories about Munchkin and Munchkinland got started. She just wishes they'd go away.

But they won't. They pass from one generation to the next, like some bad urban myth, except that these stories have a rural setting. They're vague stories about a group of tiny people who live in tiny houses with tiny windows; stories that somehow have come to center on Anna's land. It might be funny, if it weren't happening to Anna.

To be fair, Anna's 30-acre farm in Colerain Township does have an odd look. She moved here in 1940, with her husband, Percy. It was his idea to call it the Handlebar Ranch Inc. She and Percy were considered city folk then. There was no Mt. Rumpke at the southern edge of the ranch, and their road was a gravel lane. At first, Percy was in the bicycle rental business. He had 20 bikes and charged a quarter an hour. Then he got into the hayride business and bought a team of Belgian draft horses to pull his hay wagon.

Percy had an eccentric way of seeing things. Peggy Pottenger Sickmann—who grew up on a neighboring farm and has been helping out at the ranch for nearly half a century, since she was 10—says Percy was the kind who did a little bit here, a little bit there.

He built a home halfway up a steep hill of stone, hand-hewn logs, mortar, stucco, tile and boards, with a square turret and a balcony that looks down on the Handlebar Ranch Inc.

The ranch itself could be a textbook example of vintage roadside Americana. It looks like a miniature frontier village—a surreal collection of little buildings, all made from the same odd materials as the house. There are dance floors indoors and out, picnic tables, pavilions, barbecue grills and what he called a rathskeller—all decorated with Anna's hand-painted Indian totems and cartoony cowboy murals, all in a jaunty Wild West motif. Anna is still quite a talented artist. Percy died in 1990, but Anna kept up the hayride business. If you're having a party, she'll dispatch a hay wagon. Or she'll book a hayride for a fraternity or a sorority at Miami University or the University of Cincinnati. . . .

But I'm ahead of the story. Years ago—Anna doesn't remember exactly when—Percy came home with a couple of cast-iron school bells he'd bought somewhere. He put them up below the house, at the edge of the road. That was when it started.

"Kids would come in the middle of the night and ring the bells," Peggy says. "The Ritters didn't want them annoying the neighbors, so they'd come out on the balcony and yell at them. And to those kids down on the road, looking up at that balcony, Anna and Percy must've looked kind of small."

Anna is 5-foot-3; Percy was maybe 5-9. It's the only explanation for the stories that Anna and Peggy can imagine. Anna eventually turned the bells upside down and took to planting flowers in them. But even now, the stories persist. Ridiculous stories . . .

Rick Heimtold, a 20-year-old cadet with Colerain Township police, has heard the stories.

"You mean the ones about munchkinland?" he said. "Yeah, I used to go looking for it. We all did, back in high school. There were supposed to be little people there. And if you came around where they lived, they'd throw rocks at you. Those were the stories, anyway.

"So kids were always looking for it. Sometimes, you'd find it. Sometimes, you didn't. But there's all kinds of stories about little people living there."

They show up in the middle of the night in their cars, looking for Munchkins and behaving in the crummiest possible manner. If school's out, Anna has learned she can pretty well figure on a carload of them showing up the night before, screaming and yelling, making a ruckus, sometimes vandalizing her buildings and hollering obscenities.

Anna's no prude. She's no weakling either. Twice a day, she climbs the difficult hill to the barn at the top of her valley to feed a swayback horse that, she says, is older than she is.

"I've got the hide of a crocodile," she says. "But it makes me angry these stories won't go away."

Ghosts, Nazis, and Secret Passageways

When you're driving down Franklin Boulevard in Cleveland, the last thing you'd expect to see is a castle. But then again, when you're talking about the infamous Franklin Castle, anything is possible.

Rumors about Franklin Castle, which is often referred to as the most haunted house in all of Ohio, began almost as soon as Hannes Tiedemann had it built. Tiedemann, a successful German banker who had founded the Euclid Avenue Savings & Trust, was looking for a unique home that would reflect his newfound success as a banker. Tiedemann got what he was looking for. When completed, the four-story, turreted Franklin Castle had close to thirty rooms. It had a grand ballroom that took up the entire fourth floor, and even a carriage house. The outside of the house was adorned with gargoyles, and intricate carvings filled the interior. The top floor of the castle provided wonderful views of both downtown Cleveland and Lake Erie.

When it was finished, Tiedemann moved into Franklin Castle with his wife, Luise; his mother, Wiebeka; and several servants. The first few years there were happy ones for the Tiedemann family and were marked by the births of several children. Soon, however, a dark cloud came to settle over the castle.

Beginning in 1881, tragedy began to stalk the Tiedemann family. Tiedemann's mother and fifteen-year-old daughter, Emma, died within weeks of each other. Even though Wiebeka's death was from natural causes and Emma's was believed to be a result of diabetes, the deaths nonetheless gave rise not only to the story of a curse but also to rumors that Hannes Tiedemann was a controlling, evil man.

Legend says that it was during this time that the infamous hidden rooms and secret passageways were constructed inside Franklin Castle. Why they were created is open to debate. Some say they were created by Tiedemann simply as a way of taking his wife's mind off the recent death of her daughter. Others, however, say the rooms and passages were designed so that Tiedemann could commit heinous crimes, including murdering his niece, a servant girl, and even his daughter Emma without being detected. Still others believe that Mrs. Tiedemann herself had the passages created so that she could sneak past her overbearing husband undetected.

When Luise Tiedemann passed away in 1895, her death was also attributed to the curse or, worse yet, to murder at the hands of her husband, who remarried shortly thereafter. After Luise's death, Tiedemann sold Franklin Castle to a local brewer named Mullhauser and moved out. Some say that even leaving the castle was not enough for Tiedemann to escape its evil power, and in 1908 he died suddenly. Incredibly, his death brought about the end of the Tiedemann family line as the rest of the family, including

Beginning in 1881, tragedy began to stalk the Tiedemann family. Tiedemann's mother and fifteen-year-old daughter, Emma, died within weeks of each other. . . . The deaths gave rise not only to the story of a curse but also to rumors that Hannes Tiedemann was a controlling, evil man.

Tiedemann's grandsons, had all died before him.

Apparently, the curse took some time off during the Mullhausers' stay at the castle. But in 1913 it came back with a vengeance when Franklin Castle was sold to the German Socialist Party. While the castle was officially used only as a place for parties and meetings, rumors quickly spread that the Germans were actually using it as a place from which to spy. Years later, a German shortwave radio was supposedly found hidden up in the rafters. The infamous secret passageways were said to have been used by an underground group of Nazis to machine-gun a large group of people. During Prohibition, a new tunnel was allegedly constructed, running from either the basement of the castle or the carriage house all the way out to Lake Erie.

In January 1968, the German Socialists sold Franklin Castle to James Romano. Almost immediately after moving into the home, members of the Romano family began experiencing strange things. The children would often speak of a newfound friend they would play with up in the fourth-floor ballroom. Oftentimes, the children would ask their mother for extra cookies for their mysterious friend.

Mrs. Romano also began to feel the presence of Mrs. Tiedemann and to hear organ music coming from different areas of the house. Looking for explanations, the family contacted the Northeast Ohio Psychical Research Society, a local team of ghost hunters, to investigate the castle. If the stories are to be believed, one of the hunters ran screaming from Franklin Castle in the middle of the investigation. Shortly after that, the Romanos turned to a Catholic priest for help, but he reportedly refused to bless the house because of what he felt when he stepped inside.

After enduring several more years of ghostly activity, the Romanos finally decided to get rid of the place. In 1974, Franklin Castle was sold to a family who would bring the legend of the castle to the forefront: the Muscatellos.

By all accounts, Sam Muscatello was all too eager to cash in on the legends of Franklin Castle. In addition to offering tours of the house, Sam invited members of the media for walk-throughs. During a live segment on Cleveland radio, host John Webster had a tape recorder pulled from his shoulder and thrown down a staircase. Another time, during taping for a local television piece, crew member Ted Opecec witnessed a ceiling light spinning on its own.

Muscatello began searching the house for more of the alleged secret passageways. His first discovery was an old still that seemed to be left over from Prohibition days. His most shocking discovery, however, was found behind a hidden panel in the tower: Tucked neatly inside was a pile of human bones. Although few deny that real human bones were removed from Franklin Castle, whom they belonged to and how they ended up there has long been debated.

Of course, most took the bones as proof that Hannes Tiedemann was indeed involved in murderous activities.

Some, however, believed that Muscatello himself had stashed the bones there as "proof" of the hauntings of Franklin Castle. The final verdict by authorities was simply that the bones were indeed human and that they were very old.

Unable to make Franklin Castle the haunted success they had hoped, the Muscatello family finally decided to sell it. From them, it passed through a series of owners. Some tried to bring it back to its former glory, but they failed. At one point, a fire destroyed almost all of the fourth-floor ballroom.

Today, the castle looks much the same as it did after the damage caused by the fire was fixed. Windows are still boarded up. On the weedy front lawn are a few potted plants, long since dead and slowly decaying. Franklin Castle stands silent and strong—waiting for someone brave enough to ignore the bloody rumors and ghostly tales and restore it to its former glory.

Melonheads Creep Through the Woods at Night

When you get tired of hearing the same old stories about Bigfoot, Skunk Apes, and the Loch Ness Monster, head on over to Lake County and check out the Melonheads: weird humanlike creatures with enormous heads that roam the countryside in and around Kirtland and Chardon.

As for the origin of the Melonheads, the popular belief is that they were part of secret government testing that involved strange experiments on human subjects. Whatever they were testing, the result was that the subjects' heads all swelled to enormous sizes. As with any good government conspiracy, it was decided that the best thing to do would be to cover the whole thing up. A secret location deep in a woods was quickly established, and the Melonheads were all shipped there in the middle of the night.

Since they were well taken care of, the Melonheads were, for the most part, a passive bunch. However, every once in a while one of them would grow restless for contact with the outside world. Usually waiting until the cover of darkness, a Melonhead or two would slip outside their little commune and creep toward civilization. More often than not, just a glimpse of the outside world would be all the Melonheads would need to send them scampering back to the safety of their little town, which is said to be somewhere in the woods near Wisner Road.

There are a few offshoots of the Melonheads legend in which a doctor features prominently. In those versions, the doctor's name is Crowe (or Crow). In the first version, Dr. Crowe has somehow managed to acquire, either by kidnapping or through a secret deal with the mental hospital he works at, several individuals that he subjects to

bizarre experiments, most of which focus on the brain and head. Due to the severe trauma, the individuals' heads are deformed and misshapen. But since some of Dr. Crowe's experiments also included lobotomies, the Melonheads are rather docile, if not a bit slow. So though every once in a while Dr. Crowe would "lose" a few subjects for a short period of time, he would always be able to round them up rather quickly and return them to his lab.

There is also a variation on the tale, which focuses less on Dr. Crowe and more on his wife. This time, Dr. Crowe and his wife are living in an isolated cabin in the woods and have been asked to care for a group of children stricken with hydrocephalia, a disease that affects the cerebrospinal fluid in one's body and causes the head to swell. Due to the swollen heads, mean-spirited locals began calling the children Melonheads, and the name stuck.

It is said that while assisting her husband in lovingly caring for the hydrocephalic children, Mrs. Crowe began to see how the Melonheads nickname was hurting the children's feelings. Her motherly instincts kicking in, Mrs. Crowe drew the children closer to her, protecting them from the outside world. In turn, the children began to look at Mrs. Crowe as their very own mother. Unfortunately, Mrs. Crowe passed away one day, sending the children's collective world crashing down.

Feeling they were now lost, the children panicked and began running and thrashing about the Crowe cabin. Dr. Crowe attempted to calm them, but to no avail. In the ensuing melee, a lit kerosene lantern was knocked to the floor, which set the old cabin on fire, engulfing everything, including Dr. Crowe and all the children. The Melonheads

said to roam the woods in this version are the ghosts of the children who burned to death in the cabin fire.

The final legend associated with the Melonheads doesn't even mention them, but it bears discussion because again Dr. Crowe is the central figure. Besides, it's the most disturbing of all the variants. Here, Dr. Crowe performs illegal abortions in his cabin in the woods and even manages to find the time to kill a deformed baby or two in his spare time. Afterward, he would bury the tiny bodies around the knoll near his cabin. Abandoned now, the basement of the doctor's house is said to echo with the cries from the departed babies, as does the area surrounding the knoll. With that in mind, it should come as no surprise that the bridge near where Dr. Crowe's cabin is said to be is now officially a Crybaby Bridge.

No matter where they came from, most kids in the area know somebody whose sister's best friend knew a guy whose dentist saw the Melonheads. Not to be outdone by a dentist, local high school kids drive around the area late at night, looking for the Melonheads. Some say that at one time there was a family with a mentally disabled child with an oversized cranium who used to stand at the fence at the edge of his parents' property, and that all the myths and horror stories are much ado about one unfortunate kid.

At any rate, the Melonheads are most strongly associated with Wisner Road, near Chardon. They are also often sighted on King Memorial Road, especially in or near the King Memorial Cemetery. (When the road enters Geauga County it becomes Mentor Road, and the graveyard commonly called King Memorial is technically named Larned Cemetery.) Why they like it here is anybody's guess. Maybe Dr. Crowe and his wife are buried there, and they come to visit the graves. . . . Hey, we just made that up, but it sounds like as good an explanation as any.

Animal Corpses Mark Trail Through Melonheads' Woods

I live in Eastlake, not far from Kirtland. I've seen the burnt shack of Dr. Crowe and saw the chain that the "Melonheads" hung his dead corpse from. I can say as one person that the Melonheads are in fact real. Close by Kirtland, there is a small castle for picnics and BBQs and miles of hiking trails. When you walk down these trails, you can see some mutilated animals in the deep parts of the woods. I've been hiking back in the woods for as long as I can remember. Not one time while strolling have I not seen small dead animals and mutilated corpses and bones.—*Rich Gleir*

Bad Moon Rising over Melonhead Country

The story as I have heard it is that Dr. Crowe injected these kids' brains with water. This caused the heads to swell up like melons. Anyway, he kept them locked away in cages in a green barn next to his house. Now at this point the story gets a little fuzzy—either the barn burnt down in an accident and a few of the Melonheads escaped, or the barn is still there. Anyway, these Melonheads still roam the area out near the Holden Arboretum. Supposedly, they come out only at night, and if it is a full moon, they are extremely vicious and will attack any humans they see. However, they have a hard time seeing. If you wear dark clothes—blacks, reds, dark greens or blues—you will be safe. But if you have on any bright colors or white, you are a prime target.—*Justin V.*

Caught a Glimpse of a Melonhead at Mitchell's Mill

I know the Dr. Crowe story is sorta true, but there are some facts missing. First of all, Dr. Crowe did exist, but he lived in the 1940s and was a dentist. There could have been another Dr. Crowe, though. Second, full moons have nothing to do with the Melonheads' nasty behavior. I know this from experiences with them and from experiences that others have had. My first experiences with what I think were Melonheads was on the East Branch of the Chagrin River.

My brother and I were driving along Mitchell's Mill, and I saw a quick flash out of the corner of my eye. I looked right and saw something by a tree. It was very blurry, though. I was so scared I screamed, and my brother looked out of his window. "What the hell was that?" he said. I guess he saw it too, because he turned around at the spring and we headed back. This was near Mentor Road, which is off of Auburn.—*Jay*

Ditched Melonhead Along Roadside

On October 5, 2001, my stepfather, mom, stepbrother, and me were driving down Chilocothe Rd. in Chardon when we came upon this stretch of road that had fields on both sides and an irrigation ditch running parallel with each side of the road. Just then, I looked out my window and I saw him—a Melonhead! He, or it, was running along next to the ditch. Since the ditch was too wide to jump over, it was coming close (like it was about to jump), then pulling away. At the time, we were going about 45–50 mph. The Melonhead was actually keeping up with us.

He looked about the same height as me (five feet seven inches) and was wearing brown pants that were very ripped up and were held together at the seams by what looked like corn husks. Its head was a very light brown tint. It had two holes in the sides of its head, which I think were ears. Its head was swelled up, and its eyes were very big looking. Just as we turned a curve, it jumped into the woods.—*Tony*

Solving the Melonhead Mystery

My father's house rests in a secluded, thickly wooded area off of Mitchells Mill Road in Chardon. When my family relocated there in the mid-'70s, my older sister's middle school classmates turned white as a ghost when she told them where our house was.

"You live in Melonhead Country!" they exclaimed. She was then frightened with tales of Dr. Crowe, the evil man who had performed cruel experiments on hydrocephalic children to make them into cannibalistic fiends.

The legend states that Dr. Crowe's laboratory was located on Wisner Road near a bridge, but this road is actually split in half due to a washout. One half is in Chardon, one is in Kirtland, and both feature a different bridge as landmarks. I also became aware that high school students from Chardon often disguised themselves as Melonheads to frighten necking teenagers. Still, even if the reported sightings had been pranks, there had to be some fact to the myth—the story was just too bizarre to have been entirely invented by locals.

Despite the passage of several years and my own relocation to Los Angeles, I was haunted by the secrets of the woods in northeast Ohio, so I decided to get to the bottom of the Melonhead myth once and for all. A conveniently planned trip back to Ohio for the week of Thanksgiving afforded me the opportunity to solve some mysteries about my hometown.

Stories tell that Dr. Crowe was either killed by his patients or perished in the fire when his cottage burned down. Another tale has him swinging by the neck from a beam of the Arch Barn on Mitchells Mill in an apparent suicide.

I went to the library and found an article from the *West Geauga Sun* claiming that "Dr. Kroh" had been influenced by Gregor Mendl and was experimenting on humans to increase the size of their heads. His experiments failed, and in a fit of pique he piled his genetic mutations into his car and left them by the side of Chagrin River Road in Kirtland, where they presumably fled into the woods and have remained to this day.

I next visited the Health Department to look up death certificates on any Chardon residents named Crow, Crowe, or Kroh. There were records of people with these names, but none of them appeared to be doctors, and all had died of natural causes. My investigation was hindered by the fact that I could not pin these events down to a specific time period or location, assuming they had happened at all.

Just when I thought I would be returning to Los Angeles empty-handed, I tracked down an expert on local folklore who was able to give me the official versions of the Melonhead legend and the facts that it originated from.

According to her, Dr. Crowe and his wife had lived together in a cottage where they cared for children afflicted with hydrocephalus. The children adored Mrs. Crowe but weren't so keen on her husband. One night, the couple got into an argument, and Mrs. Crowe fell against a cabinet, suffering a fatal blow to the head. Thinking Dr. Crowe had murdered his wife, the Melonheads attacked and killed him. They then proceeded to tear the place apart, setting fire to the cottage in the process. Some of them survived to dwell in the surrounding woods, living off animals and occasionally attacking humans when threatened (or really hungry).

In the late '50s and early '60s, there were a few children with hydrocephalus who lived in northeast Ohio. One of them lived on Wisner Road and was enrolled in the Kirtland school district. At that time, the road was desolate, and teenagers would often go there to park. The boy and his "normal" friends, who were all preteens, would creep up on parked cars and scare away the older kids. The frightened students would tell their peers at school that they had been "chased by the Melonheads"!

Children afflicted with hydrocephalus do not live very long, and while the other "Melonheads" are now businessmen in Kirtland, the original Melonhead died of natural causes and is buried in Kirtland South Cemetery.

There was apparently a man named Crow (or Kroh) who moved to Ohio from Chicago in 1957 and lived on Wisner Road. He was working on a cure for tuberculosis. Any connection between him and the boy with hydrocephalus is unsubstantiated, but who knows? The woods along Kirtland–Chardon Road have produced many strange tragedies and mysteries. As my plane took off for Los Angeles, I could feel the magnetic pull of those mysterious woods drawing me in for further adventures.—*Ryan Orvis*

The pilot . . . said that a gray, sixty-foot-long domed, cigar-shaped object nearly collided with his helicopter at an estimated speed of 600 knots.

unidentified objects hovering over their city. Eyewitnesses described the objects as cigar-shaped. Flash-forward to June 8, 1966, when we find a man driving on Sandusky Road between Kansas and Toledo. He sees an object appear suddenly out of the blue. It appeared to be a metallic UFO, which flew low and away to the northeast. The eyewitness reported that it was completely quiet and the size of an airliner.

Next, we must mention "the great UFO wave" of October 1973. Widespread in nature, one sighting is of special interest. On October 18, 1973, in Mansfield, a city well known for its bizarre beast history, there was an encounter between a UFO and a Bell helicopter. The pilot, Captain Lawrence J. Coyne, said that a gray, sixty-foot-long domed, cigar-shaped object nearly collided with his helicopter at an estimated speed of 600 knots. Coyne made a sudden descent in order to avoid collision. The object was said to have a light, which it used to scan the helicopter. Several other eyewitnesses confirmed the encounter.

The history of cigar-shaped UFO sightings in Ohio continues into this century too. In Wilson, on December 8, 2002, at about nine p.m., a group of witnesses spotted a UFO flying over their town that then went out of view over the tree line. One witness who had exited the highway to go into the city spotted the big, bright light in the sky. Said to be about a hundred and fifty feet off the ground and two miles away, it was definitely cigar-shaped and moved with the eyewitnesses as they drove into the city. The observers, who were traveling at 60 mph, said the object was doing about 150 mph.

UFOs in the Galion Skies

In Galion, Ohio, on Nazor Road, I have three times seen something unexplainable in the sky. Each time at different distances in the sky but as close as (my guess is) about a quarter mile away and still appearing to be very large. This particular instance, which happened about five years ago, I was with a friend of mine in the backseat of his mother's car. We saw a huge saucer shape floating in the sky with bright light radiating from what appeared to be several separate lighting units (it could have been one curvy lighting apparatus going all the way around). It hovered in the sky for what seemed like minutes, although it couldn't have been that long as we were driving by. Then, as we stared gaping at this, it vanished. No light shooting across the sky. No sound. It just disappeared. Something this big doesn't do this unless, well, unless it's not from this world. I've heard other things from people in this area regarding strange sightings. It might be something to look into. —*Bess Basye*

Ohio's Classic MIB Case

Although turned into some sort of comedic relief by recent science-fiction motion pictures, the real history of ufology has been intertwined with the so-called bizarre "Men in Black" cases (or MIBs) for years. Intriguingly, Ohio was the host of a classic MIB case, which merged with the story of a giant birdlike creature called Mothman (for more about Mothman, see the "Bizarre Beasts" chapter). In fact, our story of Ohio's MIB begins with an encounter with Mothman.

On Sunday, November 27, 1966, at about ten thirty in the morning, eighteen-year-old Connie Carpenter was driving home from church when she came face-to-face with the Mothman, almost causing her to lose control of her automobile. She described it as a gray creature standing on the golf course near Mason, West Virginia. The thing suddenly flew straight at her car. She is one of the few people who actually saw the creature's face, but perhaps due to her trauma, her description—"It was horrible"— didn't include enough detail to be helpful. In 2001, when the David Grabias documentary *The Search for the Mothman* (which is included in the special-edition DVD of the movie *The Mothman Prophecies*) was being produced, Carpenter was one of the few witnesses to refuse an interview, having her husband talk on camera instead. Connie's posttraumatic difficulties appear to issue not just from her encounter with Mothman but also, and perhaps more importantly, from her brush with the Men in Black.

Connie Carpenter would have many problems after her Mothman sighting. Early in February 1967, she married Keith Gordon, and they moved across the river to a two-family house in Middleport, Ohio. They didn't get a telephone immediately because they'd had so much trouble in West Virginia. Strange people seemed to be around too. And then there's what today is characterized as her near-kidnapping by an MIB.

At eight fifteen a.m. on February 22, 1967, Carpenter left her house to go to school. As she started to walk down the street, a large black car pulled up alongside her. She later identified it as a 1949 Buick. The occupant of the car opened the door and gestured for her to come over. Thinking that the man was seeking directions, Connie approached him. He was young, clean-cut, and about twenty-five years old, wearing a colorful shirt. His hair was neatly combed, and he appeared to be tan. This suntan was an interesting detail, which has turned up in other MIB accounts. Connie said the car appeared to be brand-new inside and out even though it was a vintage model. This detail has also cropped up many times in our Men in Black investigations. Some of these old cars have that new-car smell inside, according to various MIB witnesses. As she drew close, the man grabbed her, but she struggled and ran away.

During the filming of the documentary, Connie's husband reported that she was never the same after that, that she never really went outside again, and she certainly doesn't like to talk about those days. Today, the Connie Carpenter episode figures as one of the more memorable MIB cases, particularly because it includes a Mothman encounter.

The Strange Talents of John D. Reese

One of the more wondrous and intriguing phenomena Fort liked to document was people he said had "strange talents." One such individual hailed from Ohio. But by the end of his life, Fort would have begun to tell this tale: "Upon Nov. 29, 1931, died a wild talent," he would write in chapter 27 of *Wild Talents.* According to the *New York Herald Tribune* of November 30, 1931, Fort noted, John D. Reese, a "healer," had died in his home in Youngstown.

The *Tribune* retold the story of the Ohio healer: "He never studied medicine. The only instruction he ever received was from an aged healer in the mountains in Wales, when he was a boy. Physicians could not explain his art, and, after satisfying themselves that he was not a charlatan, would shrug, and say simply that he had 'divine power.' "

Fort wrote that Reese was about thirty years old when he became aware of his talent. One day, in 1887, a man working in a mill fell from a ladder and was injured. It was "a severe spinal strain," according to a physician. The paper continued: "Mr. Reese stooped and ran his fingers up and down the man's back. The man smiled, and while the physician and the mill hands gaped in wonder, he rose to his feet, and announced that he felt strong again, with not a trace of pain. He went back to work, and Mr. Reese's reputation as a healer was spread abroad."

Fort recounts that there were "thousands of cases of successful treatments. Hans Wagner, shortstop of the Pittsburgh Pirates, was carried from the baseball field one day: Something in his back had snapped, and it seemed that his career had ended. He was treated by Reese and within a few days was

back shortstopping." The baseball player who was healed that day is better known by his nickname, Honus Wagner.

Hans "Honus" Wagner (1874–1955), called the "Flying Dutchman," played for the Pirates most of his career and went on to be a charter member of the baseball Hall of Fame. The following article appeared in the September 1939 issue of *The Bulletin,* the baseball periodical of its day: "Few years ago baseball scribes reverently passed bowlegged Pirate Wagner into baseball's Hall of Fame at Cooperstown, New York, making him first, along with Ty Cobb and Babe Ruth, to cross the threshold of diamond immortals. Nor is Honus Wagner without honor in his own city. 'Wagner Days' were common in 1902, 1903, 1909, years when the Flying Dutchman and the Pirates were bowling over the rest of the National League. There was a Wagner Day all over the circuit when he stepped out of active, major-league playing harness in 1917, and another day of kudos when he returned to the Pirates as a coach in 1932."

Today, even young baseball fans know of Honus Wagner, because his early baseball card is one of the rarest around. Sotheby's sold the pristine, 1909-issued Wagner card, produced by a tobacco company of the day, for an eye-popping $451,000 auction record in 1991. Wal-Mart discount stores offered the card as top prize in a sports card clearance raffle that grossed more than $22.5 million in the mid-1990s. The "Mona Lisa of baseball cards," the Honus Wagner T206 tobacco card was sold on eBay for $1.1 million plus a buyer's premium of $165,000 in July 2000.

But none of this would have happened without the unexplainable and "wild talent" of John D. Reese, the Ohio healer.

Weird Tales and Wicked Crimes

A number of odd, often fatal incidents occurred along the Ohio Valley during the time of the Mothman flap and the UFO wave of 1966–1967. The place does seem to be a magnet for weird tales and wicked crimes, strange deaths, and more.

The first sighting of Mothman was filed by reporter Mary Hyre. The creature was spotted on November 15, 1966, near Point Pleasant, West Virginia. Exactly thirteen months later, on December 15, 1967, Point Pleasant's Silver Bridge, which crosses the Ohio River, collapsed. Twenty-six months later (thirteen x two) exactly, on February 15, 1970, reporter Hyre died at the age of fifty-four after a brief illness. Hyre had been the Point Pleasant correspondent for the Athens newspaper *The Messenger* and during the 1960s episodes had become a close friend of Mothman investigator and author John A. Keel.

In his books, Keel mentions television personality Fred Freed. Freed is little known today, but his documentaries, *NBC White Paper,* which began in 1960, are acclaimed as groundbreaking. In September 1973, Keel and Freed began meeting regularly to discuss a White Paper that would concentrate on the UFO flaps and other activity, such as the Mothman, in the Ohio Valley. This documentary would never be made. In March 1974, Freed died suddenly of a heart attack at the age of fifty-three.

Nowadays, Keel sees himself less as a Fortean than a demonologist. Ohio transformed Keel, and he argued that "ultraterrestrials"—supernatural "transmogrifications" of paranormal energy from an unimaginable other reality—have been frightening, manipulating, and even destroying human beings from the beginning of mankind's history, especially in the Ohio Valley in 1966–1967.

Lawyer and author Julie Hilden noted in 2003 the links between the movie *The Matrix* and Ohio mayhem. The premise of *The Matrix* is that life on earth is an elaborate facade; the real world is elsewhere. We humans are nothing but slaves to an evil cyberintelligence that uses us for its own malevolent purposes. Writing in *Findlaw's Writ,* Hilden found that "two defendants in criminal cases, by offering their strange beliefs about *The Matrix* as evidence of a mental disorder, have successfully asserted pleas of not guilty by reason of insanity. In each case, the *Matrix*-based plea was accepted by the judge."

Paranormal rumors about the Cincinnati "Bone Collector"—a frightening apparition that terrorized the city in the middle of the twentieth century—still circulate too. In Cincinnati, during the height of the Bone Collector scare, some residents were seeking relief from the heat by sitting in front of their apartment building. Suddenly, they said, they saw a "huge shadow" cross the lawn in front of them, then "bounce upward into a pecan tree." A dim gray light illuminated the figure in the tree. It was a tall man with a "black cape, skintight pants, and quarter-length boots." The figure was dressed in "gray or black tight-fitting clothes." One witness thought she saw wings, but possibly this was an optical illusion caused by the cape. After a few minutes, the figure "just melted away," his disappearance followed by a "loud swoosh" across the street and the rapid ascent of a rocket-shaped object. Investigating police officers judged the witnesses as sincere and clearly frightened.

Dayton's Hangar 18

Arizona senator Barry Goldwater asked to look inside it. Presidents, tourists, and ufologists have tried to see what's there. How many aliens from the crash at Roswell, it is asked—as if the fact of the crash had already been established—are stored at a special storage facility at Wright-Patterson Air Force Base in Dayton? But the myths of Hangar 18 are hard to pin down and live on today.

According to reports, on or around July 2, 1947, a flying saucer crashed during a violent thunderstorm in a remote area of New Mexico, just northeast of Corona, west of Roswell. Military personnel from Roswell Army Air Force Base quickly cleaned up the crash site. Roswell has always been a super-secret location because it's where the military units with atom bombs were stationed. In addition to the crashed-saucer reports, unconfirmed eyewitness accounts said that four gray-skinned alien bodies—dead spacemen no more than three or four feet tall—were also recovered from the crash.

Where would these items of national security interest be taken? The remains of this spacecraft and its occupants were placed, we are told, on huge transports and quickly flown to the infamous Hangar 18 at Wright-Patterson Air Force Base.

Did any of these events actually take place? Who knows now? One thing is clear: Those who believe the story also believe that Hangar 18 at Wright-Patterson is where the dead aliens would have been stored.

Senator Goldwater, who was a brigadier general in the U.S. Air Force Reserve, did actually ask his friend General Curtis LeMay if he could take a peek in the room at Wright-Patterson where he'd heard that the alien bodies were being kept. LeMay's curt reply, according to Goldwater, was: "Not only can't you get into it, but don't you ever mention it to me again."

In the 1960s to '70s, one of the most prominent ufologists in Ohio was Leonard H. Stringfield. To find out if all the skepticism, ridicule, and jokes about Hangar 18 that came from within the ranks of ufology were justified, Stringfield decided to conduct a series of serious investigations and interviews. As ufology historian Jerome Clark points out in his books, Stringfield then began

publishing a series of monographs with credible firsthand accounts of people who said they had seen the bodies at Wright-Patterson. As Clark writes in *Encyclopedia of Strange and Unexplained Physical Phenomena* (1993), what was striking about Stringfield's informants' descriptions of pear-headed, slant-eyed, gray, four-feet-tall aliens, given in 1979, is "the anticipation of the type of being that would figure in the UFO-abduction lore of the 1980s and beyond. Humanoids of this sort are rare in the early UFO literature of occupant reports." Clark's work confirmed that others had heard or seen some very strange things in storage at Wright-Patterson.

But skeptics are hard on the story of Roswell and the grays at Hangar 18. What we do know is that while Wright-Patterson Air Force Base may not house aliens, for certain it does contain wonderful archives and alleged outer-space pancakes.

UFO investigator Gray Barker mentions in his *Book of Saucers* that he discovered an article in a 1922 edition of the Lincoln, Nebraska, *Daily Star* that quoted an eyewitness who had seen a large circular object land near his house and watched an eight-foot-tall being emerge from it.

This is significant, for as unexplained phenomena investigator John Keel has pointed out: "Dr. Jacques Vallee found a remarkably similar report from Nebraska in that same year, 1922, in a letter buried in the Air Force UFO files at Dayton, Ohio. The letter writer, William C. Lamb, was hunting near Hubbell, Nebraska; when, at 5:00 AM on Wednesday, February 22, 1922 he heard a high-pitched sound and saw a large, dark object pass overhead, blotting out the stars. He hid behind a tree, he said, and watched as the object landed. Next he saw 'a magnificent flying creature' which landed like an airplane and left tracks in the snow. It was at least eight feet tall. It passed by the tree where Lamb was hiding, and he tried to follow its tracks but never managed to catch up with it."

The point, of course, is not the Nebraska story but that evidence of this event is in Dayton. And there is one other semihumorous example that has been enjoyed in the annals of ufology.

Pancakes from Space

On April 18, 1961, Joe Simonton was having a late breakfast at eleven a.m. when some low jetlike noises disturbed him and he went outside. Joe saw a disk land, a hatch open, and a nonthreatening being get out. There were three humanoids in the silver craft that landed in Eagle River, Wisconsin, that morning. The visitors didn't speak English, and all communication took place in the form of gestures. But according to Joe, he also telepathically picked up a message to get some water in a jug for the entity. Then, according to the Air Force report: "Looking into the [saucer] he saw a man 'cooking' on some kind of flameless cooking appliance." They were fixing what Joe took to be pancakes.

Apparently in trade for the water, they gave Joe four pancakes. Each one was about three inches in diameter and had little holes throughout its surface. Joe ate one. "It tasted like cardboard," he told the Associated Press. Fortunately for future alien investigation, he restrained himself from eating the other three.

Astronomer J. Allen Hynek was dispatched by the U.S. Air Force to investigate. He took one of the pancakes away for government analysis at the Air Force Technical Intelligence Center. They found it to be made from flour, sugar, and grease. One writer, Jay Rath, says it was rumored that the wheat in the pancake was "of an unknown type."

In his *High Strangeness: UFOs From 1960 through 1979: The UFO Encyclopedia,* Volume 3 (1996), Jerome

Clark gives a more detailed rundown of the Joe Simonton case under "Eagle River CE3," on pages 168–175. Clark's report focuses on the pancakes. He notes that the "pancakes" were "still hot" when Simonton took a bite out of one of them.

The official Air Force verdict for the Simonton Pancake Incident: "Unexplained." Clark basically concurred: "There was, and is, no evidence to suggest that Joe Simonton cooked up—in the literal sense—a bogus UFO story."

Fortean investigator George Wagner tells *Weird Ohio* that he actually saw the famed Simonton "space pancakes." Guess where? That's right, at Wright-Patterson Air Force Base. In the 1970s, Wagner wrote: "My younger brother and I drove up to the United States Air Force Museum at Wright-Patterson to see Glenn Miller's trombone. Not far away from the Miller exhibit was another devoted to 1950s flying saucer contactees. Here was the 'pancake' fragment, behind plate glass, stapled (single staple) to a piece of white cardboard. The piece had a strikingly 'honeycombed' appearance, nearly as much air-holes as substance, but this may have been due to the 'outer space' food item drying out over the years. I really didn't have much experience at studying 15-year-old pancakes!"

So if you're ever at Wright-Patterson on your tour of weird Ohio, stop by. Ask if you can see the aliens, but be happy if they at least show you the "space pancakes."

Spontaneous Human Combustion: Truth or Tales?

Spontaneous human combustion (SHC) is the name used to capture the bizarre event in which human beings appear to burst into fire and flame with no possible source of ignition. Most of the records of SHC talk of these individuals as if they appear to have burned from the inside out.

SHC is first discussed in modern literature in the Charles Dickens novel *Bleak House.* In the preface to the second edition of his novel, Dickens supports the reality of the SHC death of his character named Krook by citing several real cases. In an intriguing footnote to this preface, Dickens writes: "Sometime around the year 1853, a German liquor-shop in Columbus, Ohio, mysteriously burst into flames and was consumed." In a still later footnote added to this preface, Dickens writes: "Another case [of SHC], very clearly described by a dentist, occurred at the town of Columbus, in the United States of America, quite recently. The subject was a German, who kept a liquor-shop, and was an inveterate drunkard."

What is the truth to this supposed case of spontaneous human combustion in Columbus in about 1853? No one knows, despite our attempts to track down more information in old newspapers.

Then, during 2004, artist Ashleigh Talbot assisted with the resurfacing of another old Ohio SHC case. Talbot writes of this "Fire From Heaven" by saying that he found true stories in old science journals from the Victorian era. His Ohio case goes like this:

In 1907 some roustabouts were working on the Bostick Carnival in Wilmington, Ohio and were much surprised to find a gruesome sight. They came upon a man weeping over a pile of ash, of which there were three charred bones, one resembling a hand, which clutched five coins. The distraught man regained his composure and recalled the previous night. DeGarmo Bushea claimed that he and his friend Otto Rudolph had spent the previous day off drinking in town and then returned to the lot to play cards. After Otto lost all his week's pay, he managed to win back a few coins on the final play before finally leaving. His friend stepped out for his first pipe of the morning when he saw a strange flash of light. It was there he found a blue flame spouting from Otto's stomach area much like a blowtorch. DeGarmo ran to find some water but his efforts were in vain. The bones were buried on the Carnival lot and DeGarmo worked for 23 more years in the Carnival business, and kept the five charred coins in a purse in his pocket at all times.

The phenomenon of SHC remains unexplained today, though there are ongoing investigations around the country looking into this sinister form of death by fire.

Akron's Lizard Lady

All right, the *Weird Ohio* team is not afraid to go anyplace, so here we go—back to 1910 and the case of a young woman who died a premature death. And the cause of her passing away was those darned live lizards in her stomach! Unbelievable? Apparently, it is so incredible that official records were changed after the fact because the story was, well, too hard to stomach.

Poor Akron native Lovie Herman had suffered very much in her short life. There were the stomach pains, the hemorrhages, and the occasional blackouts. She often had problems breathing. As she grew up, her skin became splotchy and her lips turned purple. By the time she was twenty, she weighed less than ninety pounds but stood five feet six and had a hearty appetite. Throughout the years, doctors had told her she had a respiratory problem, heart disease, tuberculosis, or typhoid fever. But they really didn't know. That is, until she died.

Soon after midnight on December 9, 1910, Lovie Herman passed away. As Akron reporter Mark J. Price wrote, the reported cause of death "was the stuff of nightmares."

Dr. Alex J. McIntosh, Herman's attending physician, found and then fully certified that his patient had died "due to stomach trouble caused by lizards in the stomach poisoning the entire system."

Yes. Lizards.

"Two Lizards In Stomach Cause Death," the *Akron Beacon Journal* shouted.

"There is absolutely no question about the lizards being found in the girl's stomach, for I have the two largest ones preserved in a bottle in my office," Dr. McIntosh noted. He also reported finding a batch of eggs in a tiny ball.

"Live Lizards, For 13 Years In Girl's Stomach, Slowly Poison To Death," the *Akron Press* exclaimed.

A few days before Herman's death, Dr. McIntosh said, he gave the woman a strong dose of medicine under the assumption that she was suffering from a tapeworm. That's when, he said, she could feel the green lizards "crawl up her throat." Herman's parents told the doctor that Lovie had taken a swim in a "cool, refreshing spring" near Millersburg a dozen years earlier, and it must have been there that the girl accidentally swallowed tiny lizards or possibly their eggs.

"They are each three and a half inches in length," he said. "One lizard is as well formed as any I have ever seen. I also extracted several smaller lizards from Miss Herman's stomach, but I have kept only the two largest ones. The head, mouth, and tail on both are to be plainly seen."

Reporter Price wrote: "Lova J. Herman, known as 'Lovie' to her family, had been sick since she was a child. She was treated at a Chicago sanitarium for suspected tuberculosis, but she wasn't cured. She then moved to Cleveland with her mother, Ellen, to be treated at Lakeside Hospital for suspected heart troubles. McIntosh, a Cleveland physician, deduced that Herman was suffering from a parasite because of her abnormal appetite. After making the shocking discovery of the lizards, he said, he withheld food from his patient for a few days in an attempt to starve any remaining reptiles."

Then Dr. McIntosh gave her another dose of medicine:

"Miss Herman was thought to be improving, but at midnight Thursday she died in her mother's arms just after remarking that she thought she was going to recover," the *Akron Press* of 1910 wrote.

But the medical establishment was in an uproar. This could not be. Seventeen doctors attended a postmortem exam at the funeral, including McIntosh, Summit County coroner Harry S. Davidson, Dr. Clinton J. Hays of Akron, Dr. Edgar S. Menough of Cleveland, and Dr. William S. Chase of Akron.

Dr. McIntosh felt he was right and told the media at the time: "The postmortem proved the previous diagnosis correct. . . . The lizards had eaten almost through the walls of the stomach, and a few small ones as thick as a broom straw remained." Herman's parents supported the doctor.

The other doctors did not see it that way. They said they "found nothing in the stomach" and instead talked about a possible heart condition. The Summit County coroner abruptly said: "Dr. McIntosh at the postmortem failed to enlighten sixteen other physicians present, except when we questioned him closely. . . . The only thing I could see was that the stomach was inflamed and congested. That could be caused by the action of the heart."

Cleveland health officer Clyde E. Ford denied the death certificate that Dr. McIntosh had written, saying that the explanation of lizards was "too absurd to discuss. It is simply impossible."

Beacon Journal reporter Mark J. Price summed up what happened next: "Confronted with allegations that his claims were false, McIntosh held a closed-door meeting at Ford's Cleveland office on Dec. 13, 1910, and completely retracted his lizard story. Lovie Herman's 1910 death certificate can be found on file at the Ohio Historical Society in Columbus. The cause of death has been scribbled out."

Miami's Crop Circles

Fall often brings sightings of mysterious crop circles in Ohio, and in September 2004 the Miami Valley was the place to look.

Major John DiPietro of the Miami Township Police Department spotted the pattern of interlocking circles pressed into the cornfield late in August, according to Jay Phares, Miami Township's community resource officer. DiPietro was riding in a WHIO television news helicopter scouting sites for DUI checkpoints when he saw the circles and snapped a photograph.

The photo appeared on the cover of the *Miamisburg–West Carrollton News* on September 9, 2004. The crop circles are in a field owned by the Miamisburg School District, right next door to a Miami Township fire station and service garage. Crop circle investigator Jeffrey Wilson called the design found in the field off Linden Avenue just east of the Miamisburg line "the most impressive corn crop

formation I've ever seen," and he says he has seen dozens. Although there have been larger, more elaborate designs pressed into crops like wheat or soybeans, Wilson said he's heard of only one crop circle in a cornfield that was larger than the one in Miami Township.

"It's impressive not just because of its size but because of the exactness of the geometry," he said. "I've seen lots of crop circles that were obviously hoaxes, but this one didn't have the signs of mechanical damage to the plants you sometimes see in obvious fakes. The corn stalks were laid flat but not broken, and there was some interweaving."

Wilson, who lives in Williamsburg, east of Cincinnati, is the director of a volunteer group called the Independent Crop Circle Researchers Association. He said he became intrigued with crop circles in 1989 and has been visiting sites to examine the formations scientifically since 1996.

Miami Township service administrator Jim Woolf said several people, apparently tipped off to the location via the Internet, showed up the first week in September 2004 to see the circles.

"We had license plates from northern Ohio, Illinois, all over," Woolf said. "I don't think any of my guys have been out in the field to see it, though. We had people coming from Illinois, but we didn't feel it was worth going next door for."

"The plants were all swirled down counterclockwise," Wilson said. "Along the stems of soybean plants where the branches bend off, the leaf bases had been shriveled up and browned as if they had been subjected to some sort of heat damage. . . . I think we're going to say that this one was authentic."

Ohio's fields appear to be great canvases to whoever wants to use them. The Independent Crop Circle Researchers Association expects more strange artwork in the years to come.

These images *are similar to the crop circles in the Miami Valley*

Phantom Felines

Westerville, Ohio, is a mere mile from Interstate 270, the vast ring of highway that keeps the sprawl of Columbus so neatly contained. Interstate 270, like others of its kind in America, serves as a barrier that separates suburb from city and wildlife from man. But Westerville is not a suburban community of square little houses and clipped lawns. Rather, it comprises cornfields, country roads where speed limits are difficult to enforce, scattered homes and farmhouses, and, of course, trailer parks. It is from the residents of trailer courts that we find some of the strangest reports of Ohio's mystery beasts.

When corporations push out of the cities into the countryside, grateful local officials in the new areas introduce sidewalks, stop signs, sewage systems—and zoning laws that eliminate trailer parks. This forces mobile home parks to move farther out, beyond the new city limits. In a way, the inhabitants of trailers are becoming the pioneers of our civilization. They relocate on the edges of the countryside, often with little more than a thin sheet of metal between them and the unknown. Perhaps because of this, many occupants of trailer courts find their confrontations with the unexplained more frequent than they desire.

In June 1979, an unknown large feline, a "phantom panther," was seen at the Lake Estates Home Park in Westerville. The elusive phantom panther is not new to central Ohio. Back in 1947, Stanley Belt saw one at nearby Kirkwood. In May and July 1962, near Urbana, a major "black panther" flap occurred. Over a dozen people said they saw a big midnight-black cat with a long tail and big eyes. One incident involved Mr. and Mrs. Darrell Goffs, who viewed the panther jumping eight feet from a tree, leaving behind tracks with "distinct claw marks."

But back to the Lake Estates sightings. Starting in late May 1979, Delaware County sheriff Bill Lavery began getting calls from residents who claimed to have seen a large catlike animal resembling a cougar. A big feline had already killed some sheep in the town of Delaware, and in nearby Sunbury, some people had actually spied the cat. In the midst of all of this "cougar" activity, the animal made a visit to the Lake Estates trailer court. Charles and Helen Marks, managers of the court for three years, never thought they would be involved in tracking big cats. Then suddenly, on June 10, they found huge paw prints in their backyard.

This is the way Charles Marks described the course of events: "Someone had called the police and said that the night before, they were fishin' out here (at the little lake next to the trailer court). See we got a lot of good fish in this lake here. It's stocked. He was out fishin', and he'd seen these prints. Then he called the Delaware sheriff, and they came down Sunday morning. The guy showed them the prints; he'd staked them all out and then we hightailed it out here to see what was going on." Helen Marks added, "We didn't know if it was a dead body or something. But it was these prints, some with claws, some without."

Charles Marks had some plaster of paris on hand from the time he had repaired the broken leg of a pet, so he tried his hand at making some casts of the mysterious paw prints. His wife, in the role of "operations director," told Charles to make a cast of the more exciting clawed tracks, and thus these were the ones shown to the police. For those unfamiliar with the characteristics of big cats, panthers have retractable claws, like house cats, so their claws would not appear in a print. Lions have paws that are more like dog paws, without retractable claws. This is why panthers can climb trees and lions and dogs cannot.

The authorities quickly decided that the prints the Markses had made had come from a dog, an explanation familiar to anyone with experience in mysterious feline accounts. But the couple is convinced they had discovered cougar prints, for they also came upon a patch of vegetation with clear signs that a very large animal had lain there. Helen Marks recalled, "And you could even see the tufts of grass sticking up between the place the head had rested and the five-foot-long depression where the body was."

Later that same day, three boys were out playing in their "fort" behind the trailer court, the discovery of the prints unbeknownst to them. Quite suddenly they encountered a large tan panther in a tree. Donnie Grady, twelve years of age, said the cat jumped from the tree, landed on all fours, and fled. Ricky Smith, ten, obviously taking the encounter very personally, told of how the thing "looked at me and jumped from the tree." Travis, Ricky's eight-year-old brother, said, "When it growled, I saw those BIG front teeth." The boys, residents of the trailer court, later saw the cat on a nearby roadway and then learned of the Markses' discovery of the prints.

More reported encounters with the panther took place the following week, in June. A woman on nearby Fancher Road was taking out some trash when she met the big cat—and promptly fainted. Other sightings filled the newspapers for a few days, but like many unknown creatures of the weird Midwest, this one too faded from view and the minds of the residents of central Ohio.

In May and July 1962, near Urbana, a major "black panther" flap occurred. Over a dozen people said they saw a big midnight-black cat with a long tail and big eyes.

Lions and Panthers on the Ohio Border

Sometimes these giant cats are seen in the weirdest combos. Take the story that began when a giant animal rushed a fishing party of four adults and two children at the Elkhorn Falls, located on the Indiana–Ohio border. This sighting greatly informs other encounters that came afterward in Ohio, since the creatures appear to have been traveling back and forth across the state line. The Elkhorn Falls incident occurred during the early evening hours of August 5, 1948.

According to Ivan Toney, who lived nearby, "about seven thirty p.m. a man came to the house and wanted to use the phone to call the sheriff. He said he and another man, along with their wives and two children, were fishing along the banks of the pool at the foot of the Elkhorn Falls. Their car was parked on the road near the gate leading to the falls. He said the animal came up the stream from the south. When they sighted it, they started running for the car. They reached it, but the animal lunged at the car, then plowed through the fence into the sandy bar along the stream's edge."

The creature "looked like a lion with a long tail," the witnesses asserted, with bushy hair around the neck—the well-known trait of the male of the African lion. Deputy Sheriff Jack Witherby examined the tracks and said they were like "nothing I have ever seen before." After completing his investigations, he issued a warning to those who fished along streams at night.

Two days after the Elkhorn Falls incident, two of the cats were seen together. On August 7, two teenage farm boys, Arthur and Howard Turner, saw a strange beast near a plum tree not far from the gate leading into their Richmond, Indiana, barnyard. On a rise of ground to their right, another animal stood two hundred feet away. Arthur raised his rifle to his shoulder and blasted away. Both animals wheeled around, jumped a gate, and disappeared down a lane. The Turner boys described one of the animals as "having the appearance of a lion." It was large-headed, shaggy, and brown in color. The other looked like a black panther. Tracks were found, and with the aid of their dog, Shep, the Turners and the authorities searched for the mystery cats, but to no avail.

The following afternoon, farmers northwest of Abington, Indiana, spotted two animals identical to those the Turner boys had seen. And the morning after that, others sighted the two beasts in Wayne County, Indiana. Additional sightings suggested, as Mark A. Hall—a cryptozoologist, one of those people who study unexplained animals in an attempt to either prove or disprove the existence of such creatures—would write later in the journal *Wonders* that "the movement of the pair [was] from the south around the Ohio River to the north along the Whitewater River. Their path was a U-shaped journey, returning them southward toward the Ohio River." Hall had had experience tracking strange beasts.

In June 1992, several reports were phoned in to

the Mentor Police Department in Ohio. They described a maned feline that was seven feet long, crouching low to the ground on a number of occasions. Witnesses were quoted as saying that the animal was definitely a lion. One individual, who would allow the press to use only his first name, David, said the lion had big shoulders and a mane like you would see on the animal programs on television. David confessed that he was genuinely afraid of it and wondered how it got to where it was now. The police decided that David and other witnesses had seen nothing but a "large golden retriever."

More often than not, as with the law-enforcement officers in Mentor, the urban-oriented police in America try to explain away the sightings of maned lions as being those of dogs. This was the case in Miami Township, Montgomery County, when police took a call on May 26, 1994, about a tiger on the loose. The call came from Galen Emery, of Centerville, who had seen a large animal on the prowl in a field near Washington Church Road and Spring Valley Pike at around nine twenty-five a.m. Despite the fact that the police said the cat, which Emery had videotaped, was domestic, Emery remained adamant about what he had seen. He worked in an office facing an empty field off Spring Valley Road and had often seen and taped coyotes, deer, and groundhogs from only a few hundred yards away. And he knew a thing or two about the size of objects in videos, since he is a professional video producer.

Then on June 1, 1994, the Clearcreek and Springboro police in Warren County responded to a call of a possible tiger on the loose. The call, received at 14:16, was from Debbie Couch, a resident on North Ohio 741 near Pennyroyal Road. Couch claimed that she had seen a large orange animal run from Ohio 741 into the wooded area behind the Dayton General South Airport, located just north of the Springboro city limits. As she described what

she had seen, the police began to believe that there might be truth to the "rumor" (as the press was now calling Emery's May sighting) of a Bengal tiger.

Early in November 1994, three Hillsboro residents saw a lion running through Highland and Clinton counties. It was last reported on Turner Road in Clinton County, where police said they had found footprints. "We haven't got anything that's substantiated," Sheriff Tom Horst said. "We're still looking." However, Horst had a plaster cast of a paw print that was four inches wide, and the print showed no trace of claws.

The most vivid account of these sightings comes from Clara Stroop, who said she had seen an animal sniffing around her mobile home on Turner Road, in Clinton County, the same night as the other sightings. "It looked like a cougar or a female lion," she said. She showed a visitor a small shrub at the corner of her home where the animal had stood. "It let out a great big roar and then it went off running into the woods." She watched the animal demolish her plastic trash cans and pointed out their neatly sliced remnants. A few days later, the creature came calling again, and again "it let out a great big roar," Stroop said. "I don't let my kids go out at night."

Many mystery cats, usually described as being black panthers or unknown felids with manes, remain active in Ohio to this day. But none has gotten as much press time as the lion in the Columbus, Ohio, suburb of Gahanna, first reported in the spring of 2004. A small safari, including a helicopter, was organized to track the monster cat but was never able to catch up with it. "I'm convinced it's a three-hundred-pound to four-hundred-pound African lion," Deputy Police Chief Larry Rinehart said at the start of the search. "We're scurrying. It's a heck of a day." Though the Gahanna lion continued to be seen throughout the summer of 2004, it was never captured.

Jumpin' Jehosafat!

In 1949, in the vicinity of Grove City, another type of "monster" showed up—this time a phantom kangaroo. Louis Staub, driving a Greyhound bus near Grove City in January of that year, encountered a hopping marsupial-like beast, illuminated by the vehicle's bright headlights. He described it like this: "It's about five and a half feet high, hairy, and brownish in color. It has a long pointed head. It leaped a barbed-wire fence and disappeared. It resembled a kangaroo, but it appeared to jump on all fours. I'm certain it wasn't a deer." Ohio and the mystery kangaroos had had their first meeting, but it was not to be their last.

In 1968, on the last day of May, a motorist traveling along Ohio Route 63 reported to the Ohio State Highway Patrol that he had seen a kangaroo near Monroe at two thirty a.m. The radio dispatcher took the report lightly but sent Patrolman James Patrick to check it out anyway. Patrick reported back within a matter of minutes. "The thing hopped right across the road in front of my cruiser," he said. "It sure looked like a kangaroo to me." He said the animal had hopped off in the direction of Lebanon.

Meanwhile, the director of the Cincinnati Zoo, Ed Maruska, was telling newspapers, "I doubt there's a kangaroo around here on the loose. We had a kangaroo story about two years ago. Never found one. Down the years, we've chased after reported black leopards, panthers, and even a polar bear. Anyway, anyone seeing the kangaroo, which I doubt exists, should try to keep it in sight and call the zoo."

Then sometime later, in the 1970s and 1980s, midwestern marsupial reports reached a peak in Illinois and Indiana, but the state of Ohio seems to have been hopped over. It was not until late in the 1990s that the kangaroos returned to the hills and hollows of the Buckeye State. On June 26, 1997, near Dunkinsville, another ordinary person encountered one of the critters.

Debbie Cross lives on a wooded ridge, near Peach Mountain, in the foothills of the Appalachian Mountains. To the east lies the Shawnee State Forest. Between midnight and one a.m. on the night in question, Cross was watching television when she heard her dogs barking outside. When she turned on the porch light, she observed a strange animal about thirty feet away, near the pond in her front yard.

"It was about three to four feet tall and gray in color," she later told investigators Ron Schaffner and Kenny Young. "It had large dark eyes and rounded ears that extended above the head. It had real long arms and a short tail. It made a gurgling sound. From the available light, the animal appeared to have hair or fur all over its body about one and a half inches long."

The animal looked at Cross for a few seconds, then headed toward the southern part of the pond. It kind of "skipped" when it moved, Cross noted, and appeared to walk on its hind legs while using the "knuckles" of its front arms on the ground one at a time. When her two dogs started to chase it, she called them back. The animal soon disappeared from view. Cross heard a screeching sound shortly afterward.

Mystery kangaroos remain one of Ohio's strangest, most elusive creatures. While they may be common critters in Australia, they are very out of place in the wilds of the U.S.A.

Slippery Slimy Peninsula Python

In the summer of 1944, far from the teeming jungles of the Amazon, a huge snake known as the Peninsula Python caused excitement along the Cuyahoga River in the wooded valley between Akron and Cleveland. The creature first appeared on June 8, 1944, when Clarence Mitchell saw it slithering across his cornfield. The snake left a track the width of an automobile tire, and Mitchell reported the creature to be about eighteen feet in length. Two days later, Paul and John Szalay reported a similar track in their fields, and two days afterward, Mrs. Roy Vaughn called out the fire department when the giant reptile attacked her henhouse and devoured a chicken. Now that the snake was accepted as fact, theories abounded as to where it had come from.

According to rumor, a carnival truck had crashed in a cemetery in the valley two years earlier, and it was speculated that the python might have escaped from that wreck. Of course, all investigations of "circus train wrecks" as the source of any given mystery animal report can never be tracked down; those explanations are as elusive as the giant snakes and the other animals they are meant to debunk.

The Cleveland and Columbus zoos offered rewards for the capture of the Peninsula Python, and the news services began to carry the story, which aroused nationwide and even international interest.

On Sunday, June 25, 1944, sirens went off indicating that the creature had been sighted near Kelly Hill. Countless local residents headed there in search of the python. The hunters trampled through tangled thornbush and burrs, only to learn later that it was a false alarm. Two days later, the snake leaped out of a dead willow and badly frightened Pauline Hopko. It so terrified her milk cows that they broke their halters and ran off, while her dogs cowered under her skirts. Mrs. Hopko was left holding the milk pail.

A few days afterward, Katherine Boroutick saw the snake in her backyard—it came crashing down out of her butternut tree when she was out by the river throwing out some trash. A posse found broken tree limbs and a track to the riverbed. That fall, professional searchers came several times to the area where the snake had been reported. However, hunters said they never got word fast enough to have a shot at the snake. By the first frost, residents waited for the buzzards to find a huge carcass of a snake dead of the cold, but the beast was never sighted again, dead or alive.

Today, when people hear about the Peninsula Python, they think it was only a piece of folklore told around campfires, but for those who had lived along the Cuyahoga River near Kelly Hill in the 1940s, it was all too real.

Bigfoot in Ohio

The granddaddy of American monsters is Bigfoot. And of course, there are many reports of the large hairy and stinky bipeds in Ohio.

During the late 1700s, native Americans—the Delaware of Ohio—described to the new settlers their frequent encounters with the strange hominids. As recorded in the *History of Newcomerstown*, the Delaware said that "they had to leave out foods for the wild ones of the woods to keep the peace."

The more modern history of Bigfoot in Ohio begins, so far as written accounts go, in 1869 with a news article uncovered by cryptozoologist Mark A. Hall. Dated January 23 of that year, the article was headlined "A Gorilla in Ohio" and told of a hairy creature haunting the woods near the town of Gallipolis. The creature had jumped on a man riding in a carriage, and the man's daughter, who was also in the carriage, threw a stone at the animal as it struggled with her father. The rock hit the animal's ear, and the "gorilla" departed.

In recent years, Ohio has been one of the most active areas for Bigfoot sightings. The creature has even been given a number of local names, such as Orange Eyes and Grassman. The sightings may be the result of the large number of researchers involved in Bigfoot investigations in the state. As far as we can tell, Ohio ranks second in the country, after California, in the number of "Bigfooters"—committed hairy hominid seekers. The *Weird Ohio* team itself has investigated sightings in the state many times. Read on.

Minerva Monster

One of the best examples of a Buckeye State Bigfoot dates from the 1970s from the town of Minerva. It was chronicled in some detail by homegrown researcher Ron Schaffner, who has said that the Minerva case is "by far, the most complex and interesting one" in his Ohio files.

The rumors of activity east of Minerva began surfacing in July and August 1978, when Evelyn and Howe Cayton's grandchildren and their friends came running into their house in a frightened state. Crying, they claimed to have seen a large hairy monster in a nearby gravel pit. The Caytons' daughter, Vicki Keck, and the Caytons went outside to find out what had frightened the children, and what they found was pretty scary.

They saw a huge creature covered with dark matted hair. They estimated it to be about three hundred pounds and seven feet tall. "It just stood there," said Evelyn Cayton. "It didn't move, but I almost broke my neck running back down the hill." She later observed the creature again. It was sitting in the gravel pit, picking at the garbage. She could not make out any facial features because of the long hair covering its face, but she remembered that the creature had no visible neck.

The creature returned again on the night of August 21, 1978. In Schaffner's case notes, he points out that Evelyn Cayton's family and friends saw two pairs of yellow eyes belonging to what appeared to be two panthers. But then the group saw a large upright hairy creature step in front of the large cats as if to protect them. After Bigfoot peered through a kitchen window, the eyewitnesses reached for their guns and the creature suddenly left. A strong stench still lingered in the area even after a deputy sheriff arrived to investigate.

The deputy and some other officers searched the entire area on horseback and in Jeeps but found only unusual, but not very clear, footprints. The next night, the hairy biped came back and was visible on top of a hill near a strip mine. It returned again on the following night, August 23, but when Howe Cayton fired a shot into the air, the creature departed. Schaffner and another investigator later learned that before all the Bigfoot activity, one of the Caytons' German shepherds was found dead with a broken neck.

Ron Schaffner and an associate, Earl Jones, interviewed the Caytons on two separate occasions. During their second visit, they hiked into the woods, where they spent the night. They looked for physical evidence but came up with nothing, nor did they witness anything unusual. For Schaffner, one of the most bizarre elements of the incident has always been the sighting of the phantom panthers along with the hairy hominid. He is still perplexed by that detail. Perhaps they were dogs—or juvenile Bigfoots.

In the 1970s, 1980s, and 1990s, with an explosion of interest in Bigfoot studies in Ohio, reports of other hairy, smelly creatures popped up now and then, but none were as famous as the Minerva encounters. They remain the most intriguing Bigfoot sightings in Ohio history, but by no means the last.

A flap of Bigfoot-like sightings in Logan and Union counties occurred a couple years after the Minerva ones, the strangest of which was the one reported by Union County legal secretary Donna Riegler. Driving home from work on the stormy evening of June 24, 1980, with lightning flashing, she slowed down to cross some railroad tracks and then saw it, lying on the road, all hunched over. At first she thought it was a dog, but then it stood up, and she convinced herself into imagining that it was a man. Then the creature turned and looked at her, and she realized that it was a strange upright creature, with bent hands held out, palms up. She could not see any facial features, but from what she described, it was definitely a Bigfoot. Riegler drove away, escaping as fast as she could; she stopped at the first house she saw, where she broke down and sobbed.

Monsters in the Bog

James Willis tells the following two stories, one stranger than the other, of the creatures that may lurk in the murky world of Ohio's bogs.

In 1942, the Ohio Historical Society officially listed Cedar Bog as a nature preserve, the first of its kind in the state. Today, approximately one quarter of all the plant species in Ohio call Cedar Bog home, along with over a hundred species of birds and many rare reptiles and fish. And if the stories are to be believed, the bog also has one other notable resident—Bigfoot.

Shortly after the Cedar Bog Preserve (which is actually a fen) opened, locals began whispering about spotting a huge apelike creature walking on Woodburn Road, which parallels the bog. Some claimed it was Bigfoot himself, while others said it was an albino relative. One thing they all agreed on, though, was that this creature was too big to be a man and was unlike anything they had ever seen before.

Not long after, a long metal fence topped with barbed wire was erected along both sides of Woodburn Road. Most people assumed it was meant to protect the bog by keeping people out. But there are some who believe, even today, that the fence was placed there to keep Bigfoot in the bog. Regardless of which is true, we invite you to take a trip down Woodburn Road some dark night and see for yourself if you don't feel like something is standing on the other side of the fence, just beyond the reach of the car's headlights, watching you.

And This Boggy Creek Tale . . .

According to legend, a group of teenagers from Kettering decided to venture outside the city on an impromptu camping trip. The spot they chose to camp at was alongside a creek at the far end of a large field. It was not a good decision.

The following morning, when the teenagers hadn't returned, their parents went looking for them. They came across the remains of a small campsite, the fire still smoking but no sign of the teenagers. It is said they were all attacked and killed during the night by a hideous creature nicknamed the Boggy Creek Monster. True or not, the teenagers were never seen or heard from again.

Skeptics claim that there is no Boggy Creek Monster and point to the fact that the name comes from a fictional monster created for a low-budget early 1970s horror movie called *The Boggy Creek Monster*. However, it should be noted that the movie was based on an actual creature, known as the Fouke Monster, which was said to have terrorized the residents of Fouke, Arkansas, in the 1960s. So perhaps—just perhaps—more than one of these creatures exists, and one of them has chosen to make its home along a creek on the outskirts of Kettering.

when he saw three manlike "trolls" kneeling on the side of the road, not far from a bridge over the river. About three feet tall, they had gray skin and seemed to be wearing tight-fitting gray clothes. They had froglike faces, long slender arms, and normal-looking eyes but without eyebrows. Their chests appeared to be lopsided. One of the creatures held a dark object, which emitted blue flashes. Hunnicutt tried to approach them but "must have lost consciousness," he later told law-enforcement

personnel, because he found himself driving to the police station without remembering what had taken place after he had attempted to approach the creatures. The authorities took the report seriously enough to place a guard on the bridge, and an FBI investigation was conducted. Something weird was up, though to this day nobody knows what—at least nobody who's talking.

Loveland's Frogman

In March 1972, on two separate occasions, two Ohio policemen saw what has become known as the Loveland Frogman. Ron Schaffner and fellow crypto-zoologist Richard Mackey interviewed the officers and investigated the incidents.

The first sighting occurred at one a.m. on March 3, 1972, a clear, cold night. Officer Ray Shockey was en route to Loveland, via Riverside Road, when he thought he saw a dog lying in a field beside Twightwee Road. Suddenly the "thing" stood up, its eyes illuminated by the car lights, looked at him for an instant, turned, and leaped over a guardrail. It went down an embankment and into the Little Miami River. According to Shockey, the thing weighed about sixty pounds and stood about three to four feet tall and had textured, leathery skin and a face like that of a frog or a lizard.

Shockey drove to the police station and returned with Officer Mark Matthews to look for evidence of the creature. They turned up scrape marks leading down the side of the small hill near the river, but no Frogman.

On St. Patrick's Day, March 17, 1972, Officer Matthews was driving outside Loveland when he had a similar experience. Seeing an animal lying in the middle of the road, he stopped to remove what he thought was a dead critter. Instead, when he opened his car door, the animal got into a crouched position, like a football player. Stunned, Matthews watched as the creature hobbled to the guardrail and lifted its leg over it, keeping an eye on Matthews the whole time.

He later said that he felt the creature stood more upright than Shockey had described. One local farmer told investigators that he had seen a large froglike or lizardlike creature in the same month the officers had.

The reports of the 1972 Frogman had been hard on the witnesses. "Those two officers took a lot of flack about the sighting back then," said a local businessman, who wished not to be identified, in a 1985 newspaper story about the sightings. "People made fun of them and the city." Years later, in 1999, during local media interviews, Matthews explained that he was tired of talking about the Frogman and that what he had seen was an iguana. But at the time of the sightings, both witnesses said they saw something resembling an upright manlike lizard about four feet tall.

And then there is the matter of the sketch. Officer Shockey's sister had drawn it based on Shockey's and Matthews's descriptions shortly after their encounters with the creature. A biped creature, it clearly looks like a giant frogman.

In 2001, *Weird Ohio* did a follow-up investigation, interviewing the principals, including Ron Schaffner. We asked him about Matthews's attempts to pull back from his original story. Schaffner said, "Why, after all these years, is Matthews debunking the story? I'm not sure." But four years after the sightings, both officers had showed him the sketch and said that was what the creatures they had seen looked like. If they'd seen an iguana, "why would they show us a composite drawing of this creature back in 1976 and tell us that it looked like the drawing?" asks Schaffner. "Maybe Matthews is just tired of hearing the story and all the variations."

According to Shockey, the thing weighed about sixty pounds and stood about three to four feet tall and had textured, leathery skin and a face like that of a frog or a lizard.

Bessie, the Lake Erie Monster: Horror or Hoax?

For years, people have been reporting sightings in Lake Erie of an unknown creature. Nicknamed South Bay Bessie or just plain Bessie, it is described as being gray, snakelike, and thirty to forty feet long. Though several sightings have been logged in recent years, the monster is known mostly from historical accounts.

In the July 8, 1898, edition of the *Daily Register* of Sandusky, Ohio, a reporter wrote, "For a number of years, vague stories about huge serpents have come with each recurring season from Dominion [Canadian] shores, and now, at last, the existence of these fierce monsters is verified and the fact so well established that it can no longer be questioned."

Able to live both on land and in water, this monster was a "fierce, ugly, coiling thing, call it a snake or what you will," measuring twenty-five to thirty feet in length and at least a foot in diameter. By 1912, it had become the butt of local practical jokes. A *Daily Register* article published in the spring of that year recounts an encounter between Kelleys Island residents and a large sea monster, which broke through a sheet of lake ice and headed for shore. Witnesses described a black creature with a huge head, gaping mouth, and a row of teeth. The story's last line read "April first"—the date of the story's publication and the reason for the tale.

Other times, the newspaper was at a hoax's receiving end. The July 22, 1931, edition of the *Register* stated, "Sandusky was all agog Tuesday night because it was reported that the sea serpent, supposed to be in the waters of Sandusky Bay, had been captured."

As the story had it, two vacationing men from Cincinnati saw the sea serpent while on a boat on Lake Erie. The two frightened men clubbed the animal into submission, brought it aboard, and placed it in a crate.

Harold Madison, the curator of the Cleveland Museum of Natural History, journeyed to Sandusky and pronounced the "sea serpent" to be an Indian python. The two men quickly left town. Further investigation revealed that the men, one of whom had family ties in Sandusky, worked for a touring carnival.

Still, stories of the monster persisted, either in spite of or because of the hoaxes perpetrated in its name. Intermittent sightings were reported from the 1960s through the 1990s, including one by two Huron firefighters in 1990.

By 1993, monster mania was in full swing. The national media grabbed hold of the story of the monster and ran with it. *The Wall Street Journal* took a more cynical approach. It ran an article, published on July 29, characterizing the excitement as a clever marketing ploy to draw tourists into the small town of Huron as they sped toward Cedar Point. Huron did take a particular interest in the beast and soon produced a crop of pseudo-cryptozoologists and declared itself the National Live Capture and Control Center for the Lake Erie Monster. Tom Solberg of the Huron Lagoons Marina offered a $100,000 reward for the safe and unharmed capture of the beast. The reward has never been claimed.

David Davies, a biologist for the Ohio Division of Wildlife, spends much of his time on the lake. "It's probably something closely related to a dinosaur. It looks like a brontosaurus, don't you think?" he joked when a reporter asked him what the Lake Erie Monster could be. In his serious moments, Davies thinks the animal is a large specimen of the lake sturgeon, which can live up to one hundred and fifty years and can grow to more than seven feet in length and weigh over three hundred pounds.

Caviar is actually the eggs of sturgeon. The lake's waters at Sandusky were home to so many sturgeon in the 1800s that it was known as the Caviar Capital of North

so thin and short for its height. Three long slender toes with a hooked toe or nail on the lower leg."

The legend of the Mothman hiding in plain sight is still circulating in the communities on the Ohio side of the river.

Some speculate that the flurry of Mothman sightings that began in 1966 was a warning sign that something tragic was going to happen. They believe that the dark prophecy was realized when key bar no. 13 of the Silver Bridge broke on December 15, 1967, and the bridge between Point Pleasant, West Virginia, and Gallipolis, Ohio, collapsed, taking people to their death. Tragically, a state-by-state breakdown of the dead as a result of the bridge collapse reveals that two were from Virginia, three from North Carolina, nineteen from West Virginia, and the greatest number—twenty-two victims—were from Ohio.

The creature stood between five and seven feet tall, was wider than a man, and shuffled on humanlike legs. Its eyes were set near the top of the shoulders, and it had batlike wings that glided, rather than flapped, when it flew.

What the Mothman Witnesses Saw

A reporter named Mary Hyre, who was the Point Pleasant correspondent for the Athens, Ohio, newspaper *The Messenger* during the 1966–1967 Mothman flap, wrote extensively about the local sightings. In fact, after one very active weekend, she was deluged with over five hundred phone calls from people who saw strange lights in the skies.

John Keel, who has written extensively about Mothman and other unexplained anomalies, became the major chronicler of the Mothman case and wrote that at least one hundred people personally witnessed the creature between November 1966 and November 1967.

According to their reports, the creature stood between five and seven feet tall, was wider than a man, and shuffled on humanlike legs. Its eyes were set near the top of the shoulders, and it had batlike wings that glided, rather than flapped, when it flew. Strangely, though, it was able to ascend straight up "like a helicopter." Witnesses also described its murky skin as being either gray or brown and said that it emitted a humming sound when it flew. The Mothman was apparently incapable of speech, and it gave off a screeching sound.

But there could have been a logical explanation for some of the sightings. Even John Keel (who believed the creature was genuine) suspected that a few of the cases involved people who were spooked by recent reports and saw owls flying along deserted roads at night. Even so, Mothman remains hard to easily dismiss. The case is filled with an impressive number of multiple-witness sightings that were deemed reliable even by law-enforcement officials' standards.—*Troy Taylor*

WANTED

LESTER M. GILLIS,

aliases GEORGE NELSON, "BABY FACE" NELSON, ALEX GILLIS, LESTER GILES,
"BIG GEORGE" NELSON, "JIMMIE", "JIMMY" WILLIAMS.

On June 23, 1934, HOMER S. CUMMINGS, Attorney General of the United States, under the authority vested in him by an Act of Congress approved June 6, 1934, offered a reward of

$5,000.00

for the capture of Lester M. Gillis or a reward of

$2,500.00

for information leading to the arrest of Lester M. Gillis.

DESCRIPTION

Age, 25 years; Height, 5 feet 4-3/4 inches; Weight,
133 pounds; Build, medium; Eyes, yellow and grey
slate; Hair, light chestnut; Complexion, light; Occupation, oiler.

All claims to any of the aforesaid rewards and all questions and disputes that may arise
as among claimants to the foregoing rewards shall be passed upon by the Attorney General and
shall be final and conclusive. The right is reserved to divide and allocate
the aforesaid rewards as between several claimants. No part of the aforesaid reward shall be final and conclusive ... yees of the Department of Justice.
Lester M. Gillis,

Local Heroes and Villains

They walk among us: colorful characters and local loonies. Every town across Ohio can claim at least one as its own. They might be locally famous, or even infamous, for what they're doing right now. Or maybe they earned their celebrity for something they did in the past. They might be historically significant, or just someone who marches to the beat of a different drummer. Whoever they are, the people featured in this chapter, both the admirable and the despised, have done something really strange to set themselves apart from the crowd. And so they've earned their place in our catalogue of the weird, a doubtful distinction, some might say, but one that makes for good reading.

One Gigantic Love Story

Some of our favorite heroes are circus freaks. This is the story of a love affair between two Ohio giants.

Martin Van Buren Bates was born in Whitesburg, Kentucky, in 1845, and was known as the Kentucky River Giant, eventually weighing in at 475 pounds. He joined the Fifth Kentucky Infantry during the Civil War, achieving the rank of captain. After the war, he decided to join the circus—the sideshow, to be exact. What else could a seven-foot, 8.5-inch man do?

Anna Swan was born in Nova Scotia in 1848. She grew to a height of almost eight feet and spent many years at the P. T. Barnum Museum in

Above, Anna Swan looms over an unknown male acquaintance
Left, Bates with a [normal-sized] friend

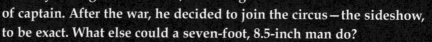

New York as a living oddity, billed—with a notable lack of originality—as the Giantess of Nova Scotia. After Barnum's museum burned down, in 1868, Anna decided to go out on her own. She and Bates met up in London, and it was love at first height—er, sight. The two were married in Europe and decided to settle down in the town of Seville, Ohio. They bought some land and, having acquired a great deal of money from their performances, had an eighteen-room mansion built to accommodate their enormous stature. Everything was constructed to their larger scale so that the lovebirds could live comfortably.

By all reports, they lived happily ever after, except for one tragedy. They had a child, born thirty inches long and twenty-four pounds. But it was a long, difficult labor, and the baby died eleven hours later. Its not-so-little body is buried in Mound Hill Cemetery.

The Giantess herself died in 1899, but her funeral was delayed because there wasn't a casket large enough to hold her. The Kentucky River Giant lived for another twenty years and remarried. He died in January 1919 and was buried next to Anna and their baby.

The larger-than-life mansion they built was demolished in 1948, but you can still visit their equally large burial plots in Seville. For the Ohio bicentennial, Seville had a historical marker erected, proudly proclaiming that the giant couple lived there. The marker lists Anna at 413 lbs. and seven feet 11.5 inches ... almost a full three inches taller than her husband!

Three Fingers of Formaldehyde for Mary Bach

You've probably heard more than one old tale of a farmer going crazy and hacking his family to bits. Well, here's one story we can absolutely vouch for. The evidence is still there for all to see, in the Wood County Historical Museum in Bowling Green.

Seems that back in 1883, farmer Carl Bach decided that his wife, Mary, just didn't complete the daily chores to his liking. So he took a corn knife to her, dismembered her body, and put the prime cuts in his barn. But it all must have weighed heavy on old Carl's head, for a few days later he decided to turn himself in and told the local authorities where to find his sliced-and-diced wife.

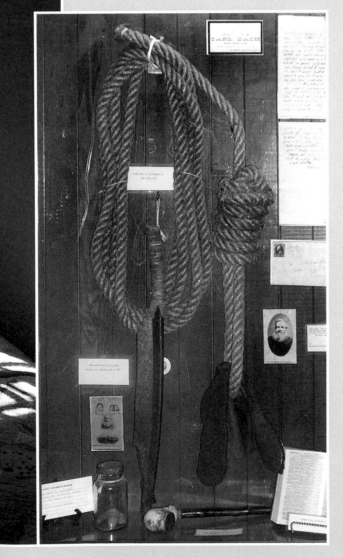

The local sheriff went to the barn and discovered the woman's body. He took three of Mary's fingers, put them in a glass of formaldehyde, and carried them back as evidence. Bach was eventually tried and sentenced to death by hanging for his crime. But rather than giving him just an ordinary execution, town officials decided that they would string Carl up in front of the Wood County Courthouse and hang him on the last day of the county fair, selling tickets for a big slam-bang grand finale. It was a well-attended event (or so we've been told), and Carl Bach did his final song and dance on October 13, 1883. It was the last public hanging the county would ever hold.

Not wanting this cherished moment to be forgotten, the townspeople decided to put a display case inside the courthouse featuring the knife that he used to hack up Mary Bach as well as the noose that hanged Carl, a ticket to the execution, and, of course, Mary's three bloody fingers in the jar of formaldehyde. They are still there today. The withered fingers are displayed on the bottom left of the cabinet; the liquid has evaporated from the jar. The corn knife used to cut off the fingers hangs above and to the right. The rest of the case is filled with memorabilia from the trial and personal mementos, including the Bible that Carl read from while awaiting execution.

If you'd like to see these gruesome reminders of what might happen if you don't complete your housework, they're on display at the Wood County Historical Museum on the grounds of the old Wood County infirmary. The infirmary was in operation from 1868 until 1971, and the museum is actually inside the old facility. And get this: In 1885, the "Lunatic House" was added to the property as a place to house the "violently insane." The museum recently restored the Lunatic House, and visitors may tour the building.

Not a Pretty Day for Pretty Boy Floyd

The year 1934 was a bad time for gangsters. John Dillinger, "Baby Face" Nelson, and Bonnie and Clyde were all shot dead that year. And on October 22, 1934, Charles Arthur "Pretty Boy" Floyd, a notorious bank robber, met the same fate right here in Ohio.

A few days earlier, Floyd had run his truck off Route 7 between Wellsville and East Liverpool. Floyd had asked two of his molls, Beulah and Rose Baird, to take the truck into Wellsville and have it fixed at a local mechanic shop. (That's right, two molls. They didn't call him Pretty Boy for nothing.) He and his gang member Adam Richetti would set up camp in the woods off Route 7.

Not what you'd called skilled at concealment, Floyd and his pal built themselves a nice campfire to keep warm. Locals became suspicious of the smoke pouring out of the woods and called the police. A shoot-out at the camp began, and Richetti was captured. Floyd escaped to a nearby farmhouse, where—at gunpoint—he forced a farmhand to drive him to Youngstown. Unfortunately (for Floyd), the car ran out of gas, but he managed to hijack another car and driver. They got as far as Lisbon when they met up with police roadblocks. After a brief gun battle, Floyd backtracked to East Liverpool and took off on foot into the woods.

Pretty Boy didn't know it, but his accomplice Richetti had squealed to the cops a day earlier that the man they were after was indeed *the* Pretty Boy Floyd. A two-hundred-man posse led by FBI agent Melvin Purvis (who had gunned down Dillinger in Chicago) was about to close in on Floyd.

The feds went to a few farmhouses and found that Floyd had been there, asking for food and to wash up. Driving by the Conkle farm in East Liverpool, Purvis spotted Floyd in a car next to a corncrib. Floyd took off on foot, running across a cornfield, and was shot in the arm and back by police officer Chester Smith. The feds gathered around him. The last words he spoke before he died were "I am Floyd."

His body was taken to the Sturgis Funeral Home in East Liverpool, where he was embalmed, and the $122 found on him was used to pay for his funeral. His bloody blue suit was torn into swatches and passed out to the roughly ten thousand people who filed by his coffin.

The official postmortem was that Pretty Boy Floyd's body had three bullets in it at the time of his death, but only two had been fired by Officer Smith. It seems nobody bothered to question that bit of information at the time.

Years later, Chester Smith confessed in *Time* magazine that Melvin Purvis was trying to get a confession out of

Floyd in the cornfield for the Kansas City Massacre, a bloody and failed attempt to free a Floyd crony named Frank Nash from federal custody. When Floyd wouldn't confess, Purvis had agent Herman Hollis execute him as he lay dying in the cornfield.

In 1993, the East Liverpool Historical Society erected a sign on Sprucevale Road where Charles Arthur Floyd ended his life of crime. You can also see the funeral home (now a bed-and-breakfast) that once had a death mask of Floyd and the metal stand that held his head while he was being embalmed. Unfortunately, on a recent visit we found that Floyd's death mask was no longer being displayed.

Adam Richetti, *pictured above, following his capture in October 1934*

The Most Famous Dead Guy in Sabina

On June 9, 1929, the body of a middle-aged black man was discovered in a ditch along the Wilmington Pike in Sabina. He seemed to have died of natural causes, but the papers found on his body led police to a vacant lot in Cincinnati. To make matters even more mysterious, when the police talked to residents of the neighborhood and gave his description, no one seemed to recognize or remember the man.

Upon arriving back in Sabina, the police decided to give the body a name—Eugene, for the last person they spoke to in the Cincinnati neighborhood. Eugene was embalmed and put up at the Littleton Funeral Home, waiting to be claimed. But his wait was to be much longer than expected. He was kept at the funeral home for over thirty years.

Somewhere along the line, someone thought it would be a good idea to give him a new suit and prop him up in a windowed shed on the funeral home property so that maybe someone would recognize him. But no one ever did.

Over the years, he became quite the character around Sabina. At Halloween, he would be put on people's front porches to scare trick-or-treaters. Sometimes, local college students would take him for a drive or bring him to a frat party. His body was remarkably well preserved, although over the years he had begun to lose a few fingers. But a look of peaceful serenity never left his face—you've got to hand it to the local embalmers.

In 1963, the Littleton Funeral Home decided it was time to lay Eugene to rest and buried Sabina's most famous dead guy in the Sabina Cemetery with a rather odd—and inaccurate—inscription on his marker: FOUND DEAD 1928, BURIED 1964.

We found the following personal remembrance of Eugene posted on a Sabina historical Web site.

I visited Sabina a number of times in the late 1950's . . . Eugene was a famous figure back then, especially at Halloween. He often appeared on the front porches of homes (with a little help from his friends) and terrorized more than a few houses.

Some of his fingers were missing but he was kept well dressed in his black suit and had a rather serene look of composure on his face. I used to spend a few minutes of each visit talking to him and asking him questions like where he came from and if he had a family. As expected, no communication was established but I did attempt to comfort him with a prayer for his soul and his loved ones at the end of each visit.—James L. Clark

Urbana Legend

While working in a pharmacy in Middletown, Ohio, in 1982, a clerk mentioned that as a youngster, her parents had taken her to Urbana, Ohio, to see a "petrified man." I expressed disbelief, but she insisted that the man was on display in a small shelter in downtown Urbana. She said his name was Eugene.

Many years later, in 1998, (without ever giving the above another thought) I took a fishing trip to the Mad River, near Urbana. I kept one very nice fish and took it to my uncle in Cincinnati, who loved fresh fish. He was a very educated and distinguished gentleman. He asked where I had caught the fish. When I told him that I'd caught it near Urbana, he asked, "Is Eugene still there?" I was stunned. Could this be a true story?

I told my uncle, then eighty-eight, that I was sure that "Eugene" could not be there, but I asked what he knew about this. He said that he had seen this man on display. He remembered a little of the story surrounding the man. He'd been told that he went only by the name Eugene and had spent some time in Urbana. Nobody knew anything about his family. When he died, he was embalmed and placed on display in the hope that someone might come by and recognize him.

I still think this is a very weird story, but hearing it from two very diverse sources, I reluctantly believe it.—*Tim Heenan*

John Cleves Symmes Explores Inner Space

Did you ever think that maybe the earth is not solid but hollow? If you did, one John Cleves Symmes of Hamilton would agree with you. And believe it or not, many people thought he might be onto something.

Captain John Cleves Symmes was a nineteenth-century philosopher and the originator of the Symmes Theory of Concentric Spheres and Polar Voids. From the mathematical patterns of interlocking spheres in nature that he had studied, he convinced himself that the world was hollow and habitable within. Symmes claimed he could show entryways to unexplored inner regions of the North and South Poles, and he lectured across the Midwest to generate interest in his theory. Maybe he was a good talker, or maybe at the time the U.S. population really considered him to be a mathematical genius. Whatever the case, he was able to persuade the public to pressure Congress into considering funding polar expeditions to start in 1822 and 1823. He almost got the vote, but the Senate never approved the money.

A man who befriended Symmes, Jeremiah Reynolds, decided to help the cause, and the two of them set a course for the East Coast with a wooden model of hollow earth, lecturing along the way. They packed halls (at fifty cents a head) at every stop.

Touring proved to be too much for Symmes, and he decided to retire to Hamilton, leaving Reynolds to lead the cause of the Hollow Earth Theory. Symmes died in Hamilton in 1849.

Reynolds again asked for help from the government, but without luck. He did, though, eventually find a rich New York investor to pay for a ship, the S.S. *Annawan*, to explore Antarctica and search for the entryways to the world within. Alas, no portals were ever found.

If you visit Ludlow Park in Hamilton, you will find a stone monument dedicated to Symmes in the 1840s by his son, Americus Vespucci Symmes, for all to wonder at (and about!). The inscription on the memorial reads: CAPT. JOHN CLEVES SYMMES, AS A PHILOSOPHER, AND THE ORIGINATOR OF SYMMES THEORY OF CONCENTRIC SPHERES AND POLAR VOIDS; HE CONTENDED THAT THE EARTH IS HOLLOW AND HABITABLE WITHIN. Appropriately, a hollow earth made of granite beckons from atop the memorial. Contrary to popular belief, this monument is NOT a grave marker. Symmes is buried, along with several of his family members, in Congress Green Cemetery, which is in North Bend, Ohio.

Since this is a travel book of sorts, we feel we should at least mention that the Symmes monument is located in a neighborhood that . . . well, let's just say it's not one of Ohio's finest. When we last visited, at one p.m. on a Sunday afternoon, it was a real challenge getting a photo of the memorial without including one or more of the local homeless people who were lying all over the place. As for the surrounding houses, well, there were a lot of business transactions going on out front—at least in front of the ones that weren't boarded up and as hollow as the earth itself.

Ohio's Unsportsmanlike Sniper

What was wrong with Thomas Lee Dillon? His friends knew he liked guns, but only a few of them had seen his cruel, sadistic side. In high school, he started recording the animals he tortured to death on a calendar alongside the names of his various sexual conquests. Years later, he would brag when his kill count reached five hundred.

Watching living things die gave Dillon a thrill that was actually physical; his breathing would shorten, and he would seemingly lose control of himself. An acquaintance once watched him finish off a wounded groundhog with a hunting knife. "He was shaking. He was in a frenzy, wild-eyed," the man reported.

Despite his weird proclivities, Dillon had a fairly normal, if unaffectionate, childhood. He was born on July 9, 1950, in Canton. His father died shortly after Dillon was born, and his mother's presence wasn't particularly comforting. He would later say that he couldn't remember her ever having hugged him, kissed him, or saying that she loved him. Lots of kids have undemonstrative parents and turn out okay, but for some reason Dillon began to evolve into a true sociopath. In high school he was known as an oddball, funny but removed from the group, someone who could be counted on to do the crazy and unpredictable. Classmates said he fired a gun from his car window, shot out windows, and took potshots at cats in his neighborhood along Thirty-Seventh Street Northwest. One classmate observed that "Dillon didn't seem to understand the concept of friendship. He never offered to do a favor or asked for one. It was always a trade—I'll do this if you do that."

After high school, Dillon attended Kent State's Stark Campus and then Ohio State University in Columbus, from which he graduated in 1972. He moved back to Canton, got a job with the water department, and married a nurse named Catherine Elsass. Around this time, he also began to shoot his neighbors' dogs. Even Dillon knew this would be frowned upon if he got caught, so to satisfy his urges he returned to his favorite sport: hunting in the Ohio Valley. By this time, his marksmanship had been improved by an Ohio Peace Officers Training course he attended in Stark County as well as nearly ceaseless target practice. All this time, Dillon's family and neighbors thought him little more than distant and eccentric. Catherine's mother described him as "a witty, kind man who has always had a yen for guns."

The Murders

The first killing happened in Belmont County on November 10, 1990. Jamie Paxton, twenty-one, left his home in Bannock that morning to go bow hunting. The next time he was seen, he was lying dead in a field near Route 9, bullet wounds in his chest, knee, and buttocks. Investigators questioned everyone who knew Jamie but came up empty-handed. The multiple wounds indicated a murder of the most cold-blooded sort, but the authorities couldn't figure why anyone would want to hurt Jamie Paxton.

His mother, Jean Paxton, addressed letters to her son's anonymous killer in the Martins Ferry *Times-Leader*. Nearly a year passed with no response, but after Jean's October 1991 plea, the killer sent a chilling letter to the paper in response:

"I am the murderer of Jamie Paxton, Jamie Paxton was a complete stranger to me. I never saw him before in my life, and he never said a word to me that Saturday. Paxton was killed because of an irresistible compulsion that has taken over my life. I knew when I left my house that day that someone would die by my hand. I just didn't know who or where. Technically I meet the definition of a serial

killer, but I'm an average-looking person with a family, job, and home just like yourself. Something in my head causes me to turn into a merciless killer with no conscience.

"Don't feel bad about not solving this case. You could interview till doomsday everyone that Jamie Paxton ever met in his life and you wouldn't have a clue to my identity. With no motive, no weapon, and no witnesses you could not possibly solve this crime."

The typed signature read: "The murderer of Jamie Paxton."

The elusive killer struck again not long after—on March 14, 1992. During the early morning, Claude Hawkins, forty-nine, was fishing at Wills Creek Dam in Coshocton County when he was shot point-blank in the back. After his body was found on federal land, the FBI was brought in to investigate. They quickly identified the connection between the murders of Claude Hawkins and Jamie Paxton. A March 26 interagency law-enforcement conference brought to light two other unsolved killings: those of Donald Welling and Kevin Loring. Welling, a thirty-five-year-old Tuscarawas County resident, had been shot through the heart from a distance of ten feet while jogging alongside a road. Loring's murder came just days after Paxton's, while he was deer hunting in Muskingum County. The "Outdoorsman Sniper" had been more active than anyone realized. Then on April 5, the killer claimed his fifth victim, forty-four-year-old Gary Bradley, who was fishing in Noble County when he was shot fatally in the back.

The Profile

The police investigation went public on August 22 with a detailed profile provided by experts at the FBI's Behavioral Science Unit in Quantico, Virginia. The FBI's workup of the shooter's personality stated that he was "a white male over 30, a gun enthusiast, avid hunter and owned at least several weapons. The killer would have above-average intelligence but was introverted and without many friends, and would resolve personal problems in a cowardly fashion. He might have a drinking problem and engage in obscene telephone calls, arson fire and vandalism by shooting out windows or tires of vehicles. He likely would take sadistic delight in mutilating and killing animals of all sorts."

Richard Fry had gone to high school with Thomas Lee Dillon and had become reasonably close to him, close enough to know that Dillon wasn't normal. When he read the FBI profile in the newspaper, he recognized nearly every trait from their time spent buddying up together.

The Dillon he knew had started out shooting road signs and setting fires before progressing to shooting rats at the local dump and finally people's dogs. After that, Fry stopped hanging out with him. Fry had also seen Dillon take shots at people on two occasions. Once during high school, Dillon shot at some other teenagers during an altercation, and another time, he took aim at a farmer at work in his field, from a great distance. It was enough to persuade Fry to tip the police about Dillon, who was living in Magnolia.

Catching Dillon

After looking into Dillon's background, the police began to follow him on the ground and from the air. On weekends, he would make round trips of more than a hundred miles into southeastern Ohio, shooting electric meters and stop signs with guns. He shot cows with a crossbow. Police were convinced that he was their man, but had no evidence.

They finally took him in on November 27 for illegal possession of a firearm, just three days before hunters were due to swarm into the area for Ohio's deer season. Eventually, after the gun used in two of the killings was connected to him, he was also charged with two counts of murder. He dodged around awhile on those charges, but on July 3, 1992, he confessed to the murders in a phone interview with television station WTOV. "I have major problems," he said. "I'm crazy. I want to kill. I want to kill."

Whatever was wrong with Thomas Lee Dillon, it cost five people their lives. Judge John Nau sentenced him to 165 years in prison—the maximum allowed by law, given the plea bargain Dillon struck. His capture was one of the first examples of a psychological profile being used successfully to identify a suspect. Dillon has never shown much remorse for his actions. From his cell in Lucasville, he writes letters and even draws cartoons about his crimes. He will never be eligible for parole.

James Ruppert's Easter Sunday Massacre

The town of Hamilton holds the distinction of being home to America's largest family mass murder, a crime that has haunted this bedroom community north of Cincinnati for thirty years. Most residents know or have heard of the modest house at 635 Minor Avenue and the horrifying details of the crime that occurred there on Easter Sunday in 1975.

Present in Charity Ruppert's home that day were her son Leonard, his wife, Alma, and their eight children, ages four to seventeen. Uncle James, Charity's other son, was upstairs in his room. James Ruppert was a gun collector and an accomplished marksman but didn't strike anyone who knew him as the homicidal type. He was generally remembered as quiet, modest, and helpful, a small, unremarkable guy. At the time of the murders, he was forty-one years old, unemployed, and still living with his mother.

After the family finished their Easter-egg hunt on the front lawn, they came inside to prepare dinner. The youngest child was in the bathroom, and one of his sisters was waiting her turn. The other children were playing in the living room. Charity was preparing food while her son Leonard and daughter-in-law sat at the kitchen table.

James Ruppert came downstairs carrying a .357 magnum, two .22 handguns, and an eighteen-shot rifle. He shot his brother first, then his sister-in-law, and then his mother. Without pausing, he walked through the rest of the house, killing the children one at a time. He did it methodically; the investigators found that he usually fired at least twice, first a disabling shot into the body, then a kill shot into the brain or heart. He moved so quickly, in fact, that no one screamed or even came close to escaping; the only sign of struggle was a single overturned wastepaper basket. One of the girls had managed to open the back door a crack, only to be gunned down before she could make it outside.

James spent three hours with the bodies before calling the police. "There's been a shooting here," he said simply, and he waited just inside the front door for them to arrive.

"We can't seem to find a motive for this," Hamilton police chief George McNally said the day after the crime. But the trial revealed a number of things previously unknown about Uncle James. Though considered a decent, even gentle, son and

Two of Ohio's most famous sons didn't make their mark until after they'd left their home state. One of them would go on to become so notorious a monster that people still recoil at the mere mention of his depraved deeds. The other would create great inventions that would revolutionize the world for the better and change the way average people live their everyday lives.

Where the Cannibal Acquired His Taste

One of the few serial killers whose crimes are famous enough to make him a household name, Jeffrey Dahmer will forever be known as the "Milwaukee Cannibal." But he got his start right here in Ohio. Dahmer was from Bath, a village in suburban Summit County, where he attended school and cautiously committed his first murder.

Dahmer was known around high school as a weird kid with antisocial tendencies but also as something of a class clown. He would act out on occasion in goofy ways, but never anything violent or dangerous. His most consistent habit, from middle school through his final arrest, was heavy drinking. Classmates remember Dahmer carrying a Styrofoam cup with him to class and refilling it with vodka from a bottle hidden in his backpack.

What no one knew was that Dahmer was developing one of the darkest and most twisted psychoses in the history of criminal pathology. In its early stages, it manifested itself as little more than ordinary homosexual isolation. But before long, Dahmer realized that he wanted more out of a relationship than just a willing partner—he wanted a partner who would never leave. His problem wasn't with rejection exactly. It was that he was so concerned about his own gratification, he made a fetish out of mind control. He would later drill holes into his victims' skulls and inject acid into their brains in an attempt to create zombified sex slaves. (Needless to say, it didn't work.)

But his Ohio murder—Dahmer's first and, for a long time, his only—was a far more straightforward exercise. In June 1978 he met the unfortunate Steven Hicks while Hicks was hitchhiking. After having sex and drinking beer together with Dahmer, Hicks prepared to go. Dahmer panicked. Rather than allow Hicks to leave, he killed him with a barbell. He got rid of the body by dismembering it and burying it in the woods behind his parents' home in plastic garbage bags.

When he graduated from high school, Dahmer was persuaded by his father to move to Columbus and attend fall classes at Ohio State University. His time there was unremarkable in every way, with the exception of his extravagant displays of alcoholism. Other students often found him passed out along North High Street with a bottle in his hand. He barely attended class and managed to flunk out without completing a single quarter. Next he joined the Army, was stationed in Germany for a brief time, and ended up back in Ohio when he was discharged early for disobedience and alcoholism. As far as we know, he didn't murder anyone during these years.

But when he moved back home after his stint in the Army, Dahmer dug up the decomposed, plastic-wrapped remains of Steven Hicks and chopped them up even further with an ax, distributing the pieces over a wider area in the woods. He would go on to murder fourteen young men in Milwaukee, compounding his crimes with bizarre acts of necrophilia and cannibalism.

After those murders were discovered, FBI forensic pathologists sifted the soil around the old Dahmer home in Bath and found chips of Steven Hicks's skeleton. There was no evidence of the strange compulsions that marked the Milwaukee murders, but it was an early instance of the kind of crime that would make him one of the most infamous Ohioans in history. Jeffrey Dahmer died in prison, murdered by one of his fellow inmates.

Edison's Ohio Roots

Every school kid knows who Thomas Alva Edison is. He's the great inventor of such modern conveniences as recorded sound, motion pictures, and the incandescent lightbulb, to name just a few of his 1,093 patented inventions. It's hard to imagine going a day without using one, if not several, of Edison's contributions to the modern world.

Most people probably associate Edison with the state of New Jersey, where he would become world renowned as the "Wizard of Menlo Park." But it was right here in Ohio that he got his start.

Thomas Alva Edison was born in Milan on February 11, 1847. From the start, he was a curious and inquisitive boy. He wanted to know exactly how things worked, constantly asked questions, and started conducting his own experiments at an early age. At school, his endless questions were deemed symptoms of some sort of handicap. When a teacher told Edison's mother that her son was "addled" — meaning he was confused or just dim-witted — young Thomas's mother took him out of school for good and began homeschooling him. In his lifetime, Edison had only three months of formal education. Edison's parents sold their home in Milan in 1854 and the family moved to Port Huron, Michigan. And the rest, as they say, is history.

So what's weird about that? Well, in addition to all of Edison's well-known inventions, there is one that is not so famous. And it not only proves that Edison was a much stranger man than most people give him credit for, but also makes us here at *Weird Ohio* proud to claim him as one of our own!

For all his greatness, Edison did have his share of faults and failures. He was fond of saying that invention was one percent inspiration, ninety-nine percent perspiration. He was not afraid of making mistakes and thought of disasters as merely opportunities to learn. "I learn just as much from my failures," he would say, "as I do from my successes."

If invention really is ninety-nine percent perspiration, we can only imagine how much he must have sweated over one particularly inspired failure.

In 1878, Edison briefly wound up associating with an organization of mystics known as the Aryan Theosophic Society, where he discussed the role of science and technology in mysticism with the group's leader, Madame Elene Blavatsky. While eventually Edison left the group (and even went on to deny ever having associated with them), these experiences got him thinking about different Eastern religious ideas, particularly reincarnation.

Perhaps because of his well-known bravado, or perhaps out of plain old ignorance, Edison saw no reason that he couldn't find a practical way to reincarnate the dead. Better yet, he believed that one could converse with the dead. His theory was that memory was the basis of a human's character and that memory was composed of small physical particles; these defined intelligence, personality, and everything else about an individual. Edison thought that these particles were from outer space and that they formed in swarms and transplanted themselves within people's minds. Death, therefore, occurred when these "little people" (Edison thought each particle had its own consciousness) disagreed among each other.

We told you he was one of us.

"They fight out their differences," the great inventor explained, "and then the stronger group takes charge. If the minority is willing to be disciplined and to conform, there is harmony. But minorities sometimes say: 'To hell with this place; let's get out of it.' They refuse to do their appointed

Madame Elene Blavatsky

work in the man's body, he sickens and dies . . . and they are all free to seek new experience somewhere else."

Edison theorized that if the exact same group of particle-sized intelligent creatures could be put back together, then a dead person's personality would return. He used photographic plates in an attempt to chart these swarms of little people but never succeeded in reanimating a person or—his ultimate goal—enabling them to talk from beyond the grave.

Eventually, Henry Ford convinced Edison to see a parapsychologist, through whom Edison found a new hobby: attempting telepathy. After this obsession took root, his attempts to talk to corpses dropped off. The inventor didn't sell out and go completely normal, however. He conducted many experiments in which he wrapped electrified coils around his own head and those of his guests in an effort to communicate telepathically.

Who knows what would have happened if Edison had lived a few more years? Perhaps instead of simple light-bulbs and summer action flicks, we could thank him for electroshock-induced telepathy with our departed loved ones. We can only hope that his formative years here in Ohio had something to do with inspiring him.

Edison's boyhood home, restored as closely as possible to its nineteenth-century appearance, is now open to the public. Located at 9 Edison Drive in Milan (near Exit 118 of the Ohio Turnpike), it is open to visitors from February through November. The museum features a collection of rare Edisonia, including examples of many of Edison's documents, family mementos, the bed Thomas Alva was born in, and even some of his early inventions. Unfortunately, though, none of these allow us to converse with the dead.

Nick Pahys Jr., DDG-CH-AdVS-A.G.E.-LDA-FIBA

Ever feel like someone isn't telling you the whole truth? Have a sneaking suspicion that you were led astray by your elementary school teachers? Well, the founder of the One and Only Presidential Museum in the World in Hartsgrove believes that your hunch is right. Nick Pahys Jr., DDG-CH-AdVS-A.G.E.-FIBA (the inexplicable string of letters following his name lends credence to the fact that he knows, well, something), wants to set the record straight: Nick Pahys Jr. is on a mission to rewrite history.

A former restaurateur and insurance salesman, Pahys is the founder and curator of the Presidential Museum, which is conveniently located above the Hartsgrove Emporium on the Geneva–Windsor Road. Pahys contends that there are lots of things you thought you knew about American history (not to mention the Bible), but you're wrong. Don't worry, it's not your fault—you've been misled.

Among the misconceptions most Americans hold dear is the fact that George Washington was our first president.

In fact, Pahys insists, he was our ninth president, since eight others were elected first, each to one-year terms, under the Articles of Confederation (our first constitution, in effect from 1781 to 1789). Washington was merely the first president elected under our new, federal constitution (you know, the one we use today), which, in Pahys's opinion, is hardly noteworthy. The museum recognizes John Hanson (a man, according to Pahys, "forgotten for a hundred and fifty years") as our esteemed first president, in an effort to give credit where credit is due.

The museum, dedicated to all fifty-one (by Pahys's count) presidents, also features presidential artifacts, portraits, trivia, and books, as well as tributes to those of our fearless leaders who hailed from Ohio. But it's really Pahys himself who makes a visit worthwhile, especially since he is available to give personal tours.

Pahys, who grew up in Cleveland, served as a Marine in Korea and is a man of devout faith. He is, therefore, by his own admission, committed to discovering and propagating the truth. He notes on his Web site, "The Lord bestows on people knowledge if they want it to make the proper choice. History is made up of the choice between believing in a lie and believing in the truth. [I] just want to arm the people with that truth so they can make the right choice!"

Certainly, Pahys doesn't have a problem with all history, just some of it. For instance, here are some other facts about American history you probably don't know (school learning be damned!): The Revolutionary War started in 1774, not 1775; the originator of the presidential great seal is John

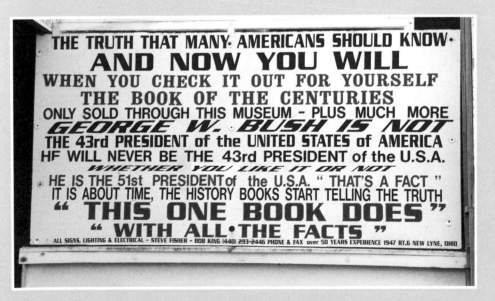

THE TRUTH THAT MANY. AMERICANS SHOULD KNOW.
AND NOW YOU WILL
WHEN YOU CHECK IT OUT FOR YOURSELF
THE BOOK OF THE CENTURIES
ONLY SOLD THROUGH THIS MUSEUM - PLUS MUCH MORE
GEORGE W. BUSH IS NOT
THE 43rd PRESIDENT of the UNITED STATES of AMERICA
HE WILL NEVER BE THE 43rd PRESIDENT of the U.S.A.
WHETHER YOU LIKE IT OR NOT
HE IS THE 51st PRESIDENT of the U.S.A. " THAT'S A FACT "
IT IS ABOUT TIME, THE HISTORY BOOKS START TELLING THE TRUTH
" THIS ONE BOOK DOES "
" WITH ALL•THE FACTS "
ALL SIGNS, LIGHTING & ELECTRICAL - STEVE FISHER - BOB KING (440) 293-2446 PHONE & FAX over 50 YEARS EXPERIENCE 1947 RT.6 NEW LYNE, OHIO

Hanson, not our friend George; the Father of our Country was of Swedish descent—yep, Hanson again.

Pahys is so dedicated to his cause that, according to an article published on www.clubconspiracy.com, he wrote to all one hundred senators asking them to help "spread the truth" (none replied); he wrote a book titled *What Every American Should Know* (self-published but touted by some as "the truest history book ever written in the United States of America"); and even contacted former first lady Barbara Bush after she joked on speaking tours that in her family, her husband is nicknamed "41" and her son "43" due to their presidential sequence. Pahys informed her

that, actually, George H. W. Bush is number forty-nine and George W. Bush is number fifty-one.

For a small fee you can become a museum member and reprogram your brainwashed mind with the correct details about our nation's past, Adam and Eve, Christ's resurrection, and various other beliefs you may hold. "For the unbelievable price of $5.50," Pahys proclaims on his Web site, "you will get the equivalency of a doctorate degree in true history, something that would take tens of thousands of dollars of expenses at one of our country's highest institutions of learning." Plus, you get tickets for a personal museum tour led by Pahys himself and a mention of your patronage inside the museum. That's a lot of bang for your buck!

Visit the museum in Hartsgrove or go online to www.oneandonlypresidentialmuseum.com for an education you won't soon forget and a chance to meet one of Ohio's most interesting characters.

Getting the Royal Treatment at the Presidential Museum

I recently stumbled across the Hartsgrove Emporium general store off of Route 534 and thought you may find it and the gentleman who runs it quite interesting. I was unaware of what lay beyond the crude presidential portraits (mind you, not men I ever knew to hold office) painted outside. I didn't know I had stumbled across the greatest story never told.

Seeing the words "Presidential Museum," I half expected to see ornate carvings inside or maybe wax sculptures. Instead, the place looked more like a tavern with various packaged goods. A gentle-looking man with white hair came at me from behind the bar with a slight waddle. The likable fellow tore into me like a patriotic marine on D-Day. He told me about his place and what I had unknowingly stumbled upon—it was, in his words, "bigger than Pearl Harbor, bigger than 9/11, because people don't realize John Hanson created the presidential seal." I was stunned at the avalanche of information he poured on me, speaking between fits of spittled passion, then fading into points spoken with the grace of an angel.

He noticed my knapsack and small camera and asked if I was media and that he was sick of them making him look like an "idiot." I told him I was just a wandering tin knocker taking the weekend to explore my state. He yelled at me, "My money, my money!" He said that if I was going to photograph anything, I was going to pay for it. He slid a folder down the bar at me that opened to hundreds of flyers and photocopied letters from various important people mentioning his name. With a stumpy finger, he would point at one and another telling me to read them out loud, to tell him what it said. He seemed to take great pleasure in hearing me read the praise he had memorized.

His name was Nick Pahys, and I had in front of me the proof that he was both a professor in history and a doctor in psychology. He showed me letters from the Queen and people who had nominated him for the Nobel Peace Prize. He told me he wasn't there to sell me something (though he did say I could buy any of his various items and charge it to my company) but that I had come across the "biggest story you will ever hear in your entire life."

It was clear he took great pride in his mission, dedicating fifty years of his life to it. The rest he told me in a flood. "Do you know the first real capital of our nation was Philadelphia, then New York, and then DC? I am building a new museum; I'll be a foundation. I sacrificed an awful lot for it all. A man of my age is doing it for future generations. I mortgaged my house for the fourth time to publish my book and to finish my museum."

He asks if my boss or company would want to be a board member and invest a quarter million dollars in his museum, but before I can answer, he reiterates, "The point I am trying to make to you is that there is no bigger story than this."

Nick told me his plans for his new museum. He plans to prove his theories by displaying all the certified letters sent back to him from various folks he has tried to contact. He claims that the returned letters from Rudy Giuliani, Arnold Schwarzenegger, and other numerous people of celebrity and influence indicate that they do not want to acknowledge that they know him. If they admit hearing from him, they would be forced to face his truths.

He mentioned some really interesting evidence that states that two versions of the constitution exist and that there is hard evidence stating that George Washington asked John Hanson for military advice; there is even a letter from G.W. congratulating Mr. Hanson on winning "the most important seat in the U.S." He urges me that he is not a religious fanatic but that he knows when God is trying to tell him something.

Nick and his museum are quite a bit to swallow. Depending on your take, he is either a self-promoting Bible-thumping zealot or a true visionary patriot. It is probably easy to name-call like that when you can't accept the truths he is showing. Personally, I admire his desire to set the world's record straight even though I admit to being a little dumbfounded on how a handful of pins, hats, shirts, and root beer can help spread his good word. Outside, I shook my head in disbelief at what had just happened. I only stopped in for a soda pop.

–Dave McCormick

Personalized Properties

It is said that a man's home is his castle, but in this
great state of ours we find that statement to be only
partially true. Yes, some of Ohio's residents actually do live
in castles, but there are others who live in equally unexpected
environments, mostly of their own design. Sometimes, these
unusual home owners are prolific artists whose work spills out
into their backyard. More often, though, these eccentric abodes are
created by folks with little or no connection to the mainstream art
world, or any other mainstream world, for that matter. They are
self-taught and self-styled and rely heavily on their own
experiences and visions for inspiration.

With some of these places we can't help but wonder what
was on the minds of the people who created them and think that,
perhaps, it's best not to know. In most cases, though, each of these
properties is clearly an extension of the home owner's soul.
These are unique individuals with a singular vision, and they have
fashioned their own slightly off-center environments in which
they happily spend their lives. Sometimes it's even a castle.

Loveland Castle

Of all the things that come to mind when someone says
"Ohio," castles aren't one of them. That is, of course, unless you've
driven through Loveland, the former home of Harry Andrews.

Andrews seems to have been a man of boundless energy and
active imagination. First, he transformed a group of young men in
his Sunday school class (which he taught for thirty years) into the
Knights of the Golden Trail, a Boy Scouts–type brood that met on

a regular basis. Then he spent more than fifty years building a medieval castle for his knights.

To those who knew him, Andrews was always a bit of an eccentric. Born in New York in 1890, he came to Ohio after returning from a tour of duty as an Army medic in Europe during World War I (opposed to modern weaponry but not warfare itself, he was a conscientious objector). It was during his military service that Andrews fell in love with the castles of Europe, particularly those in France. So deep was this love that upon returning to the United States he started making plans to build his very own castle.

Somewhere along the line, Andrews also began to feel disenchanted with modern civilization, which he felt to be seriously lacking in a code of chivalry and to be populated by a "lower grade" of people. In an effort to rectify this situation, he formed his group of Sunday school knights. Their rules were few, basically the Ten Commandments. But here and there, Andrews provided advice about clean living, based on his contention that pure young men were the only ones who could save humanity. In fact, it was this belief that led Andrews to build the castle, as he noted himself in its brochure.

"Château Laroche," he wrote, "was built as an expression and reminder of the simple strength and rugged grandeur of the mighty men who lived when Knighthood was in flower. It was their knightly zeal for honor, valor and manly purity that lifted mankind out of the moral midnight of the dark ages, and started it towards a gray dawn of human hope."

So in 1929, armed with a reverence for times gone by and a profound admiration for medieval architecture, Andrews began building a full-scale replica of a castle—a tenth-century Norman-style castle, to be exact—that he named Château Laroche, which is French for "stone castle." Over the next few decades, he devoted his life to his project. Almost single-handedly, he carried tons of stones to the construction site, an estimated fifty-six thousand loads of five-gallon pails. Many of the stones were pulled out of the riverbed of the nearby Little Miami River. He worked on his castle every weekend until he retired, in 1955, when it became a full-time endeavor.

Sadly, Andrews passed away in 1981, before

construction was officially completed. Ironically, it was the castle itself that doomed him. A trash fire on the grounds got out of control and burned him severely, eventually killing him. Still, the masterwork he left behind boasts over fifteen rooms, including a great hall, a banquet hall, an armory, a bedroom for Andrews (who lived there), a watchtower, and even a dungeon with cells. Lending credence to its status as a "true" medieval castle, Château Laroche lacks indoor plumbing.

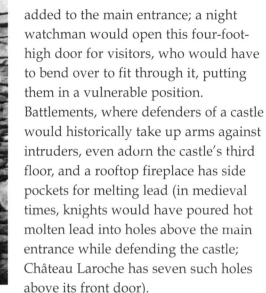

And it is a bona fide fortress. Andrews, with little faith in contemporary society, built an ax-proof door spiked with more than twenty-five hundred nails and over two hundred types of wood (cobbled together so that the grain runs in various directions, making it hard to chop through). A "night door" was also added to the main entrance; a night watchman would open this four-foot-high door for visitors, who would have to bend over to fit through it, putting them in a vulnerable position. Battlements, where defenders of a castle would historically take up arms against intruders, even adorn the castle's third floor, and a rooftop fireplace has side pockets for melting lead (in medieval times, knights would have poured hot molten lead into holes above the main entrance while defending the castle; Château Laroche has seven such holes above its front door).

Today, Andrews's fantasy is a local tourist attraction open to the public. It has been renamed Historic Loveland Castle and is touted as the world headquarters of the Knights of the Golden Trail, a group of medieval reenactors who meet monthly, dress in chain mail and armor, and address each other as "Sir So-and-So" ("Sir Harry" Andrews willed the castle to the group, so it passed to them when he died). The grounds are beautifully manicured by a group of volunteers (mostly knights sans armor) and feature a rock garden with a Loch Ness–type monster swimming through the pebbles.

Andrews never married, but he did receive, by his account, more than fifty marriage proposals from women who wanted to live in a castle. Ironically, Historic Loveland Castle is now a popular place for weddings. The castle's Web site nonetheless points out that wedding-night rentals are not available. But what about wedding knights?

Hartman's Rock Garden

When the Great Depression struck and H. G. Hartman found himself unemployed, he turned to stone. No, not like Medusa! From 1932 to 1939, Hartman built a thirty-five-foot by hundred-and-forty-foot rock garden that contains approximately two hundred and fifty thousand individual stones and which can be seen today at the corner of McCain and Russell streets in Springfield.

Hartman started with a fishpond and then filled his yard with statues, miniature stone castles with moats and

drawbridges, cathedrals complete with statues of saints, and other historic buildings. There are models of the White House, Independence Hall, Noah's Ark, Lincoln's log-cabin birthplace, Mount Vernon (including its slave cabins), and tributes to boxer Joe Louis and the Dionne Quintuplets (the only identical quintuplets known to have survived infancy at the time). Religious scenes and 1930s cultural references coexist side by side in Hartman's world. Even included is a scene from the Oregon Trail. The whole surreal environment is surrounded by a

concrete picket fence and gate that so much resemble an actual wooden fence, you'd swear it was the real thing—if it weren't for the exposed steel rebar, which is visible where the cement has chipped away.

Although now somewhat deteriorated, the Hartman Rock Garden still stands, its impressive displays adorned with flowery paintings. Since Hartman's death in 1944, the property has been maintained by Ben, his youngest son. Ben has let it be known that he would like to sell the artwork and have someone else take care of the castle. Though there are no organized tours, anyone who wants to look around is welcome to visit during daylight hours. No appointment necessary!

Zoratti's Garden

While one of Ohio's most unique personalized properties, the crowded and beautiful sculpture garden at the home of Silvio Zoratti in Conneaut, no longer exists, it was well documented by Gene Kangas in *Folk Art* magazine (volume 17, no. 3 [fall 1992]: pp. 42–47).

The following is based on excerpts from that article, which describes the author's visit to Zoratti's artistic wonderland:

'Back in 1971,' Kangas writes, 'my wife and I didn't really know what to expect when we first turned off Orange Street onto the narrow cement and grass driveway. It was flanked by two modest houses. There, prominently perched atop the small, white-frame, single-car garage down the drive, was a sizeable weathervane/whirligig featuring a painted, sheet-metal chicken and a carved dancing couple. There was no doubt that we were in the right place. From around the corner walked a lean, gray-haired, elderly gentleman following behind a tiny but noisy light-brown Chihuahua that tugged on its tight leash.

'Be careful! He thinks he's a tough little guy. His name's Tiger.' Silvio Zoratti smiled and reached out his hand.

After introductions, Zoratti led us around the corner of the house and into his backyard. By now Tiger had quieted, and was walking sedately alongside the three of us. Off to the left of the garage stood the five magnificent poles of the Presidents' Totems. They totally commanded the entrance to the petite backyard. We exchanged glances back and forth and our hearts were beginning to pound. Further beyond the manicured area of the yard, we could see more—much more.

Zoratti took us on a guided tour back into his magical garden. It was a lush, fertile oasis. Pointillistic dots of colorful flowers accented the abundant greens of beans, peppers, tomatoes, and many other well-cared-for vegetables. Further back was an earthen mound topped by stone carvings; beyond that stood luxuriant fruit trees. . . . Now, this was a garden to be proud of!

Folk artist Silvio Peter Zoratti came to the United States from his native Italy in 1919, Kangas tells us. Like so many immigrants, he entered the country through Ellis Island. And like so many others, he arrived endowed with hope, strong religious convictions, and a willingness to work hard.

Already trained as a stone mason, Zoratti took a job with the Nickel Plate Railroad in June 1923, helping to build and repair bridges, stone fences, and other structures. His work carried him across northern Ohio to the small Lake Erie town of Conneaut, where he and his wife, Beatrice, decided to make their home. They settled down and began to raise a family.

But Zoratti's interests were as widespread and diverse as his newly adopted country. His work required him to spend hours riding trains from city to city, giving the new American ample opportunity to read, think, and plan. Slowly, the idea for a garden of sculptures began to form in his mind. By the late 1950s, he would start on what was to become his life's work.

The first sculptures he did were, of course, made from stone. A lifetime of masonry experience provided him with the skills and confidence to work in what is normally considered a difficult medium. Eight of Zoratti's stone sculptures were specifically designed to be placed atop a high focal point he had created in his garden. Knowing that anything located on this ridge would be visible from every point in the garden, Zoratti decided to site his first artistic efforts there prominently. On and around it, he planted luxuriant landscaping to enliven the unique environment he was beginning to create.

Zoratti's interests were everywhere. His political and historical concerns manifested themselves in three-dimensional symbols such as *Presidents' Totems, Uncle Sam,* and *The Statue of Liberty.* His religious beliefs shone in major works like *The Nativity,* a pietà, and *St. Francis of Assisi.*

Along with the stone sculptures, Zoratti fashioned fanciful, concrete animals for his garden. There were nature walks on which the smaller creatures could be discovered, while the heads of taller animals such as deer and dinosaurs popped up in the distance. Two of his earliest works in concrete were the mascots of the Democratic and Republican parties, a donkey and an elephant, respectively. These were not merely statues, though. Built on sturdy wooden platforms and attached to substantial springs, they were also huge rocking horses, providing neighborhood children with hours of fun, riding the big beasts on imaginary journeys through the wilderness.

Nothing if not versatile, Zoratti also worked in wood. In fact, most of the sculptures he created from 1965 through the early 1980s—somewhere between three hundred and five hundred pieces—were wood. Of the hundreds of wood pieces, two stand out: *Presidents' Totems* and *The Last Supper.*

Presidents' Totems, a great example of American folk art, formed the focal point of the entrance to the backyard. Five vertical poles of varying heights featured colorful portraits of thirty-six presidents, each with its own metal name tag. This impressive group was completed in 1963 and received considerable press. In 1974, President Gerald

Ford wrote to Zoratti, saying he was "interested to read about the project and I can see you have devoted a great deal of time and considerable talent to this unique work." This signature piece was a visual testament to Zoratti's reverence for the history of his adopted country.

The Last Supper, on the other hand, was created for an entirely different purpose. The thirteen portraits were a labor of love, created after Zoratti was hospitalized for a serious illness. They were the only of his outdoor wood carvings ever protected from the ravages of time. As winter approached each year, the garden was prepared for its seasonal rest, and *The Last Supper* was covered with plastic.

In his day, Zoratti was recognized as one of Ohio's masters of folk art; his work appeared in exhibitions at the Akron Art Institute and the Art Academy of Cincinnati. A modest man, he preferred his privacy, but in 1976 several of his works were featured anonymously on NBC's *America, a Different Look: American Folk Art.* He maintained a rigid policy of not selling his artwork while it was under his control, although he gave some away to friends and family.

Unfortunately, the years took their toll on Silvio, Beatrice, and their garden. Eventually, they were forced to leave their home and move to a local nursing residence. The house was sold, and the sculptures and garden were left unattended. Today, the figures Zoratti worked over so lovingly are gone. Still, we are fortunate to have them so well documented and photographed. They are a genuine American art legacy, created by a quiet Italian immigrant.

The Temple of Tolerance

In prehistoric times, the inhabitants of what is now Ohio were known for their mound building. But there is a modern-day Ohio man with a passion for erecting similar structures in the small town of Wapakoneta. The exterior of Jim Bowsher's modest two-story home on a quiet street carefully masks what lies behind the front door and continues out into the huge backyard.

Over the past fifteen years, I've seen many amazing visionary sites, but none quite like the one Bowsher has created on South Wood Street in Wapakoneta. This writer, artist, archaeologist, and lecturer has the enthusiasm of a Tasmanian devil on amphetamines. He always has "one more story," and it's usually a good one. Jim's backyard reminds one of the ancient Stonehenge-like structures scattered throughout the British Isles. And like those famous sites, this place is also a temple, specifically the Temple of Tolerance.

The Temple of Tolerance is really two separate but

interconnected environments. The first is Bowsher's home, an incredible museum of artifacts from the America that wasn't written about in your school history books. Every nook and cranny is filled with interesting treasures, each with its own fascinating story to tell. It's like a secret Smithsonian—a Grand Central Terminal for the Underground Railroad, an invisible library of unwritten books on Freemasons, Harry Houdini, and Neil Armstrong.

In the backyard—in fact, over several backyards—is the actual Temple complex. This feels more like a place that has been unearthed rather than constructed (if that makes sense). Massive glacial boulders mound up to form the central monument, dedicated to tolerance. The main temple is a twenty-foot-high pile of boulders crowned by an altar that is fronted by ancient Irish mood-dog carvings. It is surrounded by smaller temples, a Vietnam War memorial, a meditation garden with a bench James Dean once slept on, a monument to love (in this case, erected for his wife), and a red barrel house where Babe Ruth once stopped by for a poker game. There is a stage for summer music performances and a Tree of Life that was constructed by neighborhood kids.

Throughout the grounds, you'll also find the archaeology of good and evil: boundary markers from a Shawnee Indian reservation, slab steps from a Klan meetinghouse, stone dragons from Ireland, fragments from the first baseball park in Cincinnati, even a marble countertop from a bank that John Dillinger robbed.

The theme of the Temple of Tolerance was probably most aptly put into words by Cathy J. Schreirma, a writer for *The* (Wapakoneta) *Evening Ledger,* when she wrote in an April 2001 article, "Perhaps more than anything, the Temple stands to remind us, as well as future generations, to have compassion for others as we continue to explore our dreams, follow our spirit, and search for answers in the hope of scaling new heights."

Bowsher began construction on the Temple in the late 1990s and is still adding to his unique and unusual creation to this day.

—By field reporters Larry Harris and Tom LaFaver

James Batchelor's "Odd Garden"

James Batchelor's garden is referred to in a newspaper article as "yard-art mosaic that's a little bit Mardi Gras, a little bit Looney Toons, a little bit roadside Americana." It is filled with vegetables planted in painted barrels, silk flowers, a stuffed goat chained to a bowling ball, a "life-sized, voodoo-doll-looking woman" that had to be moved to the backyard when men talking to her got angry when she didn't respond. There is also a Batchelor family "Walk of Fame" with a star-studded square for James's late wife (who didn't like the garden) and each of their nine children. People bring him things to add to his garden all the time, and he is pleased that people drive by to take a look. Batchelor's house is located at 761 Wayne Court, in the Walnut Hills neighborhood of Cincinnati.
—*Betty-Carol Sellen*

Batchelor's Place Is Not Just Weird on the Outside

Mr. Batchelor, ninety-seven years young, allowed me the privilege of seeing his garden over the summer. While the heat was too oppressive for him to join me, I was allowed free rein to explore the garden he had constructed over the past ten or fifteen years.

A stark contrast to the walls of brick and concrete nearby, the garden is full of color and life. Mixed in with his tomatoes, greens, and peppers are all sorts of odd stuffed animals and whimsical items. Various buckets and basins, all covered with splashes of paint, hold up his displays and odd arrangements.

I thought the one garden behind his house was impressive until I looked across a back alleyway to another piece of property. This area looked as if someone took a little bit of Disney World, a costume shop, and an art supply store, mixed it together in one giant bowl, and dumped it on the lawn. It is wonderful.

Back inside, I asked him about the multicolored walkway in his furthest garden with various names on it. He said very proudly and full of love that those names were his family. Then suddenly, the almost-century-old man jumped up with a gleeful secret he wanted to share with me. He opened the door to a creation he was far more excited about than his garden: His sitting room was a living altar to all his various family members. Literally thousands of faces stared back at me with smiles; they are photographic cutouts of all those he loves and who love him in return. Every inch of all four walls and all the furniture are covered with them. James Batchelor is all about his family.

On the way out, a worried elderly woman leaned over her porch to ask me if I was the gas man or the electric man. I assured her I wasn't with any utilities. I told her I was here to see James Batchelor, and she relaxed with a knowing smile.—*Ryan Doan*

Brice Baughman's *The Statues*

Brice Baughman (1874–1954) was from Black Run, Ohio. He was a stone carver who created sandstone monuments and sculptural pieces in the deep wood of his

farm near Jackson Township in Muskingum County, Ohio. He taught himself to carve animals and people from the hard rock there, a massive sandstone formation with only a shallow covering of soil. He made his first statue in 1898, of President William McKinley. Baughman, two sons, and a nephew cleared the ground around the statues and scattered picnic tables among them. The day the last statue was dedicated, more than three thousand cars passed through the park to see the site. The sculptures are still there, and there are current activities to make them more accessible. *–Betty-Carol Sellen*

Remembering the Brice Baughman Statues

I remember as a child driving through the park with Brice Baughman's statues staring down at my car. I always felt they were bigger than life and, perhaps due to their remote area in the woods, always expected them to climb off their podiums and wreak havoc on the local country folk. I recently was passing through, visiting family, and thought I would stop by to see if they were still around. The old trail "Baughman Park Road" is still there, but it is overgrown and I was met with a gate that asked to kindly not trespass. I had to see at least one statue for myself and would've gotten deeper if not for the hundreds of various beetles that flew at me. It was like they were guarding the place. People in town said that the land was bought up eleven or so years ago and is now a private residence. At least one statue is still standing, however overgrown it may be. The whole territory is just west of Frazeysburg on Ohio Route 586. *–Ray Blasi*

The People Love People Church

Walking along Lakefront Avenue in east Cleveland, you'll pass scores of houses that are either boarded up or heavily fortified against possible intruders—except one. At this unprotected home, the door stands open, inviting all to come inside. Over the front porch, a sign reading COME HOME ETHIOPIA greets visitors. WELCOME TO THE PEOPLE LOVE PEOPLE CHURCH. This is the home of the Reverend Albert Wagner, but more than that, it is where he preaches to his congregation and paints his pictures—thousands of them!

Though in his early eighties, this former boxer is still a man of imposing physical stature. He is a devout and highly spiritual person who has transformed not only his soul but also his living space into a place of enlightenment and artistic expression. The three-story house, located about fifteen minutes from downtown Cleveland, is like a massive work of art in itself. Room after room is filled with all manner of paintings on boards, carved wood sculptures, and assemblages of found and recycled objects. There are street scenes of murder, assaults, and drug deals, displayed side by side with religiously inspired works, ranting prophets, and the crucifixion of Christ. The centerpiece painting is a fourteen-foot canvas of Moses leading his people out of Egypt. A January 2001 *New York Times* article describes the painting this way:

> Gene Kangas, a local sculptor and retired art professor, who has known Mr. Wagner since 1971, remembers when the Moses figure, like the artist, had black hair and a black beard. As Mr. Wagner turned gray, he revised the figure in his likeness. Mr. Wagner stopped short of declaring himself a prophet, but said, 'Maybe somehow the Lord has permitted me to feel the joy or the pain that Moses felt, so I'm able to express his thoughts.'

In actuality, almost all of Wagner's work is autobiographical to some extent. His art is raw and folksy yet not the naïve renderings so often seen with other outsider or self-taught artists. There is a bold and stark robustness that is totally original, earning it recognition and praise in the national art community. There is also a message. The Reverend Wagner has a lot to say, and he is not shy about doing so—in his conversations, in the daylong sermons he gives in his basement church, or in the artwork that is so tightly crammed into his house.

The message, as Wagner told *LIFE* magazine in a May 1998 article, is that "we need to see the true root of all our troubles. The fault doesn't lie in American history, not in slavery times or any other injustice, but way back in antiquity. Ethiopia sinned; it's in the Bible. We committed an atrocity in God's eyes. And this is my mission now, to make my people fall down on their knees and beg His forgiveness. There is no other way."

Clearly, Albert Wagner is a man on a mission, but it

wasn't always this way. He was born into a family of poor sharecroppers in 1924 in rural Bassett, Arkansas. By the time Albert was five, his mother believed that he would be a great artist one day, if only she could afford to send him to art school. But it was not to be. He dropped out of elementary school after the third grade, and the family moved north to Ohio.

Forty-odd years later, Wagner was a successful Cleveland businessman with a fleet of moving trucks. He also had several identities, four homes, and three families, with a total of twenty children by three different women. By his own description, he was a gambler, a drinker, and a womanizer.

Then one day, at the age of fifty, all of that changed. It happened during a brutal heat wave. Wagner's car radiator overheated, and a woman at a gas station brought him two pails of water to cool the engine. At that moment, Wagner had a divine epiphany: He saw himself as a child in the cotton fields of Arkansas carrying water pails to his mother, who was toiling in the sweltering hot fields.

"Between one breath and the next, I saw the whole scene," he told *LIFE*, "myself as a child, my mother waiting, the bugs and the high cotton, the yellow sky. I went right home and I started to paint it all. I never stopped painting since."

That was more than thirty years ago, and Wagner continues to paint at an astonishingly prolific rate. If he sends paintings to a gallery, he quickly paints several more to replace them. He gave up his business and his carousing and became an ordained minister in a denomination called the Commandment Keepers. He now begins his Sabbath each Friday night at sunset and maintains a completely kosher diet.

"It didn't come easy," he admits. "Sex had me bound and chained. I was like the wolfman—the moment that

the trick of lust allured my nostrils, it was like I had fangs, my body went back to the beast. That wolf had got to die. But it took me long years to kill him."

These days, you can find the Reverend Albert Wagner most Saturdays in the basement of his home, where he gives daylong sermons, singing and playing a battered drum while retelling the story of his life, his past debauchery, and his ultimate redemption. The majority of his congregation, seated in folding metal chairs, is made up of some of his twenty children, scores of grandchildren, and even a few ex-wives and former mistresses, with whom he still has close, if somewhat complicated, relationships. Wagner chants and preaches salvation in the stifling hot cellar with all the fire and brimstone of an Old Testament prophet as family members shout back responses.

If the Reverend Wagner shows any regret about his life, it is that his own people, the African American community, have been slow to embrace his message. While white art collectors and fellow artists may hold his work in high regard, many blacks consider him to be just a crackpot, and he knows it.

The reason, according to the Reverend, can be seen in his art. For example, there is one work, a sculpture of a black man being lynched, entitled *American History,* with the words WE MUST NOT LET WHAT HAPPENED THEN ERASE US OF THE REALITY OF TODAY.

"I cannot erase history," Wagner says of it, "but history is erasing us. We're using history as an excuse."

Wagner told the *Times,* "[My people] don't like me because of what I'm saying. I'm an Uncle Tom. Everyone's an Uncle Tom who tells us to get up and make something of ourselves."

Still, though the criticism does sometimes anger him, the Reverend Wagner seems to take it all in stride as part of God's master plan for him. "Every prophet is crazy to most people," he has said. "If he wasn't, there wouldn't be no need to prophesy. . . . What do I do normally? I don't do anything normal. I'm a very strange man. Strange to myself sometimes."

Feeling the Love

I do not belong in Reverend Albert's neighborhood. Hurt by years of economic struggle, his east Cleveland region is not welcoming to an outsider wandering around with a camera. That is with the exception of Reverend Albert Wagner. He and his People Love People House of God home on Lakefront Avenue shine like a diamond in the rough, welcoming any who wish to stop in.

I am not expected when I arrive, and still they take me in. One step inside, and my jaw drops. There is not a nook or cranny that is not housing some artistic and biblical creation. The house, all three or four stories worth, is alive with art, all of which are the creation of the man I came to meet in person. The Reverend's son leads me upstairs, and I pass rooms where people sleeping on floors wake up and smile at me, rubbing their eyes. I step over paintings and under carvings of Jesus.

As I am led down the hallway, I feel like Neo from *The Matrix* coming to visit the Oracle for some divine knowledge. The son holds out an arm, palm up, and says I may enter. Inside, I meet the self-taught Wagner, who is under his blanket regaining his strength from a trip to the hospital the day before. He is simple and pleasant and not at all bothered by my visit. His eyes are soul piercing but not alarming, with a glimmer of some childlike nature he has not let go of. He tells me, "We have been looking forward to you," while sitting up to visit with me. His room is very simple with completed paintings on the walls and several sketches strewn about. Next to each painting is some note card posted with either the biblical story it represents or a quote from the Bible itself.

I wander the halls thinking there cannot be more, but there is. It is endless and amazing. After breathing in all the work and marveling at the fact that it came out of one man's passion and sense of duty, I go to thank him for allowing me the privilege. He smiles at me big and shakes my hand, saying, "Bless you, we will see you again." I certainly hope so. Reverend Albert Wagner is a humble visionary and his home a place to behold. It is a beacon of hope for those who live by him, and driving away, I felt a part of his neighborhood.
—*Ryan Doan*

Akron's Cleanup Man

P. R. Miller gives new meaning to the word "trashy" when it comes to art. That's because every piece of artwork he creates is made entirely from recycled materials—in other words, trash. Miller, who prefers the term "refuse" to "trash," calls himself the Cleanup Man. He takes junk and scrap from abandoned sites and transforms them into bugs, frogs, flowers, and other artistic creations.

Hailing from Mars (Pennsylvania, not the planet), Miller came to Ohio in 1966 to attend the University of Akron, where he earned a degree in art education. In a portent of things to come, he supported himself in college by working as a garbage collector. But Miller's ultimate career choice, he says, came from the hours he spent as a child playing in the town dump, combined with his mother's artistic influence. A survivor of colon cancer and a benign brain tumor, Miller has said that a near-death experience helped him realize his talents: "A voice told me, 'Go back, your work is not done.' I asked, 'Well, what is my job?' And then I understood that this is why we are here, to find out what we are supposed to be doing! I'm the Cleanup Man, and I'm good at it!"

Miller, who has served as artist in residence for the Norton Public Schools and exhibited his work in the Massillon Museum and other galleries, is a committed proponent of recycling and living simply. Although he was formerly the head of a demolition company in Akron, his health troubles gave him a new outlook on life. "I had forty people working for me at one time," he has said. "But my tumor put my life in perspective. I learned to open my head, to learn and observe. There's no need to drive a big, new car every year. There's no need to have a bunch of fancy clothes. We have become a nation of consumerist pigs. We've been

sold a bill of goods that tells us that we need to wear hundred-dollar shoes made by child labor in Vietnam for twelve cents an hour. The rich get richer. How much is enough?"

Miller resides in Lawrence Township in Stark County on land he calls the Frogtown Flower Farm. But while he prides himself on having revitalized the "dump" that the house and its surrounds were when he purchased it, some people would not be so quick to agree. Miller's displays of artwork fashioned from old tires, discarded bedsprings, and other throwaways crowd his property, and some neighbors consider them an eyesore. Embroiled in a lengthy legal battle over cleaning it up, Miller told the *Akron Beacon Journal* that local officials "do not know the difference between art and miscellaneous. I take miscellaneous and make art of it."

And he's not finished yet. When it was reported that the twenty-six-foot, four thousand, eight-hundred-pound *Beacon Journal* clock tower was being scrapped for a newer, LCD-display model and that, according to the

Journal, "The first person who could haul away the old one was welcome to it," Miller hastened to get in line. After some debate over the tower's fate (the *Journal* commented on May 13, 2005, that "the Normandy invasion wasn't this complicated"), it was decided that the old tower would go to Miller, who plans to use it as part of a giant flower sculpture.

Miller told the *Journal,* "The plan is to use the frame as a 28-foot-tall flower base in which will be placed a flower that I am making from the remains of the steam plant. The head of the flower will be somewhere in the vicinity of 20 feet in diameter. Depending on the bureaucratic politicians in this town, I would like to put it at the head of the canal, overlooking the Innerbelt."

A Visit With P. R. Miller, the Grizzled Wizard

He is a man who turns people's refuse into masterpieces, then sells or contributes it back to them. He is the Junkman of Akron, the Preacher of Recycling, a lifetime demolitionist, and an admitted "criminal" who practices his teaching every second of his life (having lost all ties to his biological clock when that part of his brain was removed in a tumor operation).

I would've passed his place if not for the unique art decorating the walls of the stand-alone building. Sheltered from the hot sun and with the smell of famous pork products in the air, I spent the morning with P. R. Miller and his lovely assistant, Laura.

Shirtless and ripe from a late night, P. R. is every bit part of the earth he seeks to protect. He is irreverent with his wild hair and speaks in a mix of philosophical musings and trucker language. He is totally likable.

His studio/living quarters are an array of newspaper clippings and scattered materials. He shows me wads of red glass that came out of Ford Motor Company that are the taillights of cars that didn't make it and just fell to the floor in blobs. The liquid glass would cool into amorphous shapes, and P. R. would gather them all up. It all looks like an antique shop from another reality, where things are somewhat recognizable but nothing is as you recall it.

He shows me a chair he created out of arching wire and metal bits, and I cannot believe how comfortable it is (more than any chair I have ever sat in). He says it was designed from all discarded parts, including a tractor seat and a scoop. He says he used to drink quite a bit and would pass out and find himself sprawled out on the floor. The chair was designed specifically to pass out in and is almost impossible to fall out of.

While the Grizzled Wizard's story is filled with political entanglements, civic planning, and philosophical ponderings about what God is (nothing more than the great coincidence control coordinator), P. R. is primarily an artist with a clear mission and steady determination to adhere to that dogma. He makes beautiful stuff out of things people cast away. And he does so all the while hoping people realize how much we are "f'ing up the planet."

In a pickup truck with no air-conditioning and no radio, we drive around town, where I see firsthand how symbiotic P. R.'s relationship is with the city. Every so often, you notice some giant metal flower sparkling in the sun. Maybe you note the town gazebo he created out of street lamps, with its giant plume of metalwork and sparkling compact disks. You may even see his scandalous albino frogs breeding on their migration to Cleveland. He is the Wizard of Waste Not and Want Not, and if you take some time with his work, you are sure to be influenced by his spell.*–Ryan Doan*

"But Officer . . ."

It's not easy to find a 1954 Hudson these days, but in Pleasant Hill this one is pretty simple to spot. And it's going no place fast. The Hudson is the proud property of Ivan and Noel Renner, and it's the centerpiece of Noel's business, Renner Transmissions. Noel bought the car from a man in Covington who'd had it on his lawn for years. After some negotiating, a $50 offer finally convinced the man to sell, and Noel became the owner of this priceless antique.

Well, priceless may be overstating things a bit. The car was so rusted out by the time Noel bought it that the rear end fell off when he lifted it up with his front-end loader. He decided to plant the front of the Hudson firmly in place in a fence in his business's parking lot. In the grille, he put high-intensity spotlights that are triggered by a motion sensor and manage to scare the daylights out of anyone approaching. At Christmastime, full of holiday spirit, he puts flickering red bulbs in the car's signal lights. It cheers people up, and Noel swears the car's been great for business. *–Dan McNichol*

Size Matters!

How do you make an everyday object seem more impressive and important? Super-size it! Blown up to colossal proportions, even the most mundane items can seem magnificent. The weird thing is how making something so ordinary into something extraordinary really forces us to see familiar objects as if for the first time.

Giant Rubber Stamp

The Giant Rubber Stamp in Cleveland was created by Claes Oldenburg and Coosje Van Bruggen. The twenty-eight-foot by forty-eight-foot "Free" stamp—the kind an office worker might use—was commissioned by the Standard Oil Company of Ohio in 1982. The word Free, chosen by the artists, was meant to serve not only as a representation of a typical office stamp but also as a symbol of liberty and independence that could be enjoyed by all of downtown Cleveland (except those trapped indoors in the tedium of the nine-to-five!).

The sculpture was intended for display outside the company's headquarters, but it ended up in storage in Indiana for seven years while British Petroleum assumed control of Standard Oil. No longer interested in continuing to pay to house the sculpture, British Petroleum donated it to the city of Cleveland. After some debate about where it should end up, BP offered to maintain it in its eventual home, Willard Park.

Oldenburg became famous in the early 1960s for his giant soft sculptures of everyday objects. In the late 1960s, his works became larger and moved outdoors to public spaces around the world. He began collaborating with Van Bruggen in 1976 and they married in 1977. They have created more than forty sculptures together, including *Binoculars* (Venice, CA), *Spoon & Cherry* (Minneapolis, MN), *Shuttlecock* (Kansas City, MO), and *Safety Pin, Trowel & Hankie* (New York City).

The Giant Three-Way Plug

Another Oldenburg, created in 1970, is found in Oberlin. It is made of bronze, and two identical sculptures are located in other American cities. Oldenburg has created other three-way plugs over the years using various materials, including mahogany and vinyl.

World's Largest Cuckoo Clock

Recently, we got a tip that the world's largest cuckoo clock was in an "Ohio Alpine" restaurant. This we had to check out for ourselves! Is it a restaurant? Is it a clock? Who cares!

Grandma's Alpine Homestead (formerly the Alpine-Alpa Cheese House) bills itself, or at least it used to, as a real Swiss oasis in the Ohio heartland. A huge cuckoo clock, complete with a giant bird that pops out on the hour, clog-shod dancers, and a band, is the main attraction at this cheese shop and eatery, or so we had been led to believe. Hungry tourists can sit on the Alpine-Alpa's roof to enjoy the spectacle, eat in the whimsical Alpine-themed restaurant, or bring a bit of the mountains home from the Black Forest Cuckoo Clock Shop (complete with robotic milkmaids, an automated band that, for twenty-five cents, will strike up a lively tune, and more than three hundred clocks for sale).

Well, that's what we had been told, anyway.

When we visited this odd attraction, we found it to be somewhat, er . . . different. Here's a brief history of the place. When it opened, it was part of this weird concept of "the Swiss Alps over here," meaning here in the United States. The entire building was done up to look like a Swiss chalet on the outside, and they even had actors walking around in costumes.

The building itself consists of two floors, with the cuckoo clock and some bizarre thing known as the Gnome Grotto being the only things on the second floor (which is really more like a patio). The clock shops were on either side of the main entrance as we walked in the front door. We didn't see anywhere near three hundred clocks—maybe twenty or thirty. The cheese shop is closed, although there is a sign claiming that SOMETHING NEW IS COMING SOON. So maybe they are going to reopen things, but for now, no cheese for you! On the right, there was indeed a four-piece automated band.

The restaurant is all the way in the back, where there is also a stairway to the patio area, which was used for

clock viewing. On the second floor, there are a few benches in front of the clock, and you can look through some windows down into the restaurant area.

The "robotic milkmaids" was actually just ONE robotic milkmaid. Named Trudy, she would pop out of a window above the main entrance and welcome guests to the Alpine-Alpa. She's gone now, and the window she popped out of has been boarded over with a GRANDMA'S ALPINE HOMESTEAD sign.

As for the clock itself, it has seen better days. The good news is that it still works. But the bad news is that it's just sitting out there on the roof, exposed to the elements. And there's NO advertising for it, with nary a sign anywhere. You basically have to ask where it is and be pointed up some back stairs.

The band that was along the base of the clock is now gone. The two cloggers are still there, but one of them is missing a hand and part of an arm. The Gnome Grotto is all but gone. It's basically just a fenced-off area with a small (empty) fishpond in the middle of it.

There are no longer actors walking around in costume. In fact, the place seems to be moving toward being more of an Amish attraction than anything else. There were a lot of Amish people working at the restaurant and a bunch of Amish crafts, etc., for sale in the gift shop. The place probably sounds weirdest if we try to describe it to you in one sentence: It's a Swiss-themed restaurant that serves Amish home-style cooking and has live bluegrass music on the weekend. Oh yeah, and it's got the world's largest cuckoo clock rotting away on its roof.

Really Big Rocking Chair

Outside Country Cousins, a log-furniture company in Austinburg, stands the world's largest rocking chair. Country Cousins didn't build the giant chair, and it is not known who did. Apparently, the big seat has been in Austinburg since the 1960s, rocking in the wind, seemingly waiting for a giant mother and baby to arrive for story time.

That's a Lotta Ice Cream

The twenty-eight-foot tall, twenty-foot-wide fiberglass ice cream cones (topped with cherries) that are otherwise known as Twistee Treat ice cream parlors were designed by Robert G. Skiller, the father of the Twistee Treat chain. Skiller started the corporation in Florida in 1983, but recently, franchising rights were sold to a Canadian company. Nowadays, these massive cones are being replicated across the border.

There is some controversy swirling around as to whether or not the building in Clyde is an original or a copycat. The main reason for this is, unlike the original buildings, the one in Clyde DOES NOT have a cherry on top!

Giant Graduation Cap

Created by local artist Todd Slaughter in commemoration of Franklin University's centennial celebration, this giant metal mortarboard with aluminum-rod tassel was installed over Rich Street on the university's main campus in 2002. The steel-and-aluminum sculpture, weighing almost ten thousand pounds and supported by thirteen cables and five masts, is entitled *Commencing*. Unlike traditional graduation caps, it stays up in the air indefinitely.

Root Beer for Really Thirsty People

This giant Frostop root beer mug beckons to thirsty travelers in Salem. Frostop originated in Springfield in 1926 and later expanded to over a hundred locations throughout the United States. The revolving, eight-to-ten-foot-tall mugs started popping up in the mid-1950s, first at a Frostop in Los Angeles. The Salem shop opened around 1960.

Basket Headquarters

Corporate America isn't always stodgy. The Longaberger Basket building was built in 1997 as the manufacturer's headquarters, at a cost of $30 million. The seven-story building is an exact replica of a Longaberger basket, over eight million of which are made each year and sold at home "basket parties." Synthetic plaster was used to create the building's curved, basket-weave exterior. The seventy-five-foot handles are heated to prevent ice from forming and falling onto the roof, and a gold-plated Longaberger tag was even mounted on the side.

The basket building, a replica one hundred and sixty times the size of the company's Medium Market Basket, was envisioned by David Longaberger (who, in 1974, took over the company his father had founded in 1936). Apparently, Longaberger was unhappy with the architects' attempts to render suitable plans for the company headquarters, and he figured the high-quality design of a Longaberger basket would stand the test of time. The giant basket, home to five hundred employees, was completed two years before David Longaberger's death in 1999.

Longaberger Homestead Basket

Located in the town of Frazeysburg, seventeen miles east of Longaberger's Newark offices, the Longaberger Homestead includes exhibits, basket-making instruction, restaurants, gift shops, a golf course, and a manufacturing tour. It also features—what else—the world's largest apple basket, which is twenty feet tall. We're not sure when the apples were added, but it was shortly after they decided to turn the main street of the homestead into this odd place where all the buildings featured different ways you could display Longaberger baskets in your home. Our guess is the apples were to show how you could use any giant fruits you might have lying around.

Goodyear Airdock

In Akron, once known as the Rubber Capital of the World, is the Goodyear Aerospace Airdock, the largest enclosed space in the country without interior supports. (It was once the largest in the world, but it was recently eclipsed by a structure in Germany.)

Built in 1929 by the Goodyear Zeppelin Corporation, it was originally used to construct Navy airships—including the ill-fated U.S.S. *Macon* and U.S.S. *Akron,* both of which crashed. Later, it became a construction site and a hangar for Goodyear blimps. It is 1,175 feet long, 325 feet wide, and 211 feet tall, with a volume of fifty-five million cubic feet. Each door (one on each end) weighs 609 tons. It is said that four football games could be accommodated in the twenty-two-story-high airdock and that, due to its atmosphere and enormous size, some weather conditions such as clouds and rain have been produced inside it!

Since Goodyear got out of the blimp-making business, the airdock has been used by Loral Defense Systems (who purchased Goodyear Aerospace in 1987) and subsequently Lockheed Martin, for engineering projects and storage. The airdock is not open to the public, but it can be seen from U.S. Route 224 outside downtown Akron.

World's Largest Crystal Ball

Inside the headquarters of the American Ceramics Society in Westerville is the Ross C. Purdy Museum of Ceramics, featuring the world's largest crystal ball. It was created in 1987 by Christopher Ries and Schott Glass Technologies, Inc.

The big, glassy ball is literally sitting inside the offices of the American Ceramics Society (it seems crystal balls and glass are technically ceramics). If you're interested in stopping by to see it, keep in mind that it's available for viewing only Monday through Friday during normal business hours.

Since our field trip, we're still not convinced there really is a Museum of Ceramics here. To be honest, it's just a huge area filled with employee work cubes. Along some of the walls are a few pieces of ceramics, etc.—hardly what one would call a museum. It's more along the lines of office decorations. But it does have the world's largest crystal ball sitting off by itself in one corner!

Roadside Giants

Giant Santa of Bath

The Bath Santa originally stood at a building supply store in Akron. When it closed, he was sold to a nearby restaurant, where he stood from 1984 to 1986. Today, he belongs to the Hesseman family in Bath, who celebrate the Christmas season by displaying the mammoth fiberglass Santa on their front lawn each year. Since 1986, they have bolted together his head, torso, and legs every Christmas and put him on view. He spends the rest of the year stored in a barn.

The story that was handed down to the Hessemans is that thirteen of these Santas were made in the 1940s and brought over from Germany. This Santa is identical to ones in Amherst, New Hampshire, and Cromwell, Connecticut.

The Madonna of Windsor

Behind the parking lot of the Servants of Mary Center of Peace near the town of Windsor stands this gargantuan statue of Our Lady of Guadalupe, whose appearance in the sixteenth century is credited with the conversion of seventy-five thousand Aztec Indians to Catholicism.

Although not the largest Virgin Mary statue around, the thirty-three-foot-tall Madonna is still pretty impressive. She stands on the outstretched wings of an angel perched on a cloud, bringing the statue's entire height to fifty feet. In front of her, a giant, illuminated string of rosary beads made of chain-linked metal balls surrounds a small lake. Both the statue and the Servants of Mary Center of Peace sit on an organic farm owned by Pat and Ed Heinz.

The Heinzes themselves conceived of the larger-than-life Mary, but she was just a vision until Richard Hyslin, a Texas artist, offered to donate his skills free of charge. The statue, covered with small, colorful mosaic tiles and complete with a huge metal coil from behind that conveys Mary's radiance, was dedicated in 1995.

Mary sits far back from the road, so look for her carefully if you're traveling on Ireland Road in Windsor. The center is still technically open, but it has seen better days. A lot of the "rosary beads" have been broken, and the gift shop is now closed down.

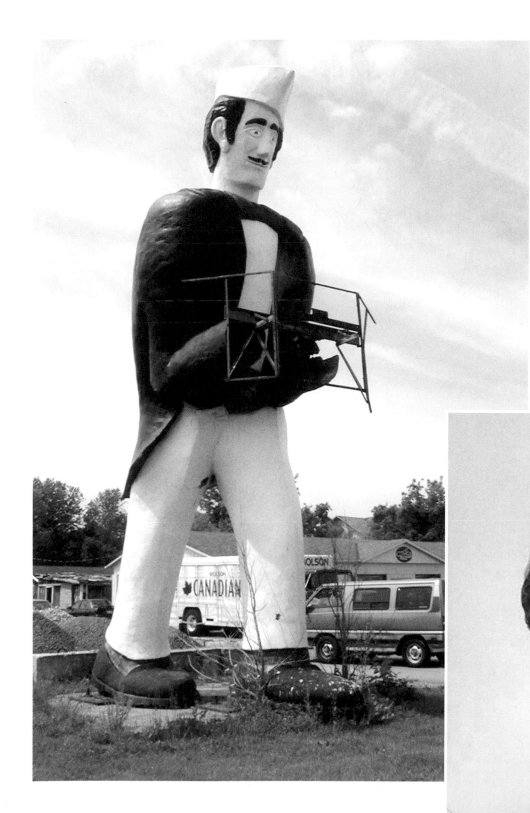

 iant Jacques of Marblehead

Giant Jacques once held a giant roast beef sandwich and lured people to Jacques' Roast Beef, a restaurant originally located in Mansfield. In the 1980s, when the owner and menu changed, Jacques held up a pizza box instead and became known as "Big Pierre." Jacques no longer has anything to hold. His hands are missing, and the building behind him is used as an RV-sales office.

Jesus Is Big in Monroe

Solid Rock Church seems a fitting name for a place that houses a colossal sculpture of Jesus, made out of plastic foam and fiberglass stretched over a metal frame. The huge Christ, which was completed in September 2004, lords over the baptismal pool outside the church, founded by evangelist Darlene Bishop and her husband, Lawrence.

The sixty-two-foot sculpture depicting Jesus's head and torso has a forty-two-foot span between its upraised hands (leading some locals to refer to him as the Touchdown Jesus) and a forty-foot cross at the base. Rendered by artist James Lynch at the request of the Bishops, the statue serves as advertising for the three-thousand-member nondenominational church and as a subject of controversy in the community. Possibly the world's largest Christ (church leaders have asked *Guinness World Records* to decide), many Monroe locals believe it is an eyesore, while others feel it will put Monroe on the map.

Differing views aside, possibly the most sensible commentary about the enormous Jesus (especially for those seeking roadside weirdness) comes from a Monroe community website, www.mainstreet-monroe.com, where one contributor observes: "There have been so many deaths on that section of I-75, perhaps when people see Jesus they will be more careful."

The statue is actually at the back of the Lawrence Bishop Music Theater, which is kind of an amphitheater and belongs to the church. If you are riding north on I-75, there is no way you can miss this thing, as it sits very close to the road. In fact, while we were there taking pictures, we heard more than one set of brakes screech to a halt and even saw a few people pull over to take pictures of their own, right there on the highway. Now, that is feeling the spirit move you!

Touchdown!

The last thing you want to see on a busy highway is Jesus in your rearview mirror. The other day I was driving north on route 71. I am a long-distance trucker and have seen my share of roadside oddities, but this one takes the cake. Near Monroe, is the largest sculpture of Jesus I have ever seen. I had to take a U-turn to see if I could get closer. Taking the exit, you can either go to a few adult stores, a truck rest area with a hot sheet motel, or try to find your way to the elaborate gates of the Solid Rock Church. The gate, with its two angles and fancy landscaping, was open, so I made myself at home. The church is more like a place where you would catch a sporting event—it's friggin' huge. There is even a digital marquee that advertises the next "godly event" and points you to their Web site (a church with a Web site?). Anyway, there is a walking path around the giant Christ, and man, do you feel small under his giant sky-raised arms. I half waited for him to rise up out of the water and start picking up cars of the unrepentant to toss them a few counties away.—*Dave Lounsberry*

The Boy with the Boot

This work was given to the city of Sandusky in 1895 by Voltaire Scott, a Sanduskian who bought it in Germany. Until Scott's death the zinc statue was displayed in Scott's Park on Wayne Street. Then it was put out to pasture in the city greenhouse for a time and in the 1930s was moved to a fountain in front of the courthouse in Washington Park.

Vandals got ahold of the *Boy* in the 1990s, and now if you want to see the original, you'll have to visit him at his home in the city hall lobby. Not to worry: A replica was cast in bronze, and he can still be found standing in the Washington Park fountain. *The Boy with the Boot* has become the unofficial mascot of Sandusky. However, his brethren hold boots in many other small towns—similar statues can be found across the United States and abroad.

Pumpkin Water Tower

Circleville, also known as the Pumpkin Capital of the World, pays homage to all things pumpkin each year at the four-day Circleville Pumpkin Show, a festival that draws more than four hundred thousand visitors annually. There, they can marvel at massive pumpkin pies (think of a pie that needs over eighty pounds of pumpkin, thirty-six pounds of sugar, thirty pounds of pie dough, and six hours of baking time), vie for the Giant Pumpkin Champion Trophy (for growing the area's largest pumpkin), compete in pumpkin tosses, and eat no end of pumpkin goodies.

Therefore, it's only appropriate that this pumpkin-crazy town has its water tower painted in the image of a giant pumpkin, complete with a stem. Thirteen hundred gallons of paint were used to make sure you never forget you're in the Pumpkin Capital of the World.

Muffler Animals

This muffler elephant can be found at National Muffler in Canton.

Mail Pouch Barn Signs

At one time, there were more than ten thousand advertisements for Mail Pouch Tobacco on barns in the Midwest, but less than half remain today. The ads were painted from the 1920s until the 1990s and the farmers who owned the barns were compensated in various ways—with cash, magazine subscriptions, chewing tobacco, or their entire barns being painted. The Mail Pouch Tobacco Company (now Bloch Brothers) was based in West Virginia. There are two painted barns remaining in Ohio, in Heath and Lisbon.

Curious Collections and Other Strange Displays

Some people might think that certain peculiarities are things to be embarrassed about, best left hidden away out of sight. Not so here in Ohio, where we proudly put our home state's oddities on display in museums, in public parks, on restaurant walls—inviting all to see just how weird we really are.

The Wall of Gum

The Maid-Rite Drive-In in Greenville must have some tasty sandwiches, leading their customers (drive-up and dine-in alike) to drool and lose their gum. How else would you explain the fact that customers routinely take chewed-up gum and stick it on the outside of the building? The entire exterior of the shop is covered with wads of gum, both on the drive-up side and the side facing the street. This less-than-appetizing display, however, doesn't seem to keep sandwich lovers away.

When the *Weird Ohio* team visited the Gum Wall, we found the site far stranger than we'd anticipated. But before we get into that, we should probably explain the lay of the land, so to speak.

Picture yourself standing in the middle of the street looking at the building. With that in mind, the front door is directly in front of you. Along the right side of the building are two windows about fifteen feet apart from each other. You order at the first window and pick up at the second. Once you have your order, you drive straight into the parking lot (unlike at other drive-throughs, you don't circle the building). The back of the building has a door that locals use as their "take-out" door.

The left side of the building is where the Gum Wall is. The ENTIRE length of wall is literally covered in gum. In fact, there is so much gum there, there isn't much room left to stick newly chewed pieces. Because of that, people have started sticking gum near the back door, the front door, and even along the order-pickup windows. But while there is indeed gum near those windows, that is not the Gum Wall. Like we said, the actual Gum Wall is on the left side of the building. All of the other pieces were just stuck there

when people started running out of room on the Gum Wall proper.

The place was hopping no matter when we visited. Cars line up at the drive-through at least five to six deep, in some cases spilling out onto the street. It's nearly impossible to get a picture of the sign and the wall together without including all those gum-chewing customers. Inside the building, there are only five or so booths and a counter lined with stools (just like at a good ol' diner). You can actually order beer here too, always a plus.

As for the menu, there are about six items listed, the big sellers being a Maid-Rite and a Maid-Rite with cheese. Basically, the Maid-Rite is browned beef on a hamburger bun with a couple of toppings (pickles, diced onions, etc.) — think White Castle, replace the patty with browned beef, make it normal size, and you've got a Maid-Rite sandwich.

But for the true connoisseur of the weird, the culinary delicacy that draws patrons to Maid-Rite is not to be found inside on the sandwich shop menu, but rather sticking to the outside walls in a gooey Technicolor display.

Allen County Museum

This collection in Lima is currently the only county museum in Ohio accredited by the American Association of Museums, and with good reason. The two-story building is filled to the gills with all sorts of historical oddities, the emphasis being on local artifacts. Everywhere one turns, there is something weird and wonderful. For instance, there's an old-fashioned hearse sitting in the middle of the transportation section and an iron lung in the medical area. Some of the museum's other exhibits include:

Swallowed Objects

By far the weirdest collection in the museum sits quietly in the basement next to the water fountain. The long, two-sectioned cabinet is filled with over one hundred objects removed from people's esophagi, lungs, and larynxes.

For whatever reason, Drs. Walter E. Yingling and Estey C. Yingling began saving assorted things their patients had swallowed. Each object has been lovingly affixed to a piece of paper bearing the name, date, and age of the person from whom it was removed. Among the collection is an open diaper pin, buttons, dentures, coins, and animal bones of assorted shapes and sizes. Some of the stranger items include a key, a pencil eraser, and even a long length of rubber hose, which is often mistaken for a horseshoe.

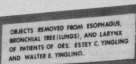

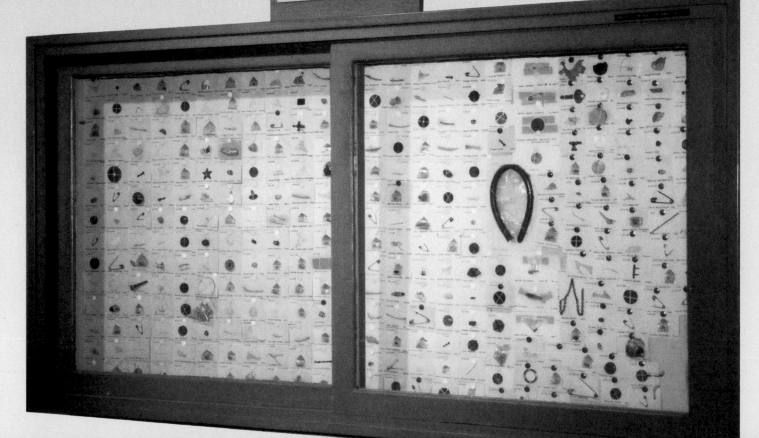

Dillinger in Ohio (pictured at right)

In August 1933, gangster John Dillinger and two accomplices robbed a bank in Bluffton, Ohio. A few weeks later, Dillinger was arrested and brought to the Allen County Jail to await trial. While this went on, several members of Dillinger's gang, including Russell Clark, Harry Pierpont, and Charles Makley, escaped from an Indiana prison and began making their way to Allen County. On the evening of October 12, Clark, Pierpont, and Makley entered the Allen County Jail and freed Dillinger, shooting and killing Sheriff Jesse Sarber in the process.

The four men were captured, and Pierpont and Makley were sentenced to death, while Clark received a life term. Dillinger was extradited to Indiana to stand trial for killing a different police officer, but again he escaped his captors, using a carved wooden gun. He swore to return to Lima to spring his friends from prison but never did.

Tired of waiting, perhaps, in September 1934 Makley and Pierpont made an escape attempt in which Makley was fatally wounded. Pierpont was eventually executed, and Clark served over thirty years of his life sentence before being released in August 1968, when it was discovered that he was dying of cancer. He died four months later on Christmas Eve.

Dillinger, who became the FBI's Public Enemy Number One after the murder of Sheriff Sarber, was shot and killed outside the Biograph Theater in Chicago on July 22, 1934.

If you visit the Allen County Museum, stop at the Sarber/Dillinger story exhibit, which recounts this story in detail, complete with a variety of memorabilia from the case—including guns, Sarber's desk, and wax figures of the key players. Among the exhibit's many weird factoids: Sheriff Sarber and John Dillinger were born on the same day, June 28, eighteen years apart.

Albino Animals (pictured below)

Taxidermied for all to enjoy at the Allen County Museum is the world's largest collection of albino animals. These pigmentally challenged stuffed creatures reside in the museum itself, away from the other, bigger game located in another building on museum grounds.

American Sign Museum

The greatest thrill in finding roadside beauty is how random it really can be. You can find yourself on a road you've never been on and suddenly come upon some landmark that just makes you stop and take notice. So imagine my delight when my wrong turn led me straight into Todd Swormstedt and his American Sign Museum, a collection of those roadside pieces of art we take for granted but that are really unforgettable.

Todd shares his shop in a building that houses a hundred and ten artists, which is great for him because he uses his signs as art. He states, "The line between commercial art and fine art is very blurred; it's probably the number of zeroes after the dollar sign that determines the difference."

The giant two-faced genie outside was impressive enough, but when the personable founder took me inside and switched on the circuit breakers, I was astounded. The place erupted into neon life, the sounds of tiny motors springing some signs into motion while others just twinkled hypnotically. Some of the pieces were familiar, but seen so close, they seemed immense and important.

Don't let the comfortable vibe of the museum fool you. Todd is very serious about this endeavor and goes about it with the same passion (if not more) as most roadside artists. He travels the country extensively to save what signs he can. He took a sixty percent pay cut to follow his dream, which he breaks down into three elements.

I guess there are probably three components that make me, not because I am special, but make me the perfect candidate for this museum. One, my background on Sign of the Times. I know sign companies all across the country. I can call them up and ask them favors to take down a sign. That is a really good edge I have on other collectors. Two, I got the collection bug. I am a collector—I've got whatever that is, that 'ism' that collectors have, that obsession. Finally, I asked myself what I really wanted to do when I didn't grow up. So this is kind of my midlife crisis project. I started this in my late forties. Don't tell me about the stuff that is gone, but tell me about the stuff I can still save.

We don't repaint signs, with rare exceptions. It's the difference between guys who restore cars and do a frame-off restoration or want to keep it stock and in original condition. We want to keep them authentic. They were made for the outdoors, so there is some wear and tear on them. It is their patina. Another part of our philosophy is that we would rather see a sign stay in its original location and be maintained than come to the museum. Then it is there for many more to see. If it can't stay in that location, it should at least stay in its original town and stay in the local historical museum. So we are third on our own list of where we think old signs should go. There are many signs that are landmark signs, that are iconic to various towns. Those signs are part of the culture of that town, and they need to remain there if at all possible.

The American Sign Museum is located at 2515 Essex Avenue in Cincinnati. Information can be found at www.signmuseum.org. Tours are available.—*Ryan Doan*

Toledo's Bun Museum

When Jamie Farr of M*A*S*H fame signed a hotdog bun at Tony Packo's in 1972, he started an enduring tradition. Well, maybe not that enduring. The bun that Farr signed crumbled soon after. But Packo, sensing he was onto something, began to have celebrities sign Styrofoam bun look-alikes. The hotdog joint is now home to more than a thousand signed "buns" whose signatories include five U.S. presidents and more than a few 1970s TV stars. Native Ohioan Farr plugged Packo's on several M*A*S*H episodes, bringing hotdog eaters from around the world to sample the fare and marvel at the bun "museum."

Jungle Jim's

Jungle Jim's International Market on Dixie Highway in Cincinnati is part grocery store, part theme park, and part cooking school under one very big roof. Four acres large, this unique shopping experience includes a small museum-type theater where patrons can learn the story behind Jungle Jim's; a display of a 618-pound block of cheese ("The Big Cheese"); an all-knowing automated fortune-teller known as "The Brain," and the opportunity to be serenaded by a variety of singing characters while they shop.

With all this going on, don't think the food is neglected. The market features more than nine hundred and fifty hot sauces (the largest retail selection in the country), a hundred varieties of honey, a pond of live fish for harvest, an olive bar stocked with olives from around the world, eight aisles of food from England alone (marked by a Robin Hood figurine standing under a giant English oak tree that spans all eight aisles), and many other delights for food lovers and weird seekers alike.

The folks at Jungle Jim's declined when we told them we wanted to feature them in this book. They don't even allow the public to take pictures inside! But you can sneak a peek at the place on their website: www.junglejims.com. Or better yet, take one of their guided tours, given by employees decked out in explorer garb!

World's Oldest Traffic Light

For some reason, Ohio is home to the world's oldest traffic light, located in Ashville. Normally, the town keeps the light—designed by local resident Teddy Boor—in its museum, but each year, on the Fourth of July, it is brought out and hung over the entrance to the local Independence Day festival. See its psychedelic swirling from red to green on the corner of Harrison and Walnut.

World's Oldest Concrete Street

George Bartholomew had a vision of a better world. Gone, he imagined, would be the bother of getting stuck in the mud on an everyday outing. Getting bruised and bumped in your carriage on an uneven dirt road would be a distant memory. Trudging around town at a turtle's speed would be gonzo.

On a mission of improvement, Bartholomew convinced the Bellefontaine City Council that paving the roads with cement, or "artificial stone," as it was then known, would be a big benefit to the town. Skeptical but willing, they let him try it on Court Avenue in 1891. Thus the area around the Logan County Courthouse became the world's first (and now oldest) concrete street. Bartholomew guaranteed the council that the pavement would hold up for five years. In 1991, when the street marked its hundredth anniversary, the town erected a statue of Bartholomew with a plaque that reads HERE STARTED THE BETTER ROADS MOVEMENT. By then, Bartholomew had proved the worth of his idea twenty times over! The statue stands at one end of the oldest street, which cars are still allowed to traverse (no heavy trucks, please).

Living Bible Museum

In the 1970s, Pastor Richard Diamond of the Diamond Hill Church toured an Atlanta wax museum with his wife, Alwilda. Divinely inspired by a scene depicting Jesus, they decided to build their own wax museum, focusing on biblical stories.

In the 1980s, the pastor and his wife started looking for wax figures to purchase. Finding that new figures were beyond their budget, they looked into acquiring used ones. A stroke of luck (or divine intervention?) put Pastor Diamond in touch with Bill Warren, a gentleman who at one time had operated an outdoor Bible walk in Pennsylvania. Since the attraction had closed, Warren had no use for his figures and was more than willing to part with them. The Diamonds bought over twenty of them, and in 1984 they began to plan their Living Bible Museum.

The church had little funding, but the entire congregation joined in, and by the end of 1986 the building was finished, completed almost entirely at the hands of the congregants. The next step was to construct various scenes in which the wax figures would be featured and to make clothing for them. Finally it was all done, and on August 15, 1987, the Living Bible Museum officially opened. To this day, it remains Ohio's only life-size wax museum.

Visitors to the museum can view an amazing collection of American votive folk art, the largest of its kind in the United States. There are also paintings, animated displays, and even a rare Bible collection, which includes a Latin Bible from the 1500s.

But what everyone comes to see here are the wax figures, and they do not disappoint.

The museum offers four different walk-through tours, each with its own unique figures: Miracles of the Old Testament, the Life of Christ, the Reformers, and Christian Martyrs. Once your choice has been made, you will be ushered into a dark room and the show will begin.

Lights, Camera, Bible!

Each tour begins with visitors standing in the dark in front of a wooden fencelike structure. Ever so slowly, the lights come up. Sound effects and mood lighting are used to act out a biblical scene, but the only voice is that of the invisible narrator on the soundtrack. The figures themselves, well, they pretty much just stand there. (The only notable exception being Lot's wife, who turns into a pillar of salt with the help of a lazy Susan.) Once the scene has ended, the lights go down, you stand in the darkness for a few moments, and then the next scene lights up, and the action (or inaction) begins. This continues over and over until the final scene, after which you are free to visit the chapel or the gift shop.

The Living Bible Museum, while nondenominational, clearly wants to teach you a thing or two about God. And if you visit, you will indeed discover things you didn't know . . . even if it's only that if and when the Lord decides to speak to you, He'll flash the lights on and off a lot while He's talking.

What's in a Name?

Imagine having this conversation: A salesperson taking your order or a customer service representative or someone like that asks for your address. You say, "Hitler Road." Strange looks, general incredulity, requests for you to slowly spell out the street name. Incredulity again.

If you live in Circleville, this might happen to you all the time. In fact, not just one but three roads there have Hitler in their name: Hitler Road No. 1, Hitler Road No. 2, and Huber-Hitler Road. Nearby, descendants of the Circleville Hitlers (responsible for the street names) are buried at the Hitler-Ludwig Cemetery.

The Hitlers are said to be among the only "true" Hitlers in the world (Adolf Hitler, history tells us, got the name from a misspelling of Hiedler, the married name of his maternal grandmother). The Ohio Hitlers were a prominent Circleville farming family who immigrated to the area in the 1700s, long before World War II. That is not to say, however, that they were spared the inconvenience of having the same name as the despised dictator of Nazi Germany. The Hitlers were often harassed, and even years after the war and far from Circleville, one member of the family was asked by an employer to change his name.

Today, residents of these roads seem content with the unique nature of their home addresses. Most, including a WW II veteran, do not feel that the name should be changed. (Some do feel a change would be good, but being good neighbors, they don't want to offend the descendants of the Hitlers still in the area.) So it seems that at least for now, the Hitler Roads shall live on in infamy.

Hitler Road

Take Route 23 south of Columbus and keep your eyes peeled. Not too far from Circleville is a rural stretch of roads that are definitely not kosher in my book. I was just driving along thinking how quaint and somewhat boring the scenery was, so you can imagine my surprise when I noticed the sign that jumped out at me. It was "Hitler Road #1!" I had to see what it was all about, and it only got weirder. Down Hitler Road #1, I came to a huge graveyard that stretched as far as my eyes could see. The eerie part was that it was named Hitler-Ludwig Cemetery. In the middle of the well-kept graveyard was some towering device with a cross on the top that rang bells in some church music. It didn't stop for as long as I was there. It was just Hitler Road, haunting bells, and miles of corn and the dead. I wanted to see a bit more before the sun set. Hitler Road 1 intersects with Hitler Road 2, which then intersects with Huber Hitler Road. Now, don't get me wrong, the area seemed peaceful, almost beautiful, but one would think you would maybe put an asterisk after a road name like "Hitler Number One." Maybe you could call it something like "Hitler Number One—asterisk—a number, not an opinion."—*Anonymous*

World's Shortest Street

McKinley Street in Bellefontaine got the short end of the stick when it came to laying out local roads. Stretching only fifteen feet, this small side street is supposed to accommodate both north- and southbound traffic. Note: Don't all go there at once! It's officially listed as a two-way street, but if two cars are to find each other on this road, one of them is going to end up on the nearby railroad tracks. It can really handle only one car at a time in each direction.

The Last Kewpee Hamburgs

Kewpee Hamburgs originated in Racine, Wisconsin, in the 1920s. The original building there was replaced with a new Kewpee in 1997, and only five other Kewpees remain: three in Lima, Ohio, and two in Lansing, Michigan.

This location in downtown Lima was built in the 1930s and seats about fifty customers. Before the parking lot was enlarged, it had a neat feature: a car turntable. Rather than backing out of the lot, a car would pull onto the turntable to be manually turned around. This Kewpee also featured a large Kewpie doll outside the building over the front door.

While it may just be a local urban legend, rumor holds that Wendy's founder Dave Thomas "borrowed" the Kewpee idea to create his own chain of fast-food hamburger restaurants. One thing Dave didn't borrow, though, was the curious and uniquely Kewpee tradition of dipping your french fries into your shake.

Lighthouse Keeper of the Steeple

If you'd like to see something really weird along the road in Ohio, I suggest you check out a site known as the Lighthouse of God Prayer Tower. Years ago, the steeple of a local church was renovated and made to look like a lighthouse. For whatever reason, the church chose to stick a mannequin up at the top of the lighthouse, standing on the ledge. He's been known to cause a lot of rubbernecking and the occasional accident or two when out-of-towners catch a glimpse of what appears to be a man standing on the ledge of a lighthouse overlooking I-71. Sometimes the church will attach signs to the mannequin, making it look like he's holding signs like SUPPORT OUR TROOPS. It's really, really weird . . . and it's been there for at least fifteen years!
—J.W.

Brick Outhouse

If you ever thought going to school was the dumps, you're not alone. Behind the Camper Elementary School in Genoa is the so-called "Little House," a brick building where students originally went to do their business. A hundred and fifty years ago, the twelve-seat outhouse served the school. Eventually, the town turned it into a community shed, and proud residents managed to get it listed on the National Register of Historic Places (the only former pit toilet on that prestigious list). While there is a historical plaque on the structure, it makes no mention of what the building was!

The "New" Blue Hole

Fans of the ever popular but now closed Blue Hole tourist attraction are in luck. Apparently, a "new" Blue Hole—with similar blue-green water, an unexplained source, and seemingly bottomless depth—has been opened at the Castalia State Fish Hatchery on Homegardner Road. Near the site of the "old" Blue Hole, the hatchery is open for self-guided tours year-round and counts the new Blue Hole as an attraction. If you don't get excited about blue holes, perhaps fish are your thing: The hatchery raises more than four hundred and seventy thousand steelhead, rainbow, and native brook trout a year to stock Lake Erie tributaries and inland lakes.

Plumbing the Unfathomable Depths of Ohio's Blue Hole(s)

The history of the Blue Holes (that's right, plural) of the Western Erie County area goes deeper than even their bottomless depths. On my first investigation, I knew of only one that was and still is open to the public. In fact, the Blue Hole of the Castalia Fish Hatchery is actually the source of the entire operation. Each day, the hole pumps three to eight thousand gallons of "dead water" (water that doesn't support plant or animal life due to its lack of oxygen) per minute into the hatchery. The water is oxygenated and used to breed Ohio's largest population of steelhead trout. While all that sounds rather scientific, the Blue Holes aren't without their mystery. On the overcast day I chose to visit the Hole, an old man whispered to me that he knew of a second Blue Hole located in the nearby town center possibly behind an ice cream store.

Later, knocking on the window of that ice cream parlor, I asked if the lady knew about any Blue Holes in the area. She pointed to the newspaper clippings on her wall and nodded across the street. Behind me was a giant stone and iron gate locked tight with several NO TRESPASSING signs. I was able to peer around the back of the entrance, where I saw, clear as day, the mounted words BLUE HOLE. In the nearby antiques store, I found a kind, informative woman and several postcards, both detailing the great heyday in history that this particular "bottomless hole" had enjoyed. It seemed that long ago, the hole was sacred to an Indian Village, and the holes were used as medicine camps. When the English army came through, they destroyed the village, and any women and children not slaughtered were made to leave. As I gathered information on the rise and fall of the tourist area, several locals meandered into the store with their own bits and pieces of history. One elderly lady was about to tell me about some scandal involving a horse and carriage disappearing into the hole, but before I could get the details, another lady touched her arm and hushed her up with a stern look. They all agreed that the hole is very much bottomless and all assured me that there are actually seven holes in the region.—*Cono Echiverri*

SPILLWAY AND PARK AT BLUE HOLE, CASTALIA, OHIO.

25—Watching the Fish in the Trout Stream at the Blue Hole, Castalia, Ohio

BLUE HOLE

NO
VEHICLES
BEYOND
THIS
POINT

Creepy Cattle on Display

The Samuel Spitler House in Brookville has been preserved for posterity as a charming example of bygone architecture, showcasing magnificent staircases, original oak woodwork, elaborate fireplaces, and the first indoor bathroom in Brookville (which Mr. Spitler, a miller and plumber, installed in 1894). All of the rooms have been restored to their former glory, and the outside has been meticulously painted green and cream, the colors that originally graced the house.

But amid the Victorian charm and preservationist details, a truly bizarre tale lurks.

In the basement of the Spitler House are the remains of Andy D-Day, a famous freak bull, and his companion, the Two-Headed Calf—or, as touted by the Brookville Historical Society on the Darke County Genealogical Researchers website, "Rare Animals." These stuffed bovines stand as a testament to what some people will do for money.

When the two-headed calf was born on the farm of Wilbur and Nettie Rasor in 1941, it became an immediate tourist attraction, despite the fact that it died soon after it was born. The Rasors, quick to catch on to its moneymaking potential, had the two-headed wonder stuffed and charged curiosity seekers a dime to see it. One

addition, they took the pair on a traveling circuit of sideshows in Florida and other states until Andy D-Day died, in 1956.

At that time, Andy's head was stuffed and mounted, and the Rasors kept both him and the two-headed calf until 1976. Finally, they donated the two to the Brookville Historical Society, and they wound up in the basement of the Spitler House museum—a comfortable distance from the rest of the home's genteel artifacts and furnishings.

These days, the animals aren't quite the attraction they were in more innocent times, and the Brookville Historical Society doesn't exactly shout their existence from the rooftops. In fact, it seems that even many people in Brookville are unaware of their presence in the basement. (However, the museum recently re-created the building where they were kept on the Rasors' farm.) Should you visit Spitler House, expect to get your dose of nonweird history along with your freak show. The museum presumes that visitors want to see all that it offers, making for an experience that ranges from the sublime to the ridiculous under one historic roof.

The only problem with Spitler House is that it never seems to be open. It is scheduled to open to the public the first Sunday of every month—weather permitting. We're not sure how the weather is a factor, since the displays are located indoors, but we've visited on bright, sunny first Sundays and the place has still been locked up tight. Truth be told, Brookville is pretty much a ghost town these days, so we recommend calling first to make sure the museum is open before you head out to rustle up a few (stuffed) heads of cattle.

of those passersby told the Rasors of a freak bull he owned in Arkansas, complete with four horns, four eyes, and two functional noses. The Rasors traveled to Arkansas to see the (still living) bull and, recognizing a good thing, purchased him and brought him back to Brookville.

"Andy D-Day" (so-called because he was said to have been born on June 6, 1944) was put on display with the two-headed calf, and the Rasors upped the price of admission to a quarter. New housing was constructed for the bull and his stuffed friend, and the Rasors sold picture postcards of the two to visitors (savvy businesspeople to a fault, the Rasors did not allow visitors to take photos!). In

Roads Less Traveled

Some roads just don't seem quite right. These strange byways possess a special kind of aura or mystique that sets them apart from other roads. Many of the tales of these unnatural pathways reflect archetypal nightmare imagery such as wandering spirits, evil cults, and violent murderers. In this respect, they might be seen as passages to the unknown or windows into our unconscious, where our darkest thoughts reside.

Throughout Ohio, we have found supposedly cursed or haunted thoroughfares whose tales have become part of the local lore. Perhaps there is really nothing strange to be found on such roads at all. Perhaps people are just entertaining themselves, traveling these dark and usually back roads and lanes purely for the thrill of scaring the wits out of themselves and their friends. Who among us, perhaps in their teenage years, didn't pile into an overcrowded car and set off for some allegedly haunted spot? Night riders on excursions like these are often so jacked up to witness something out of the ordinary that overanticipation alone might cause their eyes to play tricks on them.

Whether these roads are actually epicenters of paranormal activity, merely favorite destinations of rowdy, nocturnal joyriders, or a little of both is open for debate. Whatever the case, one fact is indisputable: There are many long and winding roads less traveled throughout Ohio. Where they will take you, who can say?

The Ohio Crybaby Bridge Tour

Most people in Ohio have heard the term Crybaby Bridge. In fact, many have heard stories related to the one and only Crybaby Bridge, which just happens to be down the road from where they grew up. That's why a look of shock and surprise comes creeping over people's faces when they hear that there are literally dozens of Crybaby Bridges dotting the rural areas of Ohio. And each one has its own dark tale to tell.

The legend, along with its variations—Crybaby Lanes, hills, barns, etc.—crops up everywhere in the state. And while the particulars may vary, the story always involves one or more tragic infant deaths and the sound of ghostly weeping when you stand at the appointed place at just the right time.

When one moves from bridge to bridge, the stories grow wilder and weirder: This is also true the longer they've been in circulation. The only constant is that a baby (or, in some cases, several babies) came to a bad end on the bridge, often at the hands of its mother. To tune in to the cries of the not-quite-departed little one, visitors to the bridge must perform some sort of ritual, something like flashing their headlights or honking their horn. In some especially powerfully haunted places, you need only to stand on the bridge at the right time to hear the cries. Or so they say.

There does seem to be something to the phenomenon—certain bridges do actually cry. Is it the way the wind cuts through underneath the span? Or could it really be an unfortunate child's cries, echoing along the creek bed for all eternity? Are any of the following stories about the "real" Crybaby Bridge? We'll leave that up to you to decide!

Clinton Road Crybaby Bridge

There are two legends associated with this bridge, neither of which requires you to do anything except stand on the bridge to hear the baby crying.

Drowning Babies

Even though Ohio was used as a stop on the Underground Railroad during the Civil War, escaped slaves weren't in the clear just because they'd crossed the state line. Often, they were pursued by everyone from bounty hunters and slave traders to disgruntled plantation owners. Should a slave find himself recaptured, he or she was sure to find the punishment to be severe, if not fatal. For this reason, many slaves chose death instead of capture. According to legend, slaves who were in fear of being taken back by their "owners" would stand on the Clinton Road Bridge and throw their babies off, hoping that, at least in death, the children could be free. If these hard-to-believe events did take place, it would certainly explain why there have been reports of people hearing what sounds like the gurgling of babies coming from the waters below the bridge.

Hidden Pregnancy

The second legend associated with the bridge involves a young woman who had recently fallen in love. Soon after the couple became engaged, the woman discovered she was pregnant. The woman was torn between grief and happiness. She desperately wanted children, but she knew her fiancé had no interest in them. Fearing the man would call off the wedding if he found out, the woman decided to take up residence in an abandoned house near the bridge and wait out her pregnancy there. It was in this house that, cold and all alone, she gave birth. Shortly thereafter, the distraught woman wrapped the newborn child in a blanket, walked onto the bridge, and threw the baby over the side. To this day, some people say that if you go to the bridge at night, you'll hear a baby crying. Right after that, the ghost of a woman carrying something in her arms will walk to the bridge and throw it over the side. Then the child's crying suddenly stops.

Egypt Road Crybaby Bridge—Salem

Despite its name, this bridge is not actually located on Egypt Road but along an old, unused road that runs off Egypt in Salem, near the Mahoning County line. There are several different variations of the story surrounding this bridge, all of which involve a young couple and their doomed, crying child.

"She Just Wandered Off"

The first version of the legend has the young couple picnicking with their child near the bridge. The couple gets into a heated argument, during which the child crawls away and up onto the bridge. The couple continue to argue as the child gets closer and closer to the edge. Finally, the child falls off into the water, but the angry couple, too embroiled in their argument, don't even notice their drowning child's cries. Today, the story goes, the abandoned infant continues to cry, forever calling out to his oblivious parents.

"Never to Be Seen Again"

In another version, the couple and their baby are once again picnicking alongside the bridge. This time, the couple is enjoying a brief nap when the child wanders off and makes its way onto the bridge. The mother spots the child just as it falls into the water, and she dives in to try and save her baby. Unfortunately, she is unsuccessful, and both mother and child perish. The father, having been awakened by the cries of his frantic wife and child, runs to the bridge, only to find both of them floating lifeless in the water. Seeing this, the husband runs screaming into the woods, never to be seen again. But the cries of his drowning wife and child continue to echo through the night, audible to anyone brave enough to stand on this dark bridge of death.

"He Just Vanished"

The final version puts a horror-movie twist on the legend. As in the other stories, the couple and their child are sitting near the bridge when something happens that causes the father to leave his family's side (usually it's the call of nature). He is gone for only a moment when he hears his child crying and his wife screaming, "No!" Rushing back to the bridge, the husband finds both his wife and child floating dead in the water. What horror had they seen? Were they pushed into the cold water below them, or was the sight before them so terrible that they jumped? We don't know. We know only that the husband ran off into the woods . . . and vanished.

The child falls off into the water, but the angry couple, too embroiled in their argument, don't even notice their drowning child's cries.

Greely-Chapel Road Crybaby Bridge—Lima

The bridge on Greely-Chapel Road near Lima is unique in that its legend deals not only with crying babies but also murdered teenagers, a carload of whom were supposedly found scattered along the road close to the bridge. They were killed by someone or something when their car stalled at this mysterious spot. The driver's body, according to legend, was hung over the stop sign, and ever since then the stop sign itself has bled, despite the fact that it has since been replaced. The crying babies, dropped into the murky waters there by another distraught mother, are almost an afterthought. Nevertheless, there are locals who have stolen onto this bridge at night and lived to regret it.

Occurrence at Greely-Chapel Road Doesn't Compute

A few weeks ago, myself and three friends went out to the bridge on Greely-Chapel Road. It was about nine-thirty p.m. As we drove down the road, there was a cop in front of us, and as we got a little ways past the bridge, we decided to turn around and go back over the bridge the way we came. We approached a stop sign, and the police car turned right (you can only go left or right). For the cop to make it back to the bridge, it would take awhile because there's nowhere to turn after that, and besides, we would have seen him. So we did a U-turn and crossed the bridge, did another U-turn, and went back over it again, and did another one again to face the way we came.

This time we stopped. I had my friend roll down his window, and I started screaming, "Hey, Mary, wanna come out and play? We wanna see your crying baby!" My friends got freaked, but I just laughed, and we started to drive off. I wanted to give

them a real scare, so I said, "Guys, I see someone on the bridge!"

Just then a car flipped on its lights and pulled out from the bridge. So my friend speeds off, doing about eighty. As the other car gained on us, I realized it was a police car—the one that was in front of us before.

After a half hour of being followed through the country, we turned back onto Greely-Chapel. When we approached the spot where the cop had started following us, he pulled us over. He came to the door and just asked for registration and stuff; he said there were "problems on the bridge lately." Then, out of nowhere, a second cop car appeared. They eventually let us go.

What was really weird is the fact that the cop car was hunter green and said POLICE on it. Lima DOES NOT have green police cars, nor do surrounding patrollers. We have since tried to reenact our night, but it still doesn't add up.—*Mindy*

LeFevre Road Crybaby Bridge—Troy

Just go to the bridge late at night and stand in the middle of it. If you wait patiently, eventually, you will hear the faint cries of a baby. Those ghostly cries are the result of an accident that took place on this bridge over seventy years ago.

In the 1930s, a couple and their newborn baby were crossing the bridge in a car one night when they were involved in a head-on collision. The force of the impact was so strong that the baby was thrown from the vehicle. The couple and the driver of the other vehicle heard the child crying but were unable to locate it in the darkness. They searched as long as they could, but eventually the crying stopped. The next day, a search party was organized, but the baby was never found. Its cries, however, can still be heard.

Euler Road Crybaby Lane—Bowling Green

Not all crybaby phenomena involve a bridge. A case in point is the stretch of Euler Road known as Crybaby Lane. It is along this dark, tree-lined road where people report hearing the ghostly cries of a baby. Legend has it that the cries are the result of a mother's hanging her baby from one of the many tree branches that hang over the roadway.

The baby's crying is supposed to be heard there at night, and sometimes the baby is seen hanging from the tree. A pretty horrifying story, whether or not it's true.

Crybaby Overpass—Cable

The small town of Cable has its own spin on the crybaby legend, an overpass that spans a set of railroad tracks. One cold November night years ago, a woman, for reasons unknown, took her baby in her arms and jumped off the overpass into the path of an oncoming train. If you happen to drive across this overpass at midnight, you will find that your car mysteriously stalls. It will not start again until you have listened to the distant whistle of a train, the cry of a baby, and the scream of a woman. Whatever drove this woman to her desperate act, she is still demanding to be heard in the land of the living.

Fudge Road Bridge—Camden

With today's economy, people are always trying to get the most bang for their buck. And as far as ghosts, monsters, and just general creepiness are concerned, you can't go wrong with a late-night drive down Fudge Road. The stories of weird events happening there might not all be true, but with so many of them circulating about this road, one of them might have some validity to it, right?

Most of the ghostly activity focuses on the steel bridge near the end of the road. In fact, there are two different versions of how the ghost of a baby came to haunt the bridge. In the first, the child is simply thrown off the bridge by a very upset mother. The second variation sounds like a mangled Crybaby Bridge story, but then again, you can't expect distraught, suicidal mothers to stick to the rules of a legend.

Anyway, it seems that a young woman's newborn baby passed away, but not on the bridge. Right after the child's funeral, the mother went to the bridge and hanged herself from it. For some reason, the mother's ghost is resting in peace while her child's spirit makes its way to the bridge where its mother died. Perhaps it hopes to find her there. If so, it seems the baby is out of luck, for it cries constantly at night. If you want to hear it, park your car on the bridge, shut off your engine and headlights, and say "Mama" three times. We're not responsible for what happens next.

Far and away, the weirdest story about Fudge Road is the one about the monster lurking in the woods near the crossing. This beast is described in many different ways, but it is always huge. The creature apparently likes to hang around under the bridge, so if you're there long enough, you're bound to hear it rustling through the undergrowth and splashing in the water. You'll know it's time to go if it starts to growl at you.

If you decide to take a drive down Fudge Road, keep in mind that it's barely wide enough for two cars to safely pass each other. It's hard enough trying to navigate it during the day, but watch out if you're doing it late at night when you've got all those ghost and monster stories swimming in your head. Something more substantial than ghostly beasts may be around that next bend in the road, like another car.

Phoebe Walks Reformatory Road

Every town in the United States has its very own eccentric. And in Mansfield, in the late 1800s, that eccentric was Phoebe Wise. The first thing people noticed about Phoebe was her taste in clothing—bright, gaudy, and out of fashion. The fact that her favorite mode of transportation was her own two feet meant that everyone had plenty of opportunities to catch a glimpse of her. Of course, the reports that she stood over six feet tall, if true, certainly would have made Phoebe stand out among a crowd even without the bright clothes.

But what really made Phoebe different from all the other women of her time was that she was outspoken and thought nothing of saying exactly what was on her mind, even if that meant going toe-to-toe with a man.

The Wise family owed an enormous parcel of land along what is now SR 545 in Mansfield. It was on this piece of land that Phoebe chose to live in an old ramshackle shack, isolated from everyone. Aside from being spotted walking along the road from time to time, Phoebe pretty much kept to herself. Until the late 1880s, that is, when she began dating Jake Kastanowitz.

By all accounts, the relationship was tumultuous from the beginning, and violent arguments were not uncommon. The violence culminated on May 22, 1898, when Phoebe shot and killed Jake. Though it was later found that she had not meant to shoot the man, the incident further supported the notion that Phoebe was not a woman to be trifled with.

The Ohio State Reformatory owned the property next to the Wise family plot, and when the state wanted to expand the prison, they approached the family to buy some of their land. Since the state had money to spare, the townspeople assumed that the family became very, very rich when the sale went through. But when Phoebe continued to live in squalor, a rumor started that she had chosen to take her share of the family's earnings and hide it inside her shack. It was only a matter of time before a group of local thugs came calling. After muscling their way into Phoebe's home, they began ripping the place apart in search of the hidden loot. When none was found, the men took what little money they found, along with some of Phoebe's jewelry. On the way out, they paused only long enough to murder Phoebe brutally.

But the story doesn't end there. As a result of Phoebe's violent death, her ghost was unable to rest in peace and is rumored to walk up and down Reformatory Road. If you go looking for her, she's pretty easy to spot. Just look for the giant woman dressed in bright, gaudy clothes.

Just flash your headlights three times, and shortly after that a ghostly white headlight will appear and move toward your car.

Phantom Motorcycle Rider Gives Yearly Shows

The legend of the Elmore Rider opens on March 21 with our hero returning from a successful tour of duty in the war. The moment he steps inside his house, he greets his parents, throws down his bags, and hops on his motorcycle, riding off to surprise his girlfriend, who lives just on the other side of a nearby bridge. As our hero reaches his girlfriend's house, he notices movement in her bedroom. Making his way to her window, the young man prepares to knock and surprise her . . . and is horrified to see her in the arms of another man. Enraged, he climbs back on his bike and peels out of the driveway, spraying dirt and rocks from his rear tire. As our hero tears down the road toward the bridge, he realizes too late that he is driving too fast to negotiate the terrain. Tires squealing, the man slides off the road and into a barbed-wire fence, decapitating himself in the process.

Today, it is said that if you go to the bridge on March 21, the anniversary of our hero's death, his ghost will appear and reenact his fateful drive to the bridge. Just flash your headlights three times, and shortly after that a ghostly white headlight will appear and move toward your car. Just before the light reaches the bridge, it will disappear.

Now, this could just be another one of those colorful but basically fictional legends. And to be honest, the story of the Elmore Rider might have faded into obscurity save for the "research" of one man: Richard Gill.

Gill has become something of a folklore hero. He is the only person to have conducted "scientific experiments" related to the Elmore Rider. According to Gill, in 1969 he and an unnamed male friend drove out to the bridge on March 21 and attempted to summon the rider. They were successful, and the light passed by their car. Excited, Gill and his friend decided to try an experiment. Stretching a long piece of string across the road, they once again flashed their lights and summoned the ghost. Once again, the ghostly headlight appeared and moved down to the section of road with the string across it. After the light disappeared, Gill went and inspected the string and found that it was still intact, even though the ghostly light appeared to have passed right through it.

Really humming now, Gill decided to go a step further and asked his friend to stand in the middle of the road to see if he could make out anything specific about the ghostly light. The man agreed and took his place in the middle of the road while Gill summoned the rider. As Gill watched, the light appeared in the distance and began moving toward his friend. As the light reached the section of road where the man was standing, Gill lost sight of him. When the light finally disappeared, Gill ran to the place in the road where his friend had stood, only to find it vacant. Eventually, Gill found his friend lying in a nearby ditch, semiconscious and disoriented. He had no recollection as to how he had gotten there. At that point, Gill wisely decided that the experiments were over for the evening.

Richard Gill's inquiring mind breathed new life into the Elmore Rider legend. As with any good road story, though, there are still questions. For example, no one has ever discovered the rider's real name or an explanation as to why you have to flash your headlights

to see him. Indeed, even the very location of the bridge in question is open to debate. But when all you need to see a ghost is a calendar and working headlights, what have you got to lose? So go ahead—drive out to the bridge of your choice in Elmore on March 21, flash your lights three times, and see what happens. Just a bit of advice, though: Try not to stand in the middle of the road.

The Phantom Bicyclist

Take Route 732 north out of Oxford and turn left onto the first country road, Buckley Road. Drive to the place where the road curves. Turn your car around and face 732. If you now turn off your engine, flash your headlights three times, and wait, you will see a white light come toward your car from across the hills.

This, according to the story, is the ghost of a bicyclist who was struck by a car and killed while riding on either 732 or Buckley Road one evening. Now he performs on command, if you're brave enough to summon him up.

Hook Man

Pond Run Road near New Richmond is said to be the stomping grounds of the Hook Man. The story begins with a couple of very bad parents who kept their disturbed kid chained in a basement. God, apparently irritated by their parenting methods, struck their house with lightning. The bodies of both parents were found, but all that was found of the boy was his hand.

Ever since then, the legend goes, a ghost with a hook for a hand has prowled Pond Run Road, which was a popular lovers' lane for years. Regrettably, today the road has been built up and lacks the ambiance it once offered young lovers, but the stories still linger.

Lady Bend Hill

Lady Bend Hill is part of Route 40, the old National Road, between Hendrysburg and Morristown in Belmont County. The third bend from the top of the hill is said to be haunted by the ghost of a woman who, after fleeing a fight with her lover, was somehow decapitated by a bolt of lightning. (We'd be interested to see how that worked.)

Anyway, now she scares the daylights out of motorists on Route 40. She appeared floating above a man driving a team of horses on a frigid New Year's Day in 1896. More recently, she has been seen walking alongside the highway in a long gown.

Suicide on the Hill

We lived in a farmhouse right at the bottom of Lady Bend Hill. I remember one morning, my mom looked outside up the hill and there was a man swinging from the tree with a noose around his neck. He had been a hobo, just passing through.—*Anonymous*

Decaying Bride-Not-to-Be

There is a bridge in East Liverpool, in Columbiana County, where the ghost of a bride-to-be waits, hoping someone will stop and help her. Sounds interesting, doesn't it? But there's a catch. You might want to read on a bit before hopping in your car and rushing out to pick up this needy bride.

This story begins in the 1800s in Sprucevale, a then-thriving canal town that would eventually fall into ruin. But as our story opens, the lovely Esther Hale is preparing for her wedding, later that afternoon. Esther has spent the better part of the morning in her new wedding dress, happily prancing around her home near Beaver Creek. Now she is carefully adjusting every inch of the dress, making sure that it is perfect. After all, this is her wedding day, the day she has looked forward to since she was a child. (An interesting side note to this story is that while there are many different versions in circulation, the groom-to-be is never mentioned by name in any of them. At first thought, his name would seem to be an integral part of the story, one that should not be left out. But then again, it might have been omitted on purpose to preserve the man's reputation. For you see, while Esther was giddily getting ready for her wedding, the young man was planning his escape.)

Once Esther is content that her dress is perfect, she sits down near the window of her home and waits for the carriage that will bring her and her beloved to the church. Esther spends the remainder of that hot summer day waiting for her future husband to arrive. But as the sun sinks and the moon climbs higher in the sky, Esther is forced to face reality: He isn't coming. And so, Esther Hale quietly stands up and locks the door of her cabin. She then pulls all of the drapes closed and withdraws from the world.

Several days later, when Esther has not been seen in town, friends go out to check on her. They find the sullen Esther amid the wedding decorations, still dressed in her gown. Her friends sit with her awhile and urge her to change clothes and come outside with them. The jilted bride politely refuses and then asks her friends to leave. Reluctantly, they oblige.

From time to time, friends continue to check in on Esther. They always find her alone, sitting among the now-yellowing decorations. And while her guests are sometimes able to get her to eat a little, they cannot get her to remove her wedding dress.

Several months later, a passerby notices that the door to Esther's cabin is open. Seeing that snowdrifts had built up inside the doorway, he notifies the authorities.

When the police arrive, they find the decaying body of Esther Hale, still in her wedding gown.

After Esther's funeral (some say she was actually buried in her wedding gown), stories began to circulate that have survived to this day. Motorists crossing Beaver Creek Bridge, near the spot where Esther's cabin once stood, claim that the decaying figure of a woman in a tattered white dress has lunged at their cars. Oddly enough, this disturbing figure is glimpsed only on the date of Esther's ill-fated wedding.

There is a dark caveat to this story that anyone considering investigating the legend should know: It is said that if Esther's ghost is able to touch you, she will become young again and you will instantly grow old and die. Just something to think about should your travels ever take you over Beaver Creek Bridge.

Faceless Figure at Dead Man's Curve

One of our state's darkest legends is that of Dead Man's Curve, a dangerous intersection in Clermont County. The road was part of the Ohio Turnpike, built in 1831, and it has a long list of victims.

In September 1969, the state of Ohio rebuilt the road into a straight four-lane highway. On October 19, 1969, five teenagers died there when their 1968 Impala was hit at more than a hundred miles an hour by a 1969 Roadrunner. There was only one survivor: a guy named Rick.

Ever since that day, the intersection has been haunted by "the faceless hitchhiker," whom Rick has seen five times. He describes it as the pitch-black silhouette of a man, a "three-dimensional silhouette." He has seen the figure hitchhiking there with its thumb out, only to have it turn, and he sees that it has no face. A psychic who was asked to investigate the intersection lasted only a few minutes before asking to be picked up. The shadow man has even been known to attack cars as they drive by.

A driverless Impala and a mysterious green Roadrunner have been seen in the area as well.

Due to rerouting, the actual location of Dead Man's Curve is in dispute, but many believe that it's the place where 222 and Bantam Road cross State Route 125, near Amelia.

Mentor's Gravity Hill Pulls Them in (and up)

Sprinkled throughout the United States are roads known as Gravity Hills. These roads seem to defy nature itself, specifically the law of gravity. Countless people say that they have parked their car at the bottom of one of these hills, put it into neutral, and sat there as the car was pulled up the hill as if by unseen hands. As the car continues up the hill, it gains speed until it reaches the summit of the hill and slides down the other side.

While almost all of the Gravity Hills throughout the U.S. have some sort of creepy legend associated with them, the strange thing about King Memorial Road in Mentor is that there is absolutely no legend associated with the road. No school bus crash there killing dozens of children, no tortured spirit of a man killed while walking on the road. Nothing. And yet, crowded carloads still find themselves pulled up the hill, any time of the day or night.

Some people say that Gravity Hills are nothing more than optical illusions, and that while it may look and feel like your car is being pulled uphill, you are in fact simply rolling downhill. There may be some truth to this, because while you're sitting in your car at the bottom of King Memorial Road, you do feel like you're in front of a small hill. And as your car is slowly making its way "up" the road in neutral, the sensation is that you are indeed going uphill. As you reach the top of the hill and start your way down the other side, it clearly feels as though you have just crested a hill. However, when one goes back to the end of King Memorial and looks toward the hill from a distance, the road appears to be going downhill.

So which is it, up or down?

Part of the allure of King Memorial Road is that it practically dares you to test it out. Of course, the local police do not take kindly to motorists sitting in the middle of the street obstructing traffic. On top of that, since your car is going only 5 mph or so, there is the very real danger of an accident. So if you decide that you just have to try Gravity Hill for yourself, be careful. Or you might end up being the first ghost to haunt King Memorial Road.

Gravity Hill near Melonheads' Home Turf

I have some info about the Gravity Hill in Kirtland Hills. I can tell you firsthand that this story is absolutely true. If you leave Chardon on Mentor Road heading northwest, past Wisner Rd. (where the Melon Heads live), the road becomes King Memorial Rd. At the bottom of the hill, you'll stop at the Little Mountain Rd. intersection, in Kirtland Hills. Go about a hundred yards past the intersection on King Memorial. Stop your car and look in front of you. It will appear that the road ahead of you is at an upward incline. Now put your car in neutral and release the brake.

Your car will start rolling forward, and it seems like you're rolling uphill. I've never tried it going the other direction, but I've heard it works both ways. The road, obviously, goes downhill, and it's just an optical illusion. I don't know what causes the illusion, but supposedly this little trick was once mentioned, and explained, in a *Ripley's Believe It or Not* book, and they actually cited this specific road. *–Chrish*

Most folks are told from a very young age that ghosts don't exist; they're just the product of superstition and an overactive imagination. But if ghosts aren't real, then why are the stories so pervasive in our culture? And why do so many perfectly normal people swear that they've had encounters with ghosts? Doubters may publicly profess a disbelief in the supernatural and the afterlife, but how many of those same folks, we wonder, secretly harbor some uncertainty about their convictions and would like nothing more than to be proven wrong?

Haunted Places and Ghostly Tales

Ghosts may be a bridge between our limited realm of the "known" and the vast expanse of what is still unknown to all of us who are living. There are many theories as to why the not quite dearly departed might linger here on earth. They may be clueless—souls who don't know that they've passed on. Or they may be tragically restless spirits, tormented by the manner of their death or the circumstances of their life. They cling to the places they once knew, refusing to leave this realm until whatever wrong that was done to them has been righted.

Ghosts have many manifestations, from glowing orbs to free-flowing floating, misty shapes that vaguely resemble people. They may appear to the living in brief flashes or may endlessly repeat a single action or movement, as if caught in an eternal tape loop. Whatever form they take, they scare the daylights out of the people who claim to have seen them.

Ohio is home to hundreds of allegedly haunted locations. Are they for real? We leave it up to you, dear reader, to decide whether the phantasms described on the following pages are simply the product of someone's overactive imagination or if there really is more to them than that.

Haunted Houses

Everyone needs a place to call home. Apparently, this is true not only of the living but also of the dead. While it may be disconcerting to share an abode with some departed former resident, let's try to remember who was there first and who is really the uninvited guest in the house.

Squire's Castle's Ghostly Lady

Just outside Cleveland's city limits lies a section of the Metroparks District known as North Chagrin Reservation. This area is home to a golf course, a wildlife sanctuary, and, according to legend, one restless ghost. Squire's Castle has been abandoned for about a hundred years, but it is haunted to this day.

Born in England in 1850, Feargus B. Squire moved to the United States with his family when he was ten years old. Always something of a self-starter, Squire didn't take long to make a name for himself. His big break came in the 1880s, when he joined Standard Oil of Ohio as a co-manager. Once Squire was on board, his career took off. He soon became very successful and very wealthy. Of all his accomplishments, he is best remembered for developing the first carrier wagon that allowed oil to be shipped by land.

In the 1890s, Squire started to think about the beautiful castles he remembered from his childhood in England and decided to build one for himself and his family here in the United States. After purchasing a 525-acre plot of land, the still relatively young oil baron had plans drawn up for a sprawling estate he called River Farm. Construction began with the gatehouse, which would come to be known as Squire's Castle.

The plans called for an enormous three-story building that, despite the fact that it was to serve only as a gatehouse, included several bedrooms, a living room, a kitchen with a breakfast porch, and even a hunting room and a library. No expense was to be spared. The plaster walls were adorned with massive amounts of woodwork, and leaded glass windows studded the building.

But construction went painstakingly slowly. Squire used the building as a summer retreat while it was being built, but it appears that he started to lose interest in the idea of a country estate. In fact, not only was the gatehouse never completed, but work on other parts of the estate never even got under way. It seems that his wife wasn't so keen about life in the country. After construction began, she started having terrible nightmares about beasts charging out of the woods and killing her and her children. When the family moved out to the estate, Mrs. Squire went along to please her husband. But once she was in the country, her nightmares got even worse, so much so that she got to the point where she was unable to sleep.

Slowly, the woman began to go insane. The longer she went without sleep, the crazier she became and the more she believed that monsters and wild,

city — never to return again.

In 1925, the property was purchased by Cleveland Metroparks, which incorporated the castle into the North Chagrin portion of Metroparks. Squire died in 1932, his dreams of a great country estate never realized. Today, all that remains of the building are the empty rooms that were once the kitchen, the great hall, the hunting room/library, two small living areas, and a porch.

As for the ghost of Squire's Castle, it is none other than Mrs.

fanged animals were after her. Every night, she took a red lantern and walked around the border of the huge estate, looking for the hungry beasts she knew were waiting just beyond the tree line to attack her family. This went on for months. Her husband tried to convince her that the family was safe, but she was obsessed with the animals.

According to legend, in the basement of the castle was an ornate hunting-trophy room, filled with heads and skins from Mr. Squire's hunting trips. Late one evening, for reasons never fully understood, Mrs. Squire ventured alone into the trophy room. She was carrying her red lantern. While she was in the room, something frightened her. Some believe it was simply the reflection of her lantern on the faces of her husband's trophies. But there are some who believe that Mrs. Squire looked into the face of something unearthly that night. Regardless of what transpired, she became so frightened that she attempted to flee the room. In the darkness, she fell and broke her neck.

Upon finding his wife's body, Feargus was overcome with grief. In fact, he blamed himself for his wife's death. He immediately stopped construction on the house, filled the basement room with concrete, and moved back to the

Squire herself. There are some who claim to have seen the light of a red lantern moving slowly around the building. They believe it is carried by the lonely ghost of a woman so frightened in life that she is forced in death to forever patrol the grounds of a place she feared and despised. She has never moved on, and in fact, she doesn't even realize she's dead. She still thinks the safety of her family depends on her nightly walks around her husband's property.

But actually, there are some flaws in the tale. To begin with, while the basement was indeed filled in with concrete after the park took control of the castle, it had never been used as a hunting-trophy room. The castle did have such a room, but it wasn't in the basement. And Mrs. Squire did not die on the property. In fact, she died many miles away, under quite normal circumstances.

Still, too many people have reported seeing "something" moving around Squire's Castle late at night. So while Mrs. Squire may indeed have died somewhere else, who's to say that her spirit isn't still making its nightly rounds? Or perhaps some other lost soul, attracted by the abandoned castle, has moved in. If so, we hope it's happier there than poor Mrs. Squire was.

Walker Funeral Home

Near the intersection of Central and Monroe in Toledo stand a pair of nondescript white buildings. They don't look particularly strange, but according to many former employees, both are quite authentically haunted by the ghosts of former clients, the dead and dying. Unexplained noises and strange, moving shadows are among the weird things said to manifest themselves here at night.

The place has had many incarnations. It has been the Walker Funeral Home, then a private ambulance company, and then it stood abandoned for two years. Today, it's an insurance company. In the funeral home days, the dead were embalmed and memorialized here, but not always in the most conventional sense.

One example involved an October 29, 1960, plane crash at Toledo Airport, which killed twenty-two people, including sixteen players from the Cal Poly San Luis Obispo football team, who had just lost to Bowling Green, 50–6. The plane carrying the California team tried to take off in a thick fog but made it just three hundred feet in the air before its left engine went out. The plane crashed into an orchard and split in two. (The sixteen deaths made it America's worst sports-related air tragedy until that time, but it would not be Ohio's last. On November 14, 1970, the entire Marshall College football team was killed in a plane crash in Huntington, West Virginia.) Some or all of the bodies of the crash victims were brought to the Walker Funeral Home temporarily and spent the night there under the watch of employees. According to stories we've heard, the ghosts of these young men may have stayed behind, along with those of some other visitors.

Victims of a plane crash who were brought there in the late '60s or early '70s still hung out in the basement and would knock things off walls, open and close doors, or just take a walk.

Former Owner Returns

I used to work in that building for the ambulance company in the early '80s, and there was a lot of spirit activity at that time. Victims of a plane crash who were brought there in the late '60s or early '70s still hung out in the basement and would knock things off walls, open and close doors, or just take a walk. The wife of the former owner of the ambulance company told me who the spirits were; she was there the night they were brought in. After the former owner (Gene Spradling) passed away, he was also seen. I was visiting a friend there one night, and Gene walked right through the hallway. My (ex) husband and I both saw it. *—Letter via e-mail*

Gino's Ghost Haunts the Office

One building is said to be haunted by the ghost of a man who had a heart attack while working there for the Walker Funeral Home. We call the ghost Gino for the man's first name. While stationed there, we heard many footsteps above us at night where his office had been. One time, we had to leave the building altogether because we heard what sounded like a basketball dribbling upstairs getting stronger and louder until paint from the ceiling began falling on us. One female that worked there woke me up screaming one night saying she felt someone touch her and then saw an older fat guy run for the stairs. This was enough to get me to leave again, and this is only one of the buildings.

The adjacent building was the site of many more hauntings I've heard about. My own experience is the only one that kept recurring. Most nights, as we were returning to quarters from a run, my partner and I would scope the parking lot for vagrants or people who shouldn't be there before we opened the bay doors. On more than one occasion, we would see a light on, on the top floor in the adjacent building, and each time, a young woman in a dress would come to the window and stare at us. One night, after seeing the figure, we got brave and called some law enforcement friends from the area to help us search the building. We went to the room that had the light on, expecting to find a vagrant camped out there. The only thing we found was a room that had untouched dust on the floor and no lightbulbs in the sockets. We got the willies and split. We never went back into that building at night. *—Anonymous*

Institutional Infestations

It's not only small homes and businesses that play host to ghostly occupants. Larger buildings like schools and theaters also rank high on the hot list of haunted habitats. While such places are usually just temporary sojourns for us, the living, they seem to be particularly attractive to spirits as permanent residences.

Big Ghosts on Campus

Ohio State University

Ohio State University (OSU) is by far Ohio's largest college, and it is second in the nation only to the University of Texas in terms of size. The main campus in Columbus is an immense, sprawling behemoth of a place, replete with a cutting-edge hospital complex, a satellite communications center, public television and radio stations, an airport, a supercomputer, a polar research center, a wildlife preserve, and a functioning farm. It also features a well-known network of steam tunnels that the administration always worries about people exploring. And like any college that's been around since 1870, it has its share of ghost stories. The legends here have been gathered from a wide variety of sources, including students, staff, and faculty. But the best known are regularly listed in the Halloween edition of *The Lantern*.

Pomerene Hall—Mirror Lake

Dr. Clark, a professor in the early 1900s, grew depressed about a failed mining investment and committed suicide. His body was found where Pomerene Hall now stands. The devoted Mrs. Clark swore never to leave him. When she died in the '20s, her ghost, wearing a pink dress, began to haunt Mirror Lake, standing at the edge of the water or floating across it. Dr. Clark haunts Pomerene, where he slams doors and engages in other ghostly activities.

Bricker Hall

When Herbert Atkinson, a member of the university's board of trustees, died in the 1950s, his ashes were placed in a wall behind a plaque in Bricker Hall. Since then, lights have flashed and the man himself has been seen drinking punch in the lobby. Bricker is on the Oval at Seventeenth Avenue, a few buildings west of Hopkins Hall.

Orton Hall

Built in 1893, Orton Hall is one of the oldest buildings on OSU's campus. It was named for Edward Orton, who served as the university's first president, from 1873 through 1881. Orton was also a professor of geology, which is why the building that was named for him houses much of the geology department as well as OSU's own geological museum. In addition to the skeletons of prehistoric turtles, ice-age sloths, and mastodons, visitors to this building are watched by a wide assortment of creepy archaeological gargoyles—plaster representations of the various types of prehistoric life found in Ohio. The ones around the bell tower are prehistoric monsters, extinct reptilian creatures that once populated the primordial sea.

Orton was built with geology in mind, using the heavy rocks native to Ohio. This makes for a gloomy Romanesque castle of a building, spooky even at the busiest time of day—which is fitting, because Orton

Hall is probably the best-known haunted place on campus.

As you might have guessed, Edward Orton himself haunts the building. He apparently spent a lot of time reading by lamplight in the top of the bell tower. Today, you can see scorch marks left by his oil lamp on the inside ceiling of the tower room. Legend says that at night you can see light flickering through the vertical slots that surround the turret. His ghost is still reading in his favorite spot, despite the fact that fourteen huge bells now occupy the space. During the day, he is reputed to chill the air and make noises in an attempt to get unruly students to behave.

Orton's other ghost is said to be that of a man with a "humped back, thick hair, and a protruding forehead" who slams doors, bangs on things, and makes noises because he can't speak. The ghost of a football player? Or something to do with the geological museum?

Canfield Hall Hosts Ghosts

"When I went to OSU, I lived in Canfield Hall. It really is a pretty sort of Gothic building and one of the oldest. We

lived at the end of the hall on the top floor, and though our room was unusually dark and creepy, I didn't mind it at first. There was a large mirror across from my bed, so if you rolled over in the middle of the night, you would see your face staring back as well as strange shadows. All of our friends said the mirror was creepy, and some people wouldn't even look at it. I hung a sheet over my bed, canopy-style, and I was fine. As the school year progressed, things started happening in the room that were a little odd. My roommate's bible kept being hidden somewhere in the room, and she would blame me for it—of course, I didn't do it!

There was a large steam pipe that went along the heads of our beds, and at night, there would be scratching inside of it. We thought it was mice and tolerated it for maybe two hours before I ran down and got the resident adviser, and of course, as soon as she stepped in the room, it stopped. This continued for months, then eventually it just stopped on its own.

Well, to me all of this wasn't scary, just the weirdness of an old dormitory. But one night, I was up alone in the room. I was on the computer until way late, and as I went into the hallway, I could tell that all the other girls were asleep because it was dark under their doors. I left my door open, and when I returned from the bathroom, I prepared for bed—closing the big, heavy curtains on the windows and turning off the light. The room was so small, it was a sort of smothering darkness, and the curtains dampened the sound so I could tell the distance of all the noises from my bed—the clock's ticking, the heater's rumbling. I remember all of this so well. I was almost falling asleep—the type of tired where you are aware of everything but your body is absolutely still—when I heard the distinct and unmistakable sound of three shuffled footsteps on the carpet stopping at my bed near my face!

I had the canopy, so I couldn't see on the other side (and I'm almost thankful for this). I lay paralyzed and panicked for nearly ten minutes when I finally burst through the canopy and turned on the lights. There was nothing there. The carpet was entirely free of even a pair of socks. But the sound was unmistakable—I can still hear it as I recount this story. I explained to myself that it was a plastic bag shifting in my closet. Of course, in the morning when I checked, there was nothing in the closet that could have fallen. I wrote it off to my imagination or some blood pumping in one ear.

A couple months later, we had some friends visit from out of town, and one girl needed to change her clothes in my room. I left her alone, but it took only two minutes before she came out with her face pale, and she wouldn't look anyone in the eye. She just said, 'I can't go in that room. It's evil.' I was offended, assuming she was talking about how messy it was. About fifteen minutes later, another girl went into the bathroom and came out without going. She told us, 'I saw a ghost in the bathroom!' She couldn't describe anything about it, only that a shadow passed behind her as she looked in the mirror. Both girls were entirely freaked out and wouldn't even set foot in my room because of its 'presence.' I wrote this off as crazy Wiccan punk girl stuff and/or snobbery at my messy room. But definitely, there was something sinister about that room—even our phone number spelled out an upside-down cross, and we would get crazy prank phone calls at all hours of the day and night."–*Anonymous*

Alpha Delta Pi

This sorority house on East Fifteenth Avenue is one of Columbus's most notorious haunted places. It is said to still be the home of a girl who killed herself before the sorority moved in. Today, she is spotted roaming the halls and looking out windows and in mirrors. Chandeliers have been known to move for no apparent reason.

Ohio University

Ohio University in Athens is probably the most haunted college campus in the entire country, if not the world. As Ohio places go, it's ancient: established in 1804, just one year after statehood. It was the nation's first institution of higher learning west of the Appalachian Mountains. The sheer number of haunted places on campus is impressive, and that's not counting the numerous other legends floating around Athens County. Fox Television even taped an episode of its *Scariest Places on Earth* program at OU. The show aired in 2001 and took a somewhat less than studious approach to the truth of the local ghost legends. All TV hype aside, it is more unusual for a college building in Athens to be ghost-free than to have some eerie legend associated with it.

Alpha Omicron Pi

A slave named Nicodemus haunts the home of the Alpha Omicron Pi sorority. Once it was the Zeta Tau Alpha house, but before that it was a private residence and a stop on the Underground Railroad. They say that when locals found out that the house at 24 East Washington was harboring fugitive slaves, they stormed it. They found only unlucky Nicodemus hiding there and shot him as he fled through an escape tunnel. For years after that, he haunted the building. Nicodemus has long been accepted as a resident of the house and doesn't seem to generate much fear in the girls who live with him, despite the desperate circumstances of his demise.

Jefferson Hall

The story goes that students were exploring the attic of this building shortly after the beginning of fall quarter in 1996. They saw a woman who looked like a schoolteacher, dressed in 1950s fashions, in an unused room, sitting at a desk. After they tried to talk to her, they noticed that she was transparent and floating above the ground. They ran to get their resident adviser and returned to find the door securely locked, with no one inside. After that, more strange things happened: Lights flipped on and off, toilets flushed by themselves. One girl in a bathroom stall watched as the rolls of toilet paper from the neighboring stalls unrolled completely onto the floor. When hers began to unroll by itself, she ran screaming from the room. A common disturbance here is the "marble sound," the clatter of someone's dropping hundreds of marbles onto the floor above you.

Crawford Hall

Crawford Hall began to experience ghostly phenomena after the Easter 1993 death of Laura, a resident who fell from her fourth-floor window. Lights would flicker and doors would slam shut or fly open, especially on the first floor. One night, a resident adviser in a first-floor room was awakened by the silhouette of a girl who had opened his door. She said, "I'm sorry, I've woken you," and closed it. The RA went into the hall, but there was no one there. He later learned that his room's window faces the spot where Laura hit the sidewalk. CD and tape players there refuse to play the Bob Marley song "Laura."

Wilson Hall

Wilson is the place most people point to when they talk about "haunted Athens." It's a relatively new building, constructed in 1965, but in that short time it has acquired an unusual number of tales, including that it was built atop one of the Athens Mental Health Center cemeteries. This is almost certainly not true, but shadowy, ghostly figures are still sighted in its halls.

Athens, Ohio, Made a Believer out of Me

They say that Athens is the most haunted place on earth, and I believe it! My older sister has attended the local college, Ohio University, and experienced recurring accounts of paranormal activity. Well, the story goes that there was a college girl who was into black magic. One night, everyone in the campus building heard chanting and deep, throaty sounds coming from this particular girl's room. People hadn't heard from this one girl in three days, so they sent a counselor up to see if she was okay. He discovered a gruesome scene: The girl had committed suicide and had written symbols all over one wall. No one was sure why she had killed herself. The next year, they painted over the blood and cleaned up the room. Everything was fine until the blood started seeping through the paint. People who stay in the room can never sleep. Bizarre paranormal activity is reported, as well as the sound of marbles rolling across the ceiling. The room is now a boiler room.

My sister was staying down the hall from the "haunted room" with some friends, and they started hearing things hitting the walls and bumping. So she and her friend Debbie were dared to go check it out. It was about three in the morning, and my sister was afraid of ghosts and things like that, but she went anyway. She and Debbie approached the door and stood there, and nothing happened. Debbie said, "Lets go, nothing is happening." But as soon as she said that, something hit the door and made the handle wiggle. This terrified her, and she and Debbie never went back to that campus building again. I honestly believe Athens is haunted.—*Steph*

Kenyon College

Bishop Philander Chase established Kenyon College on a hilltop overlooking the scenic Kokosing River Valley in 1825. The first permanent building—now known as "Old Kenyon"—went up in 1827–29. Over the years, Kenyon grew into a respected liberal arts college, and today it remains among Ohio's top schools.

Kenyon is also very much a haunted place. A large number of supernatural entities roam the buildings and grounds of its attractive campus in Gambier, Knox County— more than the average number for a private college of this size, it's safe to say.

The spirits of the nine fire victims have been seen gliding down the halls of Old Kenyon.

Old Kenyon

The most tragic event in the history of Kenyon College spawned its darkest and most enduring ghost story: the devastating fire at Old Kenyon on February 27, 1949.

Nine male students were killed in the blaze, which leveled the school's oldest and most prominent building. When it was rebuilt the following year using fireproof materials, students were moved back in. They immediately began to see and experience strange, even terrifying things. The spirits of the nine fire victims have been seen gliding down the halls of Old Kenyon, visible only from the knees up because the foundation of the rebuilt dorm is roughly ten inches higher than that of the old one. Some people have reported seeing the transparent legs of the ghosts hanging through the ceiling of a lower floor. The spooks flip lights on and off and flush toilets. Scenes of panic are reenacted in rooms where the students were trapped. Cries of "Get me out of here!" are heard, as is the violent shaking of closed doors. Screams shouting, "Wake up, FIRE!" wake students at night. Yearbooks from 1949 are sometimes found open to the page with the names of the nine fire victims with a candle burning nearby. Although the building was restored, the lives of the young men never could be, and their spirits still haunt the place where their lives ended so abruptly and tragically.

Shaffer Speech Building—Hill Theater

The Hill Theater, located inside the Shaffer Speech Building, was supposedly built on or near the site of a drunk-driving fatality. The ghost (or maybe ghosts) associated with the accident float around the building unscrewing lightbulbs and opening curtains when no one is around. We don't know why they choose these particular activities; ghosts have reasons of their own. But guards have experienced these phenomena after hours. They've also encountered the spirit of someone (a stagehand, perhaps) who fell from a catwalk and died. The sound of his body thumping against the back of the stage can still be heard.

Caples Hall

The angry ghost of a student who died in an elevator shaft pesters girls in Caples Hall. One story is that he was pushed; another is that he fell when he deliberately climbed into the shaft as part of some sort of prank. Either way, his spirit hangs around, appearing mostly to girls—perhaps out of animosity toward his girlfriend, whom he was visiting when he died. The girlfriend later felt icy hands on her face during her sleep and found her door blocked by her dresser on different occasions. It seems that their last argument, the one that led to his death, ended when she shoved her bureau against the door so that he couldn't get in. Ever since then he appears, transparent, leaning against female students' furniture. He pushes dressers against dorm-room doors and sometimes tries to harm the girls. On at least one occasion, he tried to smother a female student with her pillow.

Delta Kappa Epsilon

On October 28, 1905, Stuart Pierson was killed while pledging this fraternity. Pierson was struck by a train as he waited for DKE members on a trestle over the Kokosing River. Some people say he was tied to the trestle. Whether or not a train was expected is not certain. It is certain that there was some sort of miscalculation of the risk involved in the hazing, and the young man was killed. His father, also a DKE, was in town to witness his son's being inducted into the family fraternity. When he found out about the accident, he refused to press charges, an action—or lack of one—that might have served to incense Stuart's ghost. Every year, on October 28, his ghost is said to stare out a window as a train passes. Whoever occupies his old room is made to vacate it on this anniversary so that Stuart can reclaim it for one day. Confined to the fourth floor, he opens and closes windows and causes footsteps to be heard overhead—despite the fact that there is no floor higher than the fourth. Now that the railroad tracks have been converted into a bicycle trail, one wonders if he continues his yearly vigil.

Ghosts Perform Nightly at Akron Civic Theatre

In the 1920s, the theater business was booming in Ohio. But with so many new places popping up for a theater to succeed, it would need that certain elusive something. That's why in late 1928, when entertainment mogul Marcus Loew was contemplating the creation of a new theater in downtown Akron, only one name came to his mind: John Eberson.

Eberson, Viennese by birth and an architect by trade, had been thrust into the spotlight several years before, in 1923, when he designed the Houston Majestic in Texas. The Majestic was the first theater designed in a style that Eberson dubbed atmospheric. Drawing heavily on the architect's European heritage, atmospheric theaters were designed to literally overwhelm the senses. Ornate fountains, grottoes, and the occasional stuffed bird were incorporated into the buildings' interiors. The most amazing aspect of some of these theaters was that the ceilings were designed to look like the evening sky, complete with blinking stars.

For his design of the Akron Civic Theatre, then referred to as the Loews Theatre, Eberson turned for inspiration to the architecture of Moorish castles. When his masterpiece was completed, it included medieval-style carvings, numerous sculptures, and "antiques" of every shape and size. Today, it remains one of only a handful of theaters in the world still to have an operating moving ceiling.

During the years it has been in business, however, and even a few years before that, the Akron Civic Theatre has managed to acquire a few ghosts.

Fred the Janitor

If asked politely, theater personnel will sometimes relate the tale of Fred the Janitor, a longtime employee back when the theater was still known as the Loews. Fred supposedly died during one of his shifts at the theater, which may be the reason his ghost still shows up from time to time: to complete his final working day. Fred's ghost has been seen all over the

building, and in one instance standing just outside the main entranceway. Fred apparently has no tolerance for people who disrespect his beloved theater, especially the bathrooms. In fact, Fred's ghost is said to get so angry about people messing up his bathrooms that he will attack anyone he catches doing anything other than neatly answering the call of nature in the restrooms.

The Well-Dressed Man

A second ghostly legend floating around the theater is that of the Well-Dressed Man. Although to be honest, there's not much of a story to go with the ghost other than the fact that he has impeccable taste in clothes. He is usually seen sitting up in the balcony, which leads many to believe that he is the ghost of a former patron. Others, though, think the ghost belongs to a former actor who just couldn't bear to leave the theater for good.

Weeping Suicide Girl

The final ghost that haunts this theater appears outside the building rather than inside. Specifically, this ghost often is seen wandering along the old canal that runs behind the theater. The female spirit is thought to be that of a girl who lived nearby prior to the theater's construction, during Akron's canal days. She apparently committed suicide by jumping into, and subsequently drowning in, the canal. Her ghost is sometimes heard sobbing softly as she walks along the canal before disappearing into the drain tunnel that runs under the theater.

It is often said that life is a journey. For the following band of wandering spirits, that journey apparently continues on into the afterlife. Instead of settling down in a nice spooky castle or abandoned hospital somewhere, these lost souls spend their time eternally wandering around the state.

Blue Flame Ghost

As the story goes, in the 1930s there was a lively young woman who lived in Sugar Grove, Fairfield County. She was a happy, vibrant girl who was well liked by everyone. But all that changed when she became engaged to a young man with a reputation for being hot-tempered. Indeed, the young couple were often seen in town having fierce arguments.

Over time, people began to notice a change in the young woman. She never smiled anymore, and she grew cold and distant. Friends even said that she started to carry a knife in her purse for protection from her fiancé. It was clear to everyone who knew the couple that if things didn't change, and soon, there was going to be trouble.

One night, the young couple were parked beside the Hummel covered bridge. A bitter argument broke out, and in a fit of rage the young woman pulled out the knife and stabbed her fiancé in the throat. Blinded by rage, she continued to slash until the man's head was severed. From the trail of blood found the next day, it was concluded that the woman, for reasons known only to her, had carried the severed head up to the top of a small hill on the west side of the bridge. It then appears that she sat there with the head for a period of time before finally slitting her own throat.

The woman, bleeding severely, apparently then staggered back down the hill, still carrying her fiancé's head. She eventually collapsed and died near the bottom, where her body was found the next day, alongside the severed head.

Recently, the covered bridge was torn down and replaced with a concrete one. But there are those who claim that on certain nights, if you stand on the bridge and call out the young woman's name, a glowing blue form in the shape of a woman will appear at the top of the hill and slowly move toward you.

Unfortunately, in most retellings of the legend, the woman's name is never given, which, since you need to call her by name, makes it rather hard to get her to appear. But then again, who ever said getting a ghost to appear on command was easy?

Sad Tale of the Haunted Locks

Within Beaver Creek State Park there exists the remains of a canal system planned in the early 1800s to open up Ohio for commerce and travel. Part of this canal system involved several locks, sections of waterway that could be closed off with gates so that the water level could be raised or lowered, allowing boats to pass through. By 1850, the majority of locks were in place, and a small canal town, Sprucevale, had sprung up in anticipation of the opening of the system. All that would change, though, in 1852, when, during construction, a nearby reservoir broke, flooding the area. The flood also caused severe damage to the system, so much so that the remaining construction plans were scrapped. Shortly thereafter, the city of Sprucevale fell first into ruin and then into obscurity. But

not before adding a few ghost stories to the annals of Ohio folklore.

One of the abandoned locks has been nicknamed Jake's Lock (its actual name is Jack's Lock) after a former lockkeeper. As a lockkeeper, it was Jake's responsibility to inspect all of the locks several times a day, making sure they were not damaged in any way and that they were operating properly.

During a terrible thunderstorm one night, Jake grabbed his lantern and made his way outside to make sure the storm hadn't damaged any of the locks. As he stood inspecting the sides of one of the locks, Jake was struck by lightning and fell into the water below. His body was found the next morning floating in the lock, still clutching his lantern.

Apparently, not even death has stopped Jake from making his rounds. It is said that on certain nights, especially stormy ones, Jake's ghost returns, lantern in hand, to inspect the locks. People camping near the locks have reported seeing the light from Jake's lantern moving through the woods late at night.

Only a short distance away from Jake's Lock is Gretchen's Lock. As this story goes, Gretchen was the daughter of a Dutch or an Irish engineer named Gill, who was brought over to America to work on the lock system. Since he was going to be gone from his homeland for so long, Gill decided to bring his wife and his daughter, Gretchen, with him. Sadly, Gill's wife became ill on the trip over and passed away. Since there was no way to store the woman's body onboard, Gill reluctantly agreed to allow his wife to be buried at sea.

Once in Ohio, Gill began working on the design of the lock system. Gretchen, however, was still grieving over the loss of her mother and became quite sullen and sad. Her father tried to lift her spirits, but he was unsuccessful. All the girl wanted was to see her mother again.

Then Gretchen contracted malaria. She lingered for a short time but eventually succumbed to her illness. Distraught over not having been able to give his wife a proper funeral, Gill was adamant that his daughter be buried back in her home country. But with the canal system still not complete, he was obliged to stay in Ohio. So he decided to delay Gretchen's formal burial and simply placed her body in a coffin. He would take her back to their homeland after his work on the locks was completed. With no secure place to keep the coffin, Gill put it inside the lock itself for safekeeping.

After the work was completed, Gill removed Gretchen's coffin from the lock, loaded it onto a boat, and sailed for home. But this man was cursed, indeed. To this day, no one is sure exactly what happened, but his ship was lost at sea. It would appear that Gretchen finally got her wish to be reunited with her mother . . . in a watery grave.

The girl's body was never seen again. But in a strange twist, Gretchen's ghost has been spotted wandering near the lock in which her body was temporarily entombed, often on the anniversary of her death, August 12. As she moves along the lock, Gretchen is said to be weeping and can be heard crying out, "I want to be with my mother."

Screaming for Jake on Sprucevale Road

I received a telephone call from a friend last night who was riding with friends through Beaver Creek Park on Sprucevale Road. He said they saw a woman in an old-fashioned wedding gown, holding a lantern at eye level, across the mill at the bottom of the hill. She was screaming wildly for "Jake," so they slowed and asked her if she needed help, but she just kept screaming and shrieking for Jake! They went home and then returned, and she was still there. They said that when they were coming down the hill, they could see her lantern through the trees. And when they drove slowly past her, she was still screaming, and they could hear something else in the woods that sounded like it was coming from behind the mill. They couldn't make out any words, just sounds. They were very scared but not sure if she was a ghost or someone goofing around due to the fact that it was Halloween season and all. But it was still creepy! She never acknowledged that they were there. She just looked at them but never answered when they asked her if she needed help; she just kept screaming. My friend was on his cell phone with his wife while the woman was screaming, and his wife heard the shrill voice too. But no one knows if she was a real ghost or a real faker!—*Letter via e-mail*

Blue Limestone Park

Strange stories are told about the picturesque community park in Delaware called Blue Limestone. It borders a rail line that has lent itself to tragedy over the years, or so they say. A 1920s train accident in the vicinity, one we haven't been able to confirm as real, is nevertheless said to be the cause of many of the unexplained phenomena in the park. Strange lights are seen there, especially at night, looking very much like people. The lost spirits of train-wreck victims? Drowning victims from a nearby quarry? No one seems to agree on much besides the fact that Blue Limestone Park is haunted.

Following a rough path through the woods and crossing a small stream will bring you to a brick tunnel under the railway. It's here that many of the legends are centered. Enigmatic chunks of concrete and metal are strewn throughout the woods. Lights are often seen in the darkness beneath the tracks, and disembodied voices are heard. Sometimes a ghost train is even seen, reenacting the fatal wreck of the 1920s.

Blue Limestone's Haunted Tunnel

There are two back quarries, and the area is extremely creepy at night. Inside the tunnel, if you listen hard, it does sound like voices, though that could be a trick of the acoustics. There's some odd things with the tracks, but this could be because of the tunnel underneath them. The tracks don't carry the vibrations of a coming train and also they do not carry any of the heat from a passing one. There are a number of pieces of concrete hidden in the woods surrounding the tunnel, most of which look like they were part of the tunnel. How they got there, I don't know. They're a good thirty to forty yards away in the trees, but they look like the emplacements at the top of the tunnel beside the train tracks. —*Mike Shaffer*

Witch Woods

I live just outside of Gambier. Near my house, there are woods that are supposed to be haunted by the ghost of a witch. Well, I always thought that those stories were just made up to frighten kids. But one night, I was walking home all alone and thought I heard a voice say, "Come here." I turned around, and I heard it again, only this time it sounded like it was coming from the woods. And it was a woman's voice.

At that point, I wasn't scared. I thought it was just one of my friends messing with me. So I kept walking. But I hadn't walked more than a few feet when I heard it again, only louder. When I turned around, I saw this weird, glowing shape standing in the woods. It was too hard to see it very clearly, but it had the outline of a human. I know this sounds silly, but I starting throwing rocks at it. I guess it was because I was scared.

Well, the shape just stayed there for a few seconds and then just faded away. I wanted to go over and see if there was anything where it had been standing, but I was scared. So I just ran home. If I ever have to walk home at night again, I am taking the long way home! —*B. May*

Cemetery Safari

Every *tombstone tells a story* if we take the time to read the words inscribed on it. The departed speak to us from beyond the grave, and their words are etched in these stoic markers. Sometimes the stones tell of evil deeds or give stern words of advice. Sometimes their messages are lighthearted and loving. Some grave sites are humble and abandoned, while others are opulent monuments testifying to the pride and vanity of the people they honor.

There are fascinating cemeteries all over the state of Ohio. A walk through any one of them is like a living history lesson, taught by those who preceded us—and who know where we are all headed in the end. There are cemeteries that have given rise to legends of hauntings and curses, while others are of interest simply for the offbeat, sometimes macabre monuments to be discovered there.

Of course, there are hundreds of famous or otherwise noteworthy people buried throughout the state. We'll show you the permanent digs of some of them in this chapter, but we're placing our spotlight mainly on Ohio's less-well known former residents. They may have passed under the radar during their time here in this mortal plain, but they came into their own once they crossed over to the other side.

Erie Street's Indians

What today is called Ninth Street in downtown Cleveland was once known as Erie Street, a name preserved only in the old cemetery directly across from Jacobs Field. Passing beneath a stone arch will take you into nine shady, meticulously trimmed acres of graves that stretch all the way back to East Fourteenth Street.

Four Cleveland mayors are buried here, but Erie Street's most famous occupants are two Native Americans, both of whom lie in the shadow of the place where the Cleveland Indians play baseball. The first, Joc-o-Sot, was a Sauk chief who died after a European tour with a Wild West show. An old bullet wound, sustained in 1831 during the Black Hawk Wars, flared up, became infected, and killed him. Joc-o-Sot apparently wanted to be buried closer to his original home, in Wisconsin or Minnesota, but his handlers didn't take him that far. Now his spirit wanders the graveyard, while his mortal remains lie beneath a cracked tombstone, torn perhaps by the misplaced Joc-o-Sot's rage.

Chief Thunderwater, the other Native American buried here, worked toward

the acceptance of Indians by white men. He was sometimes called "the official Cleveland Indian" and has been incorrectly identified as the inspiration for the Cleveland Indians' Chief Wahoo. (In fact, it was Louis "Chief" Sockalexis who is widely accepted as the namesake of the mascot. Sockalexis, who played for the Cleveland Spiders circa 1912, is buried in his home state of Maine.)

People leave trinkets such as feathers and shot glasses at the graves of both Joc-o-Sot and Chief Thunderwater in an attempt to bring good luck to the baseball team across the street. It doesn't usually work.

Above, the Hayden Mausoleum. Right,
World War I air ace Eddie Rickenbacker.
Below, humorist James Thurber

Greenlawn Cemetery

Every city has its flagship municipal graveyard, and in Columbus that honor goes to Greenlawn Cemetery. The entrance is located at the end of Greenlawn Avenue, south of the Brewery District, but the cemetery covers hundreds of acres, stretching all the way to Harrisburg Pike and Cooper Stadium.

Established on August 7, 1848, Greenlawn quickly began to fill up with Columbus's citizens, including many notable locals. You'll find the namesakes of many city streets and landmarks in the older sections, as well as more governors of this state than in any other cemetery. A few of the famous names carved on the stones there are Franklinton founder Lucas Sullivant; aviator Eddie Rickenbacker; author James Thurber; industrialists Simon Lazarus, P. W. Huntington, and Gordon Battelle; George Bush Sr.'s grandfather, Samuel Bush; and Ohio governors John Bricker, James Campbell, William Dennison, George Nash, and James Rhodes.

Some of the dead lie in the central chapel and mausoleum, designed by noted Columbus architect Frank Packard. Others have their own private mausoleums. One of the most famous is the Hayden Mausoleum, located near the pond at one edge of the graveyard. The story goes that if you knock on one of the Hayden doors after dark, some members of this illustrious family will knock back.

Greenlawn is home to a number of famous monuments, including a statue of restaurateur Emil Ambos, which shows him fishing. Another statue, this one of a little boy, is dressed and redressed constantly by his grieving mother. Another child's grave receives regular seasonal decorations as well as birthday cakes and presents.

Not all of the graves are so individualized. Whole sections of uniform military tombstones memorialize the dead from each major war, while an entire neighborhood of babies is identified as Lullaby Land. Here, most graves are marked by a sleeping lamb or a small ground-level rectangle with a single name.

Presidents and Robber Barons

Lake View Cemetery in Cleveland occupies 285 acres off Euclid Avenue and contains more than one hundred thousand graves, a number that grows by more than seven hundred each year.

Founded in 1869, Lake View has gained a worldwide reputation for the quality of its statuary. The Haserot Angel, for one, is regularly sought out and photographed for its dramatic representation of "the angel of death victorious." The memorial to the 1908 Collinwood school fire, which killed 172 students and two teachers and caused the design of school buildings to be modernized around the country, is another dramatic funereal monument.

But Lake View is perhaps most famous because of its big names. No Clevelander has risen higher than John D. Rockefeller, whose controlling interest in Standard Oil made him the richest man in the world—and, adjusting for inflation, the richest man who ever lived. His family plot is here. Eliot Ness, who modernized Cleveland's

Left, John D. Rockefeller. Middle, the Garfield Memorial. Below, the Haserot Angel

7271 GARFIELD MEMORIAL, CLEVELAND, OHIO.

police force but failed to catch the Torso Killer—the city's version of Jack the Ripper—is buried here as well. And, of course, there's James A. Garfield, whose truly gargantuan mausoleum is the largest and most elaborate of any presidential resting place, built after his tragic assassination, in 1881. His flag-draped coffin rests beside his wife's in the mausoleum's lowest level, while the upper floor contains stained-glass windows, an atrium, and a wide stone balcony.

Mound Cemetery

Marietta, the first settlement in the Northwest Territory, is home to one of the oldest pioneer burial grounds west of the Appalachian Mountains: Mound Cemetery. General Rufus Putnam, who led the settlers here and founded the city, donated the plot of land surrounding this large Indian burial mound in January 1801. The first burial—of Revolutionary War veteran Robert Taylor—took place in October of that same year. In its early days, Mound Cemetery received more than twenty-five Revolutionary War soldiers, including old Rufus himself. Also here are Return Jonathan Meigs, who served variously as justice of the Ohio Supreme Court, federal judge, postmaster general under James Madison, U.S. senator from Ohio, and the fourth Ohio governor; and Abraham Whipple, the first American to fire a shot at the British on the water, beginning the naval portion of the Revolution.

The Indian mound at the center of the cemetery is thirty feet tall and can be climbed using a staircase. Signs warn that it's a major crime to leave the staircase and trample the mound, perhaps because it's a registered National Landmark. Archaeologists agree that the Hopewell Indians built the mound, even though most of Marietta's famous earthworks were built by the Adena tribe.

Famous Indian Mound, Mound Cemetery, Marietta, Ohio

Woodland Cemetery

Dayton's major cemetery is, predictably enough, the final resting place of Orville and Wilbur Wright, as well as poet Paul Laurence Dunbar, humorist Erma Bombeck, and Ohio governor and presidential candidate James M. Cox, among others. Its official name is Woodland Hills, and its two hundred acres encompass the highest point in the city: Lookout Point.

John Van Cleve, one of Dayton's founding fathers, was instrumental in establishing a new cemetery in what was then a rural area, far outside the city proper. In 1843, Dayton, then a city of twenty thousand, had outgrown its

small municipal cemetery at Third and Main streets downtown. The new interment ground was named Woodland because the property was heavily wooded. Very few of the existing trees were cut down when turning the land into a graveyard, creating a beautiful public park that just happens to be full of dead people, more than one hundred thousand at present, with more arriving all the time. In some places the hills are gently rolling, but in others they drop off steeply, and the roads carve their way through several high-sided chasms honeycombed with tombs. The distinctive entrance gateway, with attached chapel and office, was added in 1889 and is listed on the National Register of Historic Places, thanks largely to its one-of-a-kind Tiffany windows.

The many graves here include countless distinctive angels and other sculptures. Not far from the front entrance is a marker that's hard to miss. This is the grave of Johnny Morehouse and, according to legend, his dog, two of Woodland's most famous ghostly residents. The story might be rooted in nothing more than an unusual tombstone, but this is what they say: Johnny, a five-year-old boy, fell into the Miami and Erie Canal and froze to death, despite his brave dog's efforts to pull him out. After Johnny was buried, the dog lay on his grave site and wouldn't be moved. Eventually, the steadfast animal died from starvation and sadness. A special stone was carved in 1861 to commemorate the dog's devotion. Today, people leave toys, candy, and other trinkets for the faithful Fido—a ritual the cemetery management tolerates. Some grave watchers say that Johnny and his dog, reunited in eternity, roam the cemetery after hours. The two of them are sometimes spotted playing inside the perimeter fence, and barking has been heard in the vicinity of the grave.

*Right, the grave of Orville
and Wilbur Wright*

Columbus Mental Hospital Cemeteries

People who lived in Columbus before 1991 may remember the old state hospital. It was a truly massive building that stood on the north side of West Broad Street at the gateway to the Hilltop neighborhood. The psychiatric hospital system in Columbus was established in 1838, but the main building, the city's third and longest-operating "lunatic asylum," was built between 1870 and 1877.

Over the years, the Columbus Hospital for the Insane was home to some deeply disturbed people. The methods employed there were never what you'd call cutting-edge. Even while in use, the building itself deteriorated into a place of falling bricks and peeling paint. In 1991 it was demolished, and a new building was erected on the site by the Ohio Department of Transportation (a glass-and-steel monster as big as the old asylum). The hospital is just a memory now, its only permanent remnants the patient cemeteries that dot the area.

According to records, there are four cemeteries in all, but only three are still maintained. The oldest, technically known as the State Old Insane and Penal Cemetery, is at the end of a dirt path near the intersection of Harper and McKinley. It was here that the hospital started burying guests of the state who didn't have family willing to pick up their bodies. The oldest stones are the black ones belonging to the old Ohio Penitentiary. They are hand-carved with curlicues and things like angels, birds, and trees surrounding the names and death dates. It's in these rows that unidentifiable bodies from the prison's fire in 1930, in which 322 people died, were laid to rest. Their stones read simply UNKNOWN.

Unknowns also occupy space in the asylum portion here, which radiates out in a circle from a centerpiece engraved with THE COL. ASYLUM. Many patients were never identified, so severe was their mental handicap and complete their isolation. Some are listed only by their first name—all they could provide, presumably. Others have a question mark in place of a birth date.

The middle-period cemetery is the best looked after of the three, but it's hard to know that it's there. It's on the property of the Columbus Developmental Center, set into a dip in the landscape. Only a few of the graves make themselves visible from the driveway; the others are flush with the ground, mostly obscured by mowed grass. There are plenty of question marks here, along with a few unknowns. The death dates range from the 1890s through the 1950s.

The most recent cemetery, the one located behind the recently vacated juvenile detention center near I-70, has large block tombstones in one half and flat, ground-level stones in the other. These are the patients who lived at the asylum during its final years, all the way up through the early '80s. There are fewer unknowns here, but there are two enigmatic tombstones marked simply SPECIMENS. Whatever specimens they were, they must have been human at one time, but this mystery has yet to be solved.

Sometimes the most interesting aspect of a grave has little to do with the person buried in it—it's the marker itself that has a story to tell. There are odd and sometimes bizarre monuments located all over the Buckeye State, from statues that move, driven by unseen forces, to one that watches YOU move!

The Weeping Angel

One of the many ghost stories in Athens belongs to the cemetery on West State Street. This graveyard contains stones dating back to the early 1800s. Near the front gate is a stone angel statue that commemorates the unknown soldiers buried here. Legend has it that the statue sometimes moves and, more frequently, sheds tears.

The statue looks very sad indeed, with its eyes downcast and its shoulders slumped. It's easy to see how a legend like this could get started, especially since the angel stands so close to the front and can be seen when driving by. Whether the tears are real we can't say.

Glassy-Eyed Gaze

The largest nonprofit private cemetery in the United States, Spring Grove Cemetery in Cincinnati is a beautiful and visually stunning place, complete with a wonderful cross-section of statuary (including a sphinx), several ponds, and even waterfalls. It is also home to one of Ohio's strangest legends: the statue with human eyes.

As the story goes, one of the tombstones in Spring Grove is decorated with a unique bust done in the likeness of the gentleman buried beneath. What makes this bust stand out among all the others in the cemetery is that, according to legend, the man buried here had a rather strange final request. The man's will stipulated that, after his death, his eyes were to be removed and placed in the sockets of the bust on his tombstone. No one is sure why he wanted this done—or even if it was done—but the popular belief is that he wanted to keep watch over his grave for all eternity.

No Retreat for Confederate Soldier

In 1861, federal authorities authorized the construction of a Confederate prisoner of war camp in northern Ohio. Lieutenant Colonel William Hoffman visited the Sandusky area and began looking for a location for the prison, focusing his attention on the Lake Erie islands. After rejecting several of the islands because of their proximity to Canada and/or their high civilian population, Hoffman settled on the unpopulated Johnson's Island.

Using lumber from trees on the island, a stockade covering approximately sixteen acres was built, complete with a fifteen-foot fence surrounding it. Inside were thirteen two-story prisoner barracks and a hospital. Construction was completed within the year, and in 1862 the first prisoners arrived from Camp Chase in Columbus. Over the course of the next four years, over eleven thousand Confederate officers and enlisted men would come to be imprisoned on Johnson's Island.

By all accounts, life at the island prison was better than average most of the year. However, the frozen winds that blew across Lake Erie made for brutal winters, especially since the vast majority of Confederate prisoners were used to warmer climates. It didn't help matters when the green lumber used to construct the prison shrank over time, causing holes and gaps to appear in the prison walls. Inmates tried to fill the holes with newspaper, but this did little to hold back the cold. Add to all of this the fact that the limestone in the soil made for poor drainage, causing the privies to overflow with waste, and

you are left with some rather horrific living conditions.

After the prison closed down, the island was essentially abandoned. However, in the 1890s the area enjoyed a brief revival of sorts when the Johnson's Island Pleasure Resort opened up. But when Cedar Point Amusement Park moved in nearby, the resort quickly began losing money and soon fell into ruin. Eventually, Cedar Point purchased the resort and razed or moved all of the remaining buildings.

Today, while visitors to the island can see an earthen fort, all that remains of the Civil War prison is the cemetery, which houses more than two hundred graves. The centerpiece is a large bronze statue of a Confederate soldier. This statue faces north as opposed to south, which would have symbolized a retreat. However, legends abound of the statue's coming to life at night and moving.

In addition to the moving statue, there are reports of the ghosts of Confederate soldiers, which have been seen walking among the tombstones and under the trees surrounding the cemetery. A few people even claim to have heard the disembodied voices of the imprisoned men.

There is also a strange legend involving a group of Italian immigrants hired to work at the nearby quarry. It is said that although many of the workers did not speak English, for some unknown reason they began singing "Dixie."

A taunt to the unfortunate Confederates? If so, as far as we know, none of the singing immigrants earned a place in the graveyard.

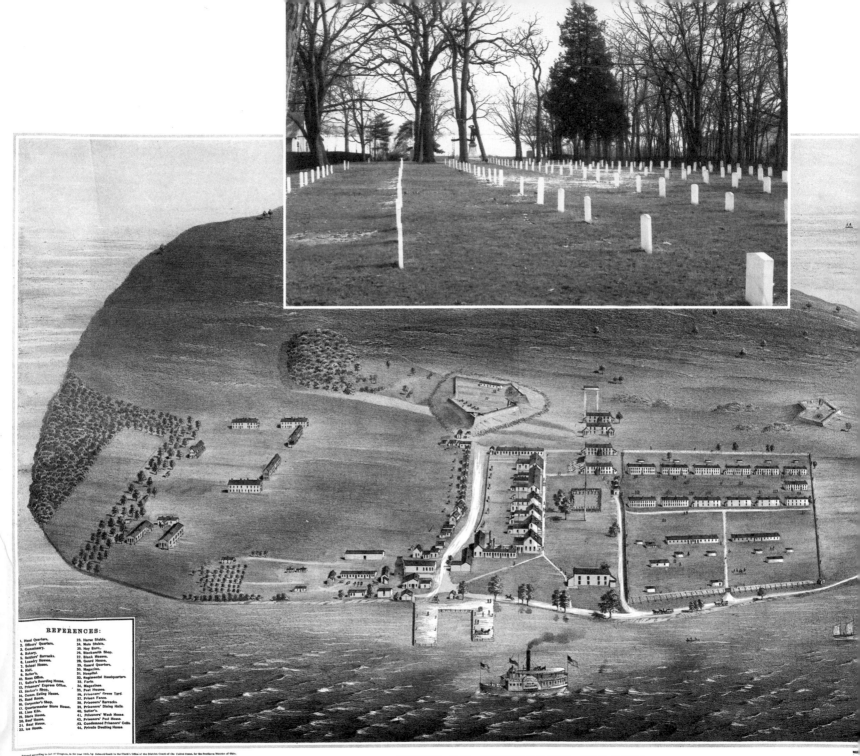

REFERENCES:

1. Head Quarters.
2. Officers' Quarters.
3. Commissary.
4. Bakery.
5. Soldiers' Barracks.
6. Laundry Houses.
7. School House.
8. Hall.
9. Sutler's.
10. News Office.
11. Sutler's Boarding House.
12. Prisoners' Express Office.
13. Barber's Shop.
14. Comm. Eating House.
15. Band Room.
16. Carpenter's Shop.
17. Quartermaster Store House.
18. Lime Kiln.
19. Store House.
20. Boat House.
21. Boat House.
22. Ice House.

23. Horse Stable.
24. Main Stable.
25. Hay Barn.
26. Blacksmith Shop.
27. Block Houses.
28. Guard House.
29. Guard Quarters.
30. Magazine.
31. Hospital.
32. Regimental Headquarters.
33. Forts.
34. Magazines.
35. Post Houses.
36. Prisoners' Green Yard.
37. Prison Fence.
38. Prisoners' Barracks.
39. Prisoners' Dining Halls.
40. Sutler's.
41. Prisoners' Wash House.
42. Prisoners' Post House.
43. Condemned Prisoners' Cells.
44. Private Dwelling House.

Entered according to Act of Congress, in the year 1865, by Edward Gould, in the Clerk's Office of the District Court of the United States, for the Southern District of Ohio.

VIEW OF JOHNSON'S ISLAND,

NEAR SANDUSKY CITY, O.

SKETCHED BY

EDWARD GOULD.

The Rolling Stone of Marion Cemetery

There are many sites within Marion Cemetery that make it a popular destination for those who entertain themselves by visiting graveyards. Even from outside the gates one can see the breathtaking Marion County World War II Memorial, which was officially opened during a Memorial Day ceremony in 2001. The structure, made up of eight-foot-high walls with a thirteen-foot centerpiece, is one of the largest in the United States and features the names of the almost six thousand Marion County residents who lost their lives in World War II. There are also quite a few notables buried here, including playwright Saxon Kling, as well as several figures from Warren G. Harding's short-lived term as the twenty-ninth president of the United States. Charles Sawyer, who served as Harding's personal physician, is here, as is Carrie Phillips, who was involved in a scandalous love affair with Harding. Harding himself was briefly interred at Marion before being moved in the 1920s to the nearby Harding Memorial, where he rests, presumably in peace, with his wife.

But the number-one tourist attraction isn't any of those listed above. Rather, it's a giant stone sphere that just won't stay still.

In 1896, members of the wealthy Charles B. Merchant clan decided to spruce up the family plot in Marion Cemetery. They wanted to make it a focal point, as prominent in the cemetery as they were in town. They commissioned a design that started with a series of small black granite spheres arranged in a large circle to mark their plot. In the center of this circle was erected a five-foot-tall granite monument engraved with the family name. On top of that was placed an enormous fifty-two-hundred-pound black granite sphere, which was polished once it was in place.

All in all, the Merchant family plot was a stunning site that quickly became a popular attraction in the cemetery. It wasn't until a few years later that people began to notice something weird was going on with the giant sphere—hard as it was to believe, the two-and-a-half-ton sphere appeared to be moving. The motion wasn't visible to the naked eye, but there was no denying that it was happening. All one had to do was look at the sphere to see that the unpolished portion of the orb, the part that had originally been in contact with the base of the monument, was now fully visible. What's more, there were no markings on the sphere to suggest how it had been moved. It was as if it had been gently lifted from its base and turned ever so slightly. But that was impossible. Or was it?

Concerned, the Merchant family hired workers who used a crane to lift the sphere and return it to its original position on the base of the monument. That seemed to do the trick . . . for a while. But as the years rolled on, it wasn't long before the unpolished portion of the sphere began poking out once more. Several other attempts were made to reset the sphere, but all efforts proved fruitless. Experts were called in to try to figure out why the strange movement was occurring but could provide no reason, at least none that science could explain.

That was just fine for curiosity seekers, who began flocking to the cemetery in droves to catch a glimpse of the mysterious ball. Of course, many were disappointed when their visions of a wildly spinning two-ton piece of granite were dashed by the sight of the virtually motionless sphere. Still, it did still attract the attention of *Ripley's Believe It or Not,* which featured the monument in 1929.

As more and more people visited Marion Cemetery, the number of explanations for the sphere's movement also increased. Everyone seemed to have a theory, which ranged from gravitational pull to bizarre tales of the monument's being cursed or even possessed. Whatever the reason, the sphere continues to move even today, creeping along at an

average of two inches a year. In fact, the unpolished portion is now fully exposed and is slowly making its way toward the top of the sphere. It's not uncommon to encounter people in the cemetery taking measurements and scrawling down numbers in a notebook as they track the stone's progress. So it seems that the Merchant family got its wish: Their family plot has become a focal point of the area—just not in the way they had envisioned.

Three Witches' Graves

Sitting by themselves in the middle of a field in Columbiana are three lonely tombstones. The first reaction on seeing them might be to assume that the graves are lonely because they're in the middle of nowhere. Perhaps a cemetery was meant to be established here but was abandoned for some reason.

But that assumption would be wrong. According to legend, the three women buried under those stones were placed here with the express intention that they be left alone, far from the living—and the dead, buried elsewhere. For, you see, these gravestones are said to mark the graves of three powerful witches who practiced their craft for years in Germany before immigrating to the United States.

When the women arrived in Ohio, rumors of their powers began to spread. If a cow died, the townspeople knew the three immigrants were to blame. A family struck down with an illness? Those witches were at it again. The locals began to fear the powers of the women and would do anything to avoid being in their presence. Even in death, no one wanted to have anything to do with them, so they were buried along an isolated stretch of land in the hope that no one would ever stumble upon their graves.

Even in death, the three witches still have power. If you don't believe it, just drive your car up the road until you get to the graves, park, and then walk up to the stones. Wait there a few minutes, and then go back and try to start your car. If the engine turns over, consider yourself lucky. It's said that when the spirit of any of the three witches doesn't take an immediate liking to a visitor, she will disable his car. To break the spell, you must push the car far enough away from the graves to escape her realm of power. Considering how strong the spirits of those three women are rumored to be, you'll probably be pushing that car a long, long time.

The Witchy Warlock Grave

Wolfe Cemetery in Haydenville is said to be haunted by a witch or a warlock who was supposedly burned and buried there. His or her grave is said to be the big one with the flat top, and if you touch it you may get sucked into a scary netherworld of witches and warlocks. We're not making this up; it's a popular legend with the local high-schoolers, who dare each other to drive up the steep incline into Wolfe Cemetery at night, park, and run out to touch the prominent slab tombstone in the center. The braver kids sometimes party up here, dancing on the flat gravestone, which has left it cracked and nearly illegible without rubbing materials. So far nobody has been seen getting sucked under. But you never know.

There seems to be no getting around it—whenever the topic is cemeteries, the conversation turns to ghosts. And why not? Graveyards are, after all, not only where the mortal remains of the deceased are interred for all eternity. They are also the places that we, the living, go to when we want to honor and remember the dead. So we must believe that some trace of those departed souls is still here with us, lingering around their graves.

Maybe there is. Throughout Ohio, there are tales of spirited cemeteries filled with spooks and specters that cry out to be recognized, sometimes in the most hair-raising ways.

The Moving Tombstones at Elizabeth's Grave

The official name of the cemetery is Mount-Union Pleasant Valley, but no one calls it that. Instead, the cemetery, located in the northwest of Ross County in Chillicothe, is referred to by the name of the ghost who is supposed to haunt it. As far back as anyone can remember, the entire area was referred to simply as Elizabeth's Grave.

So who was Elizabeth? Well, some say she was a simple farm girl who lived all alone in a cabin near the cemetery. Others believe Elizabeth was the wife of a wealthy landowner who owned the property in and around the cemetery. And you wouldn't be able to call this legend complete if there wasn't at least one version that declared Elizabeth to be a witch.

Whichever story you choose to believe, they all include Elizabeth's meeting an untimely end near a tree at the back of the cemetery. In the tamest version, she simply commits suicide by hanging herself there. In other tellings, the hanging is carried out by the townspeople, who for some reason drag Elizabeth kicking and screaming to the tree at the back of the cemetery. But the strangest version has the townspeople becoming angry because Elizabeth, a woman, was going to inherit large portions of land from her husband. So they did what any benighted town folk would do in that situation: They took Elizabeth out to the cemetery tree and decapitated her.

The one weird constant in the story is that while

Elizabeth is buried at the front of the cemetery near the road, her tombstone always moves itself to the back. It is this aspect of the legend that's led to some of the most violent and disrespectful vandalism we've ever witnessed. Near the back of the cemetery there are literally piles of tombstones. Is there an Elizabeth among them? Actually, there are three. But there are also two Marys, a Susan, four Johns, two Michaels, and a vast array of broken stones that bear only partial names or no name at all.

One look is all it takes to know that ghosts had nothing to do with this sad pile; it was caused by human hands. In an apparent attempt to "prove" that Elizabeth's tombstone moved, visitors (to use a polite term) have uprooted tombstones bearing the name Elizabeth and dropped them at the back of the cemetery. When all of the Elizabeths were gone, people apparently started dragging any tombstone they could find back there. Sadly, the actions of these individuals have only fed the stereotype that people interested in ghost stories and weird tales are really just bent on desecrating cemeteries and other landmarks.

So the question remains: Who was Elizabeth and why does she haunt the place? As far as who she was, if she ever existed at all, she could be any of the three Elizabeths whose tombstones were senselessly thrown in the back of the cemetery. In fact, given the many versions of the tale, she could be all three of them. As for why she might be haunting the cemetery, one need only look at the senseless vandalism here and it's easy to see why she'd be furious.

The Horseshoe Grave of Otterbein Cemetery

A very distinctive mark on the back of an otherwise unremarkable tombstone in Somerset's Otterbein Cemetery has turned it into something of a mecca for ghost hunters. So many people have taken an interest in the grave of Mary Henry (who died February 28, 1845) that the pieces of her broken gravestone had to be set in a metal frame and surrounded by a low iron fence to protect them from souvenir hunters.

What the hunters are after is a piece of the so-called Bloody Horseshoe that is permanently imprinted on the back of the gravestone. It looks like a horseshoe was laid on the stone, left to rust, and removed. For what reason, we don't know. But that hasn't stopped the stories from circulating.

Here's the tale: James K. Henry, who lived in Perry County when John Tyler was president, had a horse named Bob. He also had two different women who wanted to marry him: Mary Angle and Rachel Hodge. One night, James was out riding Bob and trying to decide between the two women. He thought and thought and finally fell asleep, still undecided. When he awoke, he found that Bob had carried him to Mary's house. Taking it as a sign, he asked her then and there to marry him, and she accepted. Rachel was a (grief stricken) bridesmaid at the wedding.

The newlyweds rode around in a carriage pulled by Bob, now a wedding present from James to his wife. The couple was happy, by all accounts, and things seemed to be going well. Bob the horse had chosen the right bride for his master.

Then Mary got pregnant, but what should have been a blessed event turned into tragedy. On February 28, 1845, Mary Angle Henry died in childbirth, her baby stillborn.

James had his wife buried in a corner plot at Otterbein Cemetery.

He waited more than three years, until December 7, 1848, to marry Rachel Hodge. One can only imagine the thoughts of the second-choice bride. She wore a black dress to the wedding and afterward stood with James at his dead wife's graveside, where an icy winter wind almost immediately drove them back to their carriage, drawn by Bob.

That was the beginning of the supernatural occurrences at Mary Henry's grave site. A week after the wedding, the cemetery caretaker came knocking at James and Rachel's door, summoning them to see what had happened to the tombstone of the first Mrs. Henry. When they got to the cemetery, they saw that a sharply defined horseshoe was emblazoned in the granite of Mary's tombstone. Had Bob galloped out to the grave of his former mistress, perhaps to bring tales of the traitorous James and his happiness with his new wife, Mary's old rival?

Strange wailings were heard in the cemetery that night, and a blazing ball of blue light was seen hovering above Mary's burial plot. The next morning, James went out to the barn to begin his chores for the day. When he didn't return on time, Rachel ran out to the barn to check on him . . . and found him dead in Bob's stall. The imprint of a horseshoe, identical to the one on his first wife's gravestone, had been punched into his forehead.

Now Mary haunts the grave site in the form of that same blue ball of light, and the clip-clop of an invisible horse's hooves can be heard on the road nearby. The bloody horseshoe will not go away, no matter how hard anyone scrubs. You can see it for yourself on Otterbein Road, just off State Route 22 near the Fairfield County line.

Ghosts of Egypt Valley

There is a place in northwestern Belmont County and southern Harrison County — roughly surrounded by Hendrysburg, Holloway, Sewellsville, Flushing, and Piedmont Lake — that has a bad reputation locally. Anyone in the area will tell you not to visit the Egypt Valley Wildlife Refuge at night. Navigating the maze of poorly mapped gravel roads is hard enough in broad daylight; the essential oddness of the place comes across even when you can see where you're going. A night trip is inadvisable for a number of reasons.

The Indians knew this valley even before the U.S. Army Corps of Engineers dammed the creek that became Piedmont Lake and the state declared it a protected animal sanctuary. Various tribes used it as a hunting ground, but they took care to be on their way home long before dark. Even in those days, it was known to be one of the thin places between this world and the next.

Many ghosts and other creatures of the night are said to roam Egypt Valley, but the primary legend here involves the ghosts of Thomas Carr and Louiza Catharine Fox, the first murderer hanged in Belmont County and his victim, respectively.

The facts of the case have achieved something like ballad status. They're detailed in a booklet available at the Barnesville Public Library, and the spot where Louiza Fox lost her life is marked with an engraved plaque.

In 1869, Louiza Fox was thirteen years old, living with her family in this corner of the Ohio Valley. Back then, Belmont County was sparsely populated and extremely remote.

Louiza was being courted by Thomas

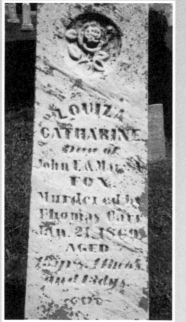

D. Carr, a "notorious character" and local coal miner, when she was still an adolescent. Carr had met her when she'd come to work as a domestic servant at the home of his employer, Alex Hunter. Carr wanted to marry the girl, and her parents apparently consented. However, they later rescinded their promise, and the wedding was canceled. They changed their minds because of Carr's reputation for violence, as well as the fact that he was much older than their daughter. Louiza apparently went along with their wishes.

Carr was enraged when he learned that his fiancée wanted to end their engagement, so on the night of January 21, 1869, he waited behind a fence on the road she took home from work. Eventually, she walked by with her little brother, Willy. Carr approached them and sent Willy home, saying that he wanted to talk to Louiza. Instead, he kissed her good-bye, then slit her throat with a razor and stabbed her fourteen times. He deposited her lifeless body in a nearby ditch. He spent that night in a coal bank while the Foxes, alerted by Willy (who had seen the whole thing from a distance), got a posse together to search for him.

Carr made a halfhearted suicide attempt the next morning by slashing his own throat and even trying to shoot himself, but it wasn't enough to do the job. When he was found and arrested, his wounds were treated, and he was taken to the jail in St. Clairsville.

An "intensely exciting" five-day trial ensued. Carr, according to some questionably melodramatic reporting, laughed when his death sentence was read aloud and said that he did "not care a damn if it was to be tomorrow." In his sentencing, the judge described Carr as "petulant, ill-natured, irritable, of a nervous temperament, and possessed of a heart fatally bent on mischief."

On March 8, 1870, while waiting to be hanged, Carr made a full confession, which included the admission that he'd murdered fourteen other people and had attempted to kill at least five more.

His execution took more than a year to carry out because of a "legal technicality." Finally, on March 24, 1870, Thomas D. Carr became the first person to be legally hanged in Belmont County. Louiza Catharine Fox's narrow gravestone, located in Salem Cemetery in the heart of Egypt Valley, mentions the circumstances of her premature demise: MURDERED BY THOMAS CARR JAN. 21, 1869 / AGED 13 YEARS 11 MONTHS AND 13 DAYS.

Louiza is the ghost most often reported to be wandering around the valley. She lingers near her marker, crying, or walks to the spot, just a mile away, where she lost her life. The plaque at the top of a small rise on Starkey Road resembles a gravestone and gives the basic details of what happened there on that cold night in 1869.

People who visit this place in the hope of communing with Louiza Fox might also encounter the dark spirit of Thomas Carr, who is said to walk these hills. He was buried on the grounds of the St. Clairsville courthouse, where he was executed, but that hasn't stopped him from visiting the place where he spent his final free days.

As horrific as the Carr-Fox murder story is, it's not the only haunting associated with Egypt Valley. Close to the murder plaque is the site of another ghostly occurrence: the phantom house. It appears to travelers with seven red candles burning in the windows but always fades away when approached.

Other stories center around the Circle Cemetery, which borders the preserve near a lake with a steep ledge. Supposedly, a dozing truck driver drove into this graveyard and lost his arm when his truck rolled over the cliff. Although the trucker lived, his arm was never found, and now the severed limb roams the cemetery, apparently using its fingers as legs like Thing from the Addams Family. You can hear its skittering walk on still nights. You might also hear the "devil dogs," evil canines that may or may not guard the cemetery. You have to wonder how the severed arm avoids getting chewed on by one of the dogs.

A Flying Nightmare

We visited Salem Cemetery, but nothing eventful happened. We then decided to try Circle Cemetery. Right before entering, there was a big black-and-white dog lying on the side of the road. He just watched us enter. We decided to circle the cemetery before entering to make sure nobody else was there. Going back around, the dog was still there, staring at us. We went up into it, got out, and started looking around. Everyone was drawn to one stone. While looking, we saw a big puddle of blood on and around the stone. Then we saw a big black thing standing maybe six or six and a half feet tall. It flew straight up into the sky. Its wingspan was maybe between six and ten feet wide. We ran to the truck and left the place immediately.—*Anonymous*

Bloody Claw Marks

On September 13, 2003, me and a group of friends were getting ready to go fishing when we heard the story of Circle Cemetery from a friend who had visited the place before. That's when we decided to visit this so-called haunted cemetery. We drove up to it and pulled over and began to walk up to "the circle." Then we stepped up to a marble headstone, and the air got real cold. We weren't really scared—that is, until we heard the dogs bark. But they suddenly stopped, and we calmed down a little bit. Then, out of nowhere, our sides started to burn, and we lifted our shirts. Three claw marks were stretched across my side like a dog's paw. Two of my other friends suddenly had burning sensations on their face and arms. When they looked down, they had prick marks, and my one friend had a cut above his eye with blood coming out of it. That's when we decided to leave the cemetery.—*Letter via e-mail*

Circle the Stonewall Cemetery and Watch the Ghosts Appear

An extremely unusual graveyard is situated just south of Lancaster near the intersection of Stone Wall and Cemetery roads in Fairfield County. Completely enclosed by a six-foot-high, twelve-sided stone wall, it's a monument to family love.

Nathaniel Wilson II settled in the area in the very late 1790s. The son of a Scottish immigrant, Nathaniel was raised in a devoutly religious household, which taught him that the dead should be not only revered but respected as well. Wilson instilled those beliefs in his own family. So when he passed away, in March 1814, Nathaniel's son, Nathaniel III, decided that the simple plot in Lancaster's old city hospital—where his father's body had been laid to rest—just wasn't good enough. He thought his father and family deserved better. So he set about making plans to construct a truly memorable memorial. It took some time, but construction on the family cemetery finally began in 1838, starting with the wall.

The stones—native sandstone likely taken from a nearby quarry—measured eighteen inches in thickness and were carefully shaped so that they would fit together perfectly. Like his father, Nathaniel III was a very religious man, and it is said that at both the quarry and the cemetery, he read aloud from the Bible. One of the passages he read said that Solomon's temple was built of stone "made ready before it was brought thither so that neither hammer nor ax nor any iron tool" would be used in the construction of it. Nathaniel wanted his cemetery wall constructed in the same fashion. Incredibly, all the corners of the wall were created without mortar, by using mitered stones and butting them together. Mortar was not used on any of the other stones, either; they were simply stacked firmly in place. Today, the cemetery wall stands as one of the best examples of dry masonry in the state of Ohio.

There are other amazing facts about the stone wall that are a testament to the love, care, and planning that went into its creation. For one, it was constructed so that the entrance faces Polaris, the North Star. Stand at the back of the cemetery on a clear night and you will find that Polaris is positioned directly above the center keystone of the cemetery arch.

Sadly, Nathaniel III would never see completion of the Stonewall Cemetery. After he died, on May 12, 1839, his son, Gustin, took up where his father had left off and completed the wall several months later. Several family members are buried inside, but it took some time for the original ancestor to get there. In 1907, when the old Lancaster Cemetery was in the process of being moved, the bodies of Nathaniel II and his wife, Elizabeth, were finally relocated to the Stonewall Cemetery and placed in unmarked graves.

Despite the family devotion associated with this place, ghostly tales still whirl around it. The legends say that if you climb to the top of the wall at night and walk around it thirteen times, the spirits of the dead will appear and drag you inside the locked cemetery. In some cases, it is said that the gates of hell themselves will open, and demons will pull you down into the netherworld. One can only wonder what Nathaniels II and III would think of such goings-on.

Abandoned
in Ohio

There may be no places in Ohio weirder than abandoned buildings. What terrible things happened in these dark, vacant places that caused the occupants to flee and never return? What is the meaning of the unsettling pieces of lives they left behind—a broken table on the floor, a rusting bedpost, a scrap of paper? Abandoned sites inspire legends of gruesome murders and tormented souls who still linger in their old homes. These tales are all the more poignant if the abandoned building in question really does have a history of human suffering, such as an insane asylum.

There is no denying that people will conjure up all manner of fantastic stories and project them onto places that have been left to rot. But have the stories sprung forth from our overactive imaginations, or is there really something weird going on behind some of America's forlorn façades?

Whether they are big, old vacant houses, forgotten institutions, or even whole towns that time has passed by, abandoned places possess an aura that is both foreboding and captivating at the same time. Stepping into a world that others once inhabited and then deserted is a weird and unnerving sensation. One cannot help but wonder what these once-vibrant places were like in their day. And there is often a sense of sadness and loss that they are no more.

However, keep in mind that it may not be easy, or even legal, to visit some of Ohio's abandoned sites. Many are on private property where trespassing is illegal. Others are downright dangerous (if not life threatening) to enter. So sit back and read on. Let the intrepid *Weird Ohio* team take you on a tour of some places that are probably best not explored on your own. Come with us now as we rush in where wiser men would fear to tread.

Welcome to Hell Town

What can you say about a place called Hell Town? As the commercial goes, with a name like that, it has to be good. Right? Well, honestly, it's hard to say. Hell Town, while one of Ohio's most famous horror/supernatural legends, is also one of the most confusing. It's a good example of the way folklore can get really complicated and convoluted.

Hell Town is the nickname given to the northern part of Summit County. There's no single haunted farmhouse here, no headless train conductor or ghostly children running around in the woods. Hell Town is home to six or seven separate legends, each with dozens of variations in its own right. All of which has led this area in and around Boston Township to be grouped into one oversized haunted place and given the evil-sounding name.

Hell Town is a dark place where ghosts, cults, and even a serial killer are said to lurk. People will tell you that the entire area is cursed, warning that it is dangerous to be there after dark. Needless to say, we were intrigued and wanted to learn more. In the summer of 2001 we made our first visit to the place known as Hell Town. You may be surprised at what we found.

The areas most often associated with the legends here are Boston Township and Boston Village, as well as portions of the townships Sagamore Hills and Northfield Center. In most of the stories, all of these areas are combined into one large region, which is referred to as Boston Mills.

First settled in 1806, Boston stands as the oldest village in Summit County. The first mill was built in the village in the early 1820s. Several years later, the construction of the Ohio and Erie Canal brought more people to the area, and over the next few decades mills began to flourish, most notably a paper mill. When a railroad station was

constructed in the town in the early 1880s, the station was named Boston Mills, in reference to the paper mill, and the name stuck.

Over the years, little changed in the small town. Then, in the late 1960s, a nationwide movement expressing concern over the destruction of our forests began. In 1974, in an effort to save the forests, President Gerald Ford signed legislation that enabled the National Park Service to purchase land and use it to create national parks. As a result, on December 27, 1974, hundreds of acres, including land within the township of Boston, were officially designated a National Recreation Area.

What many people did not realize until it was too late was that this legislation gave the federal government the right to buy houses and land from the current owners—whether the owners wanted to sell or not—in order to clear the way for the park. Almost immediately, the government began acquiring houses throughout Boston Township and the surrounding area. In what can only be described as a mass evacuation, residents began leaving, and entire towns were swallowed up by the Cuyahoga Valley National Park. These events were so tragic that they were featured in the 1983 PBS documentary *For the Good of All.*

Once a house was bought by the government and the owners had left, it was boarded up and covered with a U.S.-government–issued NO TRESPASSING sign. Then it would sit vacant until the government arranged for it to be torn down. In some cases, houses were intentionally burned to serve as training exercises for local fire departments. It was not uncommon in those days to drive down a street and find boarded-up homes sitting next to the burned-out hulks of other residences. To anyone unaware of the events taking place, it easily could have seemed as if the population of an entire town had disappeared eerily into thin air.

These events have left behind a feeling of melancholy. Even the towns that survived, perhaps suffering from something like survivor's guilt, now seem lonely and sad. There also is a weird tendency for deep fogs to roll into the valleys and hollows around here. This, and the sad history of the area, has given rise to many strange tales.

Traveling to the End of the World to See Hell Town

I have traveled to the End of the World. I speak of the end of the world I have come to know, the one that is the scariest place I have ever visited, Hell Town.

Formally known as Boston Township, Hell Town is a little rural town, partially abandoned, and home to many mysteries. I have experienced much in my explorations there, some of which I don't care to remember and some of which I can never hope to explain.

Hell Town is not truly abandoned. It does have residents, but they are a strange and frightening breed. I have gone exploring the woods and cemetery of the area in the late night and wee morning hours and have returned to my car to find strange people looking into its windows. This has happened twice—once at two a.m. and once at four-thirty a.m. Both times, the people fled as soon as they saw me approaching the car, before I had a chance to speak to them. Both times, they were dressed all in black.

A part of me is glad that I didn't get to converse with them, because I have heard too many tales about the ways of Hell Town residents. Supposedly, they are all Satanists and worship at the town's two evil churches. I have been to both of these churches, however not inside them. One, the Mother of Sorrows, has upside-down crosses hanging from it.

I have also been to the Boston Cemetery, where a ghost has been seen sitting on a bench. This cemetery is as dark a place as I have ever been. The graves date back to the early 1800s. I didn't see the ghost when I visited, but I did hear strange

growls and howls from the depths of the graveyard. This was more than enough to convince me to leave.

The End of the World is a road that has a large hill and dip. It is easily one of the steepest thoroughfares I have ever traveled. I have heard that if you travel this road at a certain speed, it has a frightening, even deadly, aftermath. I have never opted to test the fates by speeding on it though. I have traveled it at normal speeds and can attest to the fact that it is still a dangerous-looking, freaky road that leaves me feeling very unsettled.

Numerous bodies have been found dumped in the woods of Hell Town. This place is truly evil, as I have seen with my own eyes.—*Randall Chilesworth*

Mudhouse Mansion Keeps Its Secrets Hidden

Do you believe in Bloody Mary? You know, the woman who appears in your bathroom mirror and scratches your face if you say her name three times? Well, ask enough people in central Ohio and you just might find out that if Bloody Mary does exist, her mailing address is the Mudhouse Mansion in Lancaster. With its empty windows and isolated location, the Mudhouse Mansion practically screams haunted house. And, appropriately enough, that's what it is.

Of course, if you don't believe in Bloody Mary, there are plenty of other spooky things going on at the Mudhouse Mansion. Consider the legend that says a former owner cruelly mistreated his servants, including locking them all in the basement for extended periods of time. One night, the story goes, the servants had finally had enough and decided to dig their way out of the cellar. That being accomplished, they slaughtered the mansion owner and his entire family and left in a hurry. The ghosts of the murdered family are said to haunt the house to this day.

Then there's the story of the owner, a different one this time, catching his wife in an affair and shooting her to death, then committing suicide. He, too, is said to still roam the house at night, opening doors and sneaking around corners, looking for his treacherous wife and her lover.

There are very few facts known about the Mudhouse Mansion, starting with when it was built. *Weird Ohio* has heard some conflicting reports. One says it was constructed in the 1840s, another in 1900. A clue comes from the architecture, which includes a Second Empire mansard roof of a sort that was common during the Ulysses S. Grant administration, from 1868 through 1877. But the roof could have been built anytime, so that's not definite proof. Whenever it went up, the house and its surrounding property were purchased in 1919 by Mr. and Mrs. Hartman. When they passed away, it was transferred to their daughter, Lulu Hartman Mast. It has remained in the Mast family ever since, but it isn't lived in by them now. In other words, it's not exactly abandoned, just uninhabited.

The Mudhouse Mansion has three levels. Most of the upper floors still contain furniture. Some of it is in decent shape, though the vast majority is broken, stained, and piled up crazily. In the kitchen are cancelled checks from 1930, but in a second-floor bedroom there are school-

books published in the late '60s.

If you're thinking about visiting Mudhouse Mansion, be aware that the house and property are heavily posted with NO TRESPASSING signs and that the area is patrolled regularly by the Mast family, police, and even neighbors. Jeannie Mast, the woman responsible for the building and the land surrounding it, has taken a zealous approach to prosecuting trespassers, even hiding in the weeds with a sheriff's deputy on a weekend night once in a while. That's a little weird in itself, don't you think?

Abandoned Hospitals, Prisons, and Asylums

Mansfield Reformatory

Anyone driving around the outskirts of Mansfield has probably seen the enormous Gothic structure that seemingly rises fully blown out of the mist, distracting motorists and scaring generations of kids. It's the Ohio State Reformatory at Mansfield, no longer in operation but still managing to attract a lot of attention.

The original purpose of what would become the Ohio State Reformatory was a home for "middle of the road" criminals: those too old for the Boys Industrial School in Lancaster but not hardened enough for the Ohio State Penitentiary in Columbus. In September 1896, the building admitted its first inmates, who were immediately set to work completing the sewer system and other parts of the building. Construction would not be fully completed until 1910.

Even though the reformatory was not home to convicted criminals (the most famous inmate being Henry Baker, who would later gain infamy for taking part in the great Brink's Robbery of 1950), it had its share of violent episodes. In November 1926, Philip Orleck, a parolee, returned to the reformatory and shot officer Urban Wilford to death while trying to help another prisoner escape. Orleck was eventually captured and executed in the electric chair at Ohio State Penitentiary.

On July 21, 1948, one of the strangest and saddest events in the history of OSR occurred. In an act of revenge, two former inmates, Robert Daniels and John West, snuck back onto the property surrounding the prison and kidnapped OSR farm superintendent John Niebel, along with his wife and daughter, all of whom resided in a small farmhouse near the facility. Daniels and West took the family out to a nearby field and

killed them all. Several days later, the two were cornered by police. In the ensuing firefight, West was shot and killed while Daniels was taken into custody. He died in the electric chair in January 1949.

But not all of the misery at Ohio State Reformatory was the result of men's violence against their fellow man. Some of it was a result of the conditions the inmates were forced to live in. By the time the Reformatory celebrated its fortieth anniversary, its facilities were badly inadequate. Cries of overcrowding and inhumane living conditions were heard far and wide. The young reform school residents weren't complaining, though. They knew if they did, they were buying themselves a ticket to visit one of the worst areas of the reformatory: the Hole.

Solitary confinement, or the Hole, was the one place no inmate wanted to end up. In solitary, you were placed in a tiny room all alone . . . in the dark. As to when you came out, well, that was for the guards to decide. It's no wonder stories abound of prisoners going insane while they were in solitary. Some are said to have attempted (and in some cases, succeeded) to hang themselves inside the cell. One allegedly even set himself on fire.

By the time the 1970s rolled around, the state had already declared that the Ohio State Reformatory no longer met the guidelines and standards for correctional facilities, and as the 1980s came to a close, so did the Ohio State Reformatory. In 1994, demolition of the outer wall and some of the outbuildings began to take place. But not before Hollywood came calling.

While OSR was in operation, several movies, including 1976's *Harry and Walter Go to New York* and 1989's *Tango and Cash,* used the facility as the setting

for some scenes. However, it wasn't until 1994, when the film crew for a little movie called *The Shawshank Redemption* showed up, that Hollywood really began to take notice of OSR. The reformatory was heavily featured in the film, with close to thirty scenes being shot inside the facility or on the grounds. Several years later, scenes from *Air Force One* were also filmed at OSR. More recently, music video producers have turned their eyes to the old reformatory, and the building has been featured in videos by Godsmack and Lil' Wayne.

As part of an effort to save OSR, the Mansfield Reformatory Preservation Society was formed, which now leases the property. Today, steps are under way to restore the remaining structure to its original stature. The building was added to the National Register of Historic Places in 1987, and the reformatory's six-tier east wing is listed in *Guinness Book of World Records* as the world's largest freestanding steel cell block.

Several ghosts are said to haunt the prison. The most common occurrence seems to be voices heard around the old superintendent's quarters. Regular ghost hunts are held there, during which participants are allowed to roam freely, and unsupervised, throughout much of the prison, taking pictures and trying to make contact with the other side. Some claim to have succeeded.

Though it's still rough and unrenovated, with no plans to be turned into anything else, the reformatory is not, strictly speaking, abandoned most of the time. It does sit empty throughout the winter, but the rest of the year, there's usually somebody looking after the place, doing research, or conducting tours. Unlike so many other historic landmarks in Ohio, this one looks like it will be around for a while.

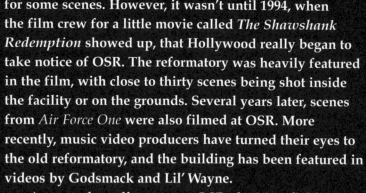

The Permanent Stain at Ridges Asylum

At one time, large public mental institutions served every part of the state, but today the only one that still stands in anything resembling its original condition is the Athens Mental Health Center, also known as the Ridges.

In 1867, state and federal governments purchased over a thousand acres of land in Athens with the sole intent of creating a mental health facility there. For the design of the facility the state turned to Thomas Story Kirkbride, a Quaker physician with a then-progressive vision of how the mentally ill should be treated.

Kirkbride had recently introduced his Kirkbride Plan—a standardized method by which mental asylums should be constructed and patients should be treated.

It was Kirkbride's belief that the two should go hand in hand and that asylums should not be just buildings but rather large, self-sufficient communities, therapeutic in themselves.

Originally known as the Athens Asylum for the Insane, this massive institution first opened its doors on January 9, 1874. Giant asylums in the Kirkbride style were going up all over America at this time, partly because of the number of Civil War veterans suffering from what we now call post-traumatic stress disorder. In the cemeteries

woman with profound mental disabilities who somehow managed to lock herself in a ward that had been abandoned for years. She disappeared on December 1, 1978, and wasn't found for over a month, until January 12, 1979. She was dead on the floor then, a victim of heart failure, probably due to exposure in an unheated ward during the coldest part of winter. As she was dying, oddly enough, she took off her clothes, folded them neatly beside her, and lay down on the concrete floor.

When the authorities attempted to move her body, they found that it had left a permanent stain of her outline on the concrete floor. The stain was probably caused by a combination of the natural decay of the body coupled with its position in front of big bay windows that allowed sunlight to shine down on it. Despite constant scrubbing, the stain would not come up. Even more disconcerting, people walking past the asylum at night would sometimes see the ghostly image of a woman staring down at them from the window of the room where the body had been found.

You can still see the stain today. People sometimes leave flowers and other trinkets around it. Some say that Margaret Schilling's spirit wanders the building at night. They say that other patients, especially those who died at the hospital, also wander around at night.

Tours of the former asylum are a popular Halloween event. (So popular, in fact, that one year's tour had to be cancelled because of the huge turnout.) Other parts of the grounds are off-limits, however. Ghosts are sighted most often in the main asylum cemetery, which occupies the downslope of the hill behind the hospital. Only the patients whose families paid for professional stones are identifiable. All the state provided was a plot and a simple, narrow gravestone marked with a number but no name. Hospital records tell which number belonged to whom, which is why several of the unmarked stones are accompanied by veterans' plaques. Due to missing records, however, the identities of male patients numbers 1 through 63 are lost to history.

In total, roughly two thousand people were interred in the Athens State Hospital burial grounds before 1972. Apparently, Ohio University also buried the cadavers used in its medical classes here. To see the two more recent graveyards, you need to double back toward the Dairy Barn Arts Center and climb a hundred or so wooden stairs set into the hillside. But it's here, in the oldest and closest cemetery, that the restless spirits are most active.

Several gravestones are arranged in a perfect circle on the hillside for no apparent reason and in no apparent order. (It has been speculated that this was a prank pulled by OU students sometime in the 1920s.) This circle is supposed to be a mecca for witches and practitioners of all sorts of black arts who hold séances here and use it as a "circle of power." Also unique is the presence of half a dozen additional grave markers on the other side of the creek, that runs alongside the graveyard. Crossing a wooden footbridge will take you to these final resting places, right where the woods begin. Some say these are the graves of murderers, unable to be interred in the same hallowed ground as the other dead. Their spirits are particularly violent and vindictive, but it's okay because they cannot cross the running water of the creek.

She Does Herself In Nightly at Roseville Prison

With so many bad guys running around Ohio, Columbus's Ohio State Penitentiary was always on the verge of bursting at the seams. In order to alleviate that situation, officials decided to move the less violent criminals to satellite facilities throughout the state. These facilities could serve a second purpose, as manufacturing plants using prison labor. Roseville, in southeastern Ohio, was chosen as the site of one of these satellite prisons.

Oddly enough, while the facility was referred to as the Roseville Prison, it is actually in a different county from the town of Roseville. The prison, which also functioned as a brick-manufacturing facility, is on the outskirts of Roseville, in neighboring Muskingum County.

The prison building still stands, and its walls still surround it, topped in two places by guard posts. The primary surveillance tower is still across the street. Next door are two houses obviously related to the prison, built from the same brick, though renovated and recently occupied by renters.

Inside the prison, there are cells on the ground floor of the main building. The doors still close, though the guts were wisely ripped out of the locks when the place was abandoned. The upper floors are big, empty chambers that once contained shops and dormitories but are now used for nothing but Paintball, if the splatters on the walls are any indication. The bricks were made in the high-roofed outbuildings attached to the main structure. The buildings are connected by a multigated hallway, which also contains the broken-down prison shower. Though the furnaces have been removed from the work buildings, the concrete canals that were once used to channel cooling water to the nearby creek are still intact, and the mud along the bank is still stained brick red.

The exercise yard seems surprisingly narrow and claustrophobic, looked down on by one of the guard towers, but inmates obviously had access to the sunny main field out front. A faded scoreboard even shows where they used to play baseball.

The biggest building still contains the leftovers of a haunted house tour conducted here some years ago, fittingly enough, since Roseville Prison is supposed to be haunted. A ghostly young woman in a white dress is said to repeat her suicidal jump from the roof each night. That's strange, because when the prison was in operation, it housed only men. Those who refuse to let the legend die, however, simply state that in life this woman was a local who chose the roof of the abandoned prison as the spot to make her journey from this world to the next. Apparently, she got trapped somewhere in between the two, as her ghost is still seen today.

This Odd House

If you've heard rumors of an abandoned house in Logan shaped like a giant golf ball, you didn't hear wrong. It's a bizarre building, but it's very real. The structure, about two stories tall, seems to be made of poured concrete. So why would anyone want to live in something like this?

People in Logan have been asking that question since the early '70s, when a Mr. Stewart built it. It came to be known as Stewart's Folly, but for a while the builder had high hopes for it—he intended it to be a revolution in weatherproof housing. The round house is a prototype for a new, highly durable type of home that is sold along hurricane-prone coasts and through Tornado Alley. Because of its lack of corners and flat exterior surfaces, the wind resistance on the building is almost nil, making it ideal for parts of the country where high winds cause problems for home owners. The basic shell is also fireproof, as were the original Lexan windows, though the interior could burn. And it came with special fire escape plans that involved sliding through escape hatches and windows onto a rear scaffolding.

The house was begun in 1971 and completed in 1973. Two wooden shells were built—inside and out—and the concrete was poured in from the top. It hardened, the molds were removed, and the main part of the structure was done, with walls five inches thick on the sphere and eight inches thick at the base. The interior has two floors on top, a porch, and a basement with a built-in garage.

The place has seen better days. It was never wired for power, and Stewart never moved his family into it as he had intended. When it was finished, he had an offer of $350,000 for the round house, which he refused. Unfortunately, he never got an offer that good again. He stopped working on it and began to use it for storage, until some thieves broke in and stole several of his tools.

Mr. Stewart died without ever seeing his innovations put to the test. Equally unfortunate is the fact that the original blueprints and design notes were lost in a fire. That makes the Logan round house a true original, never to be duplicated.

Today, Mr. Stewart's son owns the house. He lives close by, in Logan, and drives out to check on the building from time to time, but nothing has been done with it for more than a decade. The slightly amusing warning scrawled on the garage door (ALL TRESPASSERS WHO SURVIVE THE HAZARDS THAT OTHER . . . TRESPASSERS CREATED WILL ALL BE PROSECUTED TO THE LIMITS OF THE LAW) has done little to keep locals away. Time and weather have also broken holes in the upper floors and dropped most of what was left into the basement.

But it's worth a trip from anywhere to see something like this. It's a truly original piece of architecture and a testament to the determination of one Hocking County man with a dream, some concrete, and a whole lot of spare time on his hands.

Octagon House

This strange home has legendary status in Circleville. Also known as the Crites House, presumably for a family who once lived there, it was constructed in the shape of an octagon with eight outside walls. For a long time it sat at the back of a residential area not far from Route 23 and within sight of the famous pumpkin water tower.

This style of architecture was fairly common in Ohio in the nineteenth century, and we have to admire the ingenuity of its builders. Inside, weird architecture reigns. The rooms surround an open "hallway" in the center with a spiral staircase, and all of the rooms open onto each other. The closets are shaped like pie wedges with sloped ceilings. By climbing the staircase all the way, you can poke around in a smaller octagon-shaped attic just below the peak of the roof.

The Octagon House was almost lost when Wal-Mart wanted to build on the site in 2003. But thanks to the efforts of the Roundtown Conservancy, it was pried up from its original foundation and moved via flatbed truck to a location behind the Super Center, safe from development.

Hotel and Motel Vacancy

Luxury High-rise for the Homeless

The Seneca is a landmark building that, strangely for downtown Columbus, stands empty. It's located on the southeast corner of Broad and Grant streets, and at ten full stories it's a minor part of the city skyline.

At one time, this was a luxury hotel, featuring suites of rooms, offices, and banquet facilities. It was built in 1917, designed by noted Columbus architect Frank Packard. Many Columbus residents remember

when the Seneca was one of the best places to stay in town. Decades ago, the OSU Faculty Club was located here. Later, the building was turned into offices for the Ohio Environmental Protection Agency. It was abandoned in the early '90s, a victim of the downtown blight that affected so many cities.

But wait! Rumors are rife that the Seneca will rise again, that it will be restored and turned into a luxury apartment house. In the meantime, though, it is a full-out abandoned site.

Gaining entrance into the building has not been difficult. Holes have been conveniently kicked in the wall of the rear loading dock by vagrants who sleep in the rooms upstairs. As you climb through the floors, the condition of the building improves; in fact, the top floor looks like it could be moved into right away.

The bottom floors, though, especially the bottom three, are in miserable condition. Trash litters the former club offices along the main hallway, and the front lobby is mostly disassembled, with the chandelier on the floor and the glass behind the bar broken into sections. The front desk is still there, a sad reminder of the building's glory days. Beside it is the receiver for a ten-story mailbox drop and an antique elevator. Papers from the EPA still fill the drawers.

The Bon Air Motel

The crumbling Bon Air Motel stands on Route 30 near Williamstown and Mt. Blanchard in Hancock County, close to the Hardin County line. Route 30 is part of the old Lincoln Highway, which was America's first transcontinental road. Completed in 1920, the Lincoln Highway stretched from New York City to San Francisco. In Ohio, it cut across the north-central portion of the state, missing every city of any size. This stretch of old highway is home to several interesting abandoned places that lost their customer base when the fancy new interstates were built. The Bon Air is probably one of the hardest to miss—the old neon sign still stands near the road with the words TRUCKERS WELCOME at the top.

The motel itself is L-shaped. Near the place where the two sections meet is the old night check-in—a covered drive-through with a boarded-up window. Today, it doesn't drive through to anything but the field in the middle of the property. The main office, at the center of the longer section, is still mostly intact. It's more of an apartment than a motel room, with multiple bedrooms and a full kitchen, where the motel manager's family lived.

The rooms are bare now, but you can still see roughly what they once looked like. Most of the furnishings are gone, but in one there's still a table next to the spot where the telephone line came through the wall. No one has called for quite a while.

Now Showing: An Abandoned Drive-in Tour

Among the many distinctions of the great state of Ohio is the fact that it is home to more drive-in movies, open and closed, than any other state in the Union. Most of these old "ozoners", a.k.a. drive-ins, are fondly remembered by folks who caught a double feature there many summers ago and perhaps stole a kiss on a first date. Ah, is there anything other than a drive-in that can conjure such nostalgic images of Americana? Perhaps for this reason, seeing these drive-ins in their current state of abandonment is an especially dismal experience. They speak to us of innocence, of simpler times and irreplaceable youth.

Heath Drive-in

Located just south of Heath on Route 79 stands what was Licking County's last operational drive-in. For decades, it was a huge draw, showing movies on three different screens. Today, one tattered and tilting screen remains. The concession stand still contains a popcorn popper and a refrigerator, as well as a sliding rack for the food selection. Upstairs, the projection booth is much as it must have been in the good old days, minus the projector. Interesting to note are the numbered reel rack as well as the toilet employed by the projectionist, who was expected never to leave his post.

On the outside are restrooms and the projection booth, which is at the front of the building at ground level. The sound box is still on the wall with its guts stripped out.

Linden Air Drive-in

The entrance to the Linden is a long, gated-off driveway on Cleveland Avenue south of Morse Road, marked by a colorful sign that's still eye-catching despite a couple of decades of disrepair. This theater once had something to brag about: It was one of the few Ohio drive-ins to remain open all year long, including during the worst part of winter, when cigarette-lighter-powered heaters were issued at the ticket booth.

Now the Linden is nearly forgotten in its scrubby field behind an auto accessories place and a trucking company. Surprisingly, the screen is in very good shape.

The screen at the Linden Air Drive-in

Hocking Theater Drive-in

Like a thousand other defunct drive-ins, the Hocking Theater outside Logan is still there only because nobody seems to need to tear it down. In this case, the owners—the Logan Lions Club—have put the concession stand to use as a storage shed. The Lions also use the land to store their club vehicles: a tractor and an unhitched concession vendor's trailer. You can still see the doors to the his and hers restrooms.

Pulling into the old movie theater driveway, the first thing you pass (besides the marquee) is the ticket booth. It's hidden behind an evergreen bush nobody trims anymore. The booth looks fairly all right from the outside—though it is unpainted and missing its window glass—and inside it's surprisingly intact. Still present is the seat, complete with armrests, where the box office person used to sit, as well as the old wooden money drawer. And the screen is still standing, peeling away at the back of the field.

Miles Drive-in

Cleveland's best-kept drive-in secret is this single-screen ozoner on Miles Road. A holdout in the drive-in world, it closed as recently as 2000. So much of it is left intact that the new owners are interested in renting it out.

The marquee and sign are still standing, and the driveway is relatively clear of the garbage, cracks, grass, and weeds that mark so many forgotten theaters. The concession stand is in excellent shape, though the interior is somewhat trashed. Still, it's structural integrity that matters, and there aren't any holes in the walls or caved-in ceilings here. And the speaker poles are mostly still around, though the metal speaker boxes are gone.

Chippewa Lake Amusement Park

Despite the fact that no one has been able to buy a ticket here since 1978, people continue to plan trips to Chippewa Lake Amusement Park to see the sights and enjoy the rides—in a way. None of the rides still operate or even have many moving parts anymore, but their stark emptiness can be fascinating.

Nearly every attraction that was here when the park closed almost two decades ago is still around in some form. The most prominent feature—the skeletal wooden roller coaster that winds its way around three sides of the property—was nameless, though it was usually referred to as the Big Dipper or the Big Coaster. A smaller steel roller coaster, the Little Dipper, lies in rusted pieces in the woods, along with what's left of the Wild Mouse.

One truly constant feature of the grounds at Chippewa Lake is the vegetation; not only are the paths and roads overgrown with weeds and high grass, but entire trees have grown up through roofs, between rails on the coaster tracks, and on the ride platforms. The Ferris wheel is barely visible between the leaves of a huge tree that has grown up through the middle of it, taller than the wheel itself.

Competition from the nearby Cedar Point, which was just beginning to assert itself as one of the world's leading parks, was a major factor in Chippewa Lake's demise. The 1978 season was Chippewa Lake's last. Everything of value that could be moved out was sold at auction, and the rest was left to rust and rot amid the wild vegetation.

Today, a small housing community, situated in the shadow of the Big Dipper, lines what was once the park's driveway. The roadside sign and ticket booth now point the way to the Chippewa Lake Community. There's not much glory left here in the ruins of one of Ohio's early amusement parks.

Going Underground

Cincinnati Subway

In the early years of the twentieth century, when the river trade was flourishing and the city was one of the largest in the nation, Cincinnati decided to build a subway. The major impetus was the draining of the Miami and Erie Canal, along which the subway would be built. The idea really originated in 1884, when the Cincinnati *Graphic* printed an illustration showing trains chugging along underground in an old canal bed covered with a new street. After their remarkably brief golden era, canals quickly became a nuisance. Many were partially drained, and their muddy bottoms were used as refuse dumps, which made only the mosquitoes and garbage companies happy. Since the Miami and Erie cut right through the heart of the city, it was a particular eyesore in Cincinnati.

In 1912, a plan was made to build a sixteen-mile rapid transit rail system in a loop around the city, with a branch going underground and heading downtown. There were several delays—World War I among them—but the two-mile underground portion of the subway was finally completed by 1923. By then, inflation had caused the budget for the long-awaited system to skyrocket. Central Parkway, which was built atop the underground tunnels, opened in 1928, and that seemed to be as much as Cincinnatians were willing to do to fill their transit needs at the time. Then, in 1929, any consideration of paying for more construction evaporated when the stock market crashed and the country plunged into the Great Depression.

Over the years, Cincinnati grew, but not nearly as quickly as the subway's conceivers had hoped. (Today, it's only the third-largest city in the state.) A 1948 study finally mothballed the subway for good, though efforts to do something with the tunnels have been ongoing for more than half a century. Ideas have included a bomb shelter, a shopping and nightlife district, and a massive wine cellar. The latest proposal is for another underground rail line.

Many people have heard of the subway, but one of the Queen City's best-kept secrets is the fact that sections still remain, including all four of the stations put in during the initial construction. (We suggest you visit these tunnels just by reading about *Weird Ohio*'s visit. These are not good places to go to.) One entrance is near Hopple Street. Two tunnels run side by side at this point, separated by a wall with regular openings. Bolted-down wooden tracks run the entire way; they rise on one side corresponding to curves in the tunnel so that the trains could bank. The west tunnel is taken up by a huge water main, and walking in the east tunnel is sometimes made difficult by foot-deep stagnant water. Anyone who walks far enough in, however, will come to the stations.

The first one resembles what it was supposed to be: a subway platform. There is a small room with windows, presumably for a ticket seller, and a wide flight of stairs covered at street level by a metal sheet. Cars passing on Central Parkway rattle the covering and echo through tunnels few drivers even know exist.

A second station is walled off, perhaps collapsed or filled in. The third was turned into a bomb shelter in the 1950s, complete now with some broken, moldy food-ration canisters. The shelter is divided into rooms where people could sleep, eat, and play board games until the nuclear winter was over. In one of the rooms, metal-framed bunks are still standing.

The fourth, largest subway station is double-wide and was intended to be a turnaround for the cars that never ran. It was festooned with flags and banners and was supposed to be revealed to the city in the '20s. The city never got a look at it, however, and now it's hidden beneath downtown. Maybe someday Cincinnati will find a use for this weird underground resource.

We can only hope that some of Ohio's great abandoned landmarks will be spared the wrecking ball and survive to inspire and awe future generations. These sites offer invaluable glimpses into our history and fuel the imagination with their tantalizing mysteries. Some are truly remarkable architectural and culture achievements, others more modest undertakings, though no less visionary in their own right.

In the end, though, like the best-laid plans of mice and men, they all fell into ruin just the same. But even in their final days, these hollow and haunted edifices speak to us in voices that are hard to ignore. They are voices that echo down crumbling corridors and emanate through shattered windowpanes. They seem to be telling anyone who cares enough to listen that you just don't know what you've got until it's gone.

INDEX
Page numbers in **bold** refer to photos and illustrations.

A

Abandoned places, 254–277
Abbott, Benjamin W., 248–249, **248, 249**
Adam, E. Reginald and Rhea H., 51–52
Adams, George Jeffrey, 209
Adams, George Willison, 209
Adams, John J., 209
Adena burial mounds, 34–35
Airdock, giant, **152–153**, 153
Air Force Technical Intelligence Center, 74
Albino animals collection, 167, **167**
Aliens. See UFOs and aliens
Allen, E. A., 41–42
Allen County Museum, 166–167, **166, 167**
Alligator Mound, 36–37, **37**
Alpha Delta Pi house ghost, 214
Alpha Omicron Pi house ghost, 215
American Sign Museum, **168**, 169, **169**
Ancient mysteries, 30–43
Andrews, Harry, 120, 122–123
Andy D-Day, 180–181, **180**
Aryan Theosophic Society, 116
Athens Asylum for the Insane.
   See Ridges Asylum
Athens Mental Health Center.
   See Ridges Asylum
Atkinson, Herbert, 212

B

Bach, Carl and Mary, 103
Baker, Henry, 261
Barker, Gary, 73
Barnum, P. T., museum, 101–102

Bartholomew, George, 171
Batchelor, James, garden of, 134–135, **134, 135**
Bates, Martin Van Buren (Kentucky River Giant), 101–102, **101**
Baughman, Brice, 136, **136**
Beaver Creek Bridge, 198–199, **199**
Beavers, giant, 43, **43**
Bessie. See South Bay Bessie
Bicyclist, phantom, 197
Big Bird. See Mothman
Bigfoot, 88–90, **89, 90**
Bizarre beasts, 80–99
Blavatsky, Madame Elene, 116, **116**
Blood Bowl, 18–19, **18, 19**
Bloody Horseshoe grave, 247, **247**
Bloody Mary, 258
Blue Holes, 178, **178–179**
Blue Limestone Park, 226, **226**
Boggy Creek Monster, 90
Bon Air Motel, 270
Bone Collector, 71
Bowsher, Jim, 131–133, **131**
Bricker Hall ghost, 212
Brick outhouse, 175
Bridges
   Beaver Creek, 198–199, **199**
   Crybaby, 48–49, **49**, 184–191, **184–185, 187, 188, 189, 190–191**
   Dean's Hollow, 192
   Devil's Heartbeat, 192
   Screaming, 193
   Troll, 91, **91**
Bun museum, 170, **170**
Bush, George H. W., 118
Bush, George W. and Barbara, 118

C

Calf, two-headed, 180–181, **180**
Canfield Hall ghosts, 213–214
Caples Hall ghost, 218
Carpenter, Connie, 68
Carr, Thomas, 250–251
Castalia State Fish Hatchery, 178
Cats. See Felines, mysterious
Cayton, Howe and Evelyn, 88–89
Cedar Hill Cemetery, **240**, 241, **241**
Cemeteries. See also Graves; Monuments
   Boot Hill, 176–177, **177**
   Cedar Hill, **240**, 241, **241**
   Circle, 251
   Columbus Mental Hospital, 236, **236**
   Congress Green, 107
   Erie Street, 230, **230**
   Greenlawn, 231, **231**
   Johnson's Island, 238, **238, 239**
   King Memorial, 60
   Lake View, 232, **232**
   Marion, 242–243, **243**
   Milan, 248–249, **248, 249**
   Mound, 233, **233**
   Mound Hill, 102
   Mount-Union Pleasant Valley, 245–246, **245, 246**
   Otterbein, 247, **247**
   Salem, **250**, 251
   Spring Grove, 237, **237**
   State Old Insane and Penal, 236
   Stonewall, 252–253, **252–253**
   West State Street, 237, **237**
   witches' graves, 244, **244**
   Wolfe, 244
   Woodland, 234, **234, 235**

Cemetery safari, 228–253
Ceramics museum, 154, **154**
Château Laroche. *See* Loveland Castle
Chidester's Mill, 48
Chippewa Lake Amusement Park, 275, **275**
Circle Cemetery, 251
City of the Dead. *See* Mound City
Civic Theatre (Loews Theatre), 219–220, **219, 220**
Clark, Russell, 167
Cleanup Man, 140–142, **140, 141, 142**
Cochran, Malcolm, 160
Columbus Mental Hospital cemeteries, 236, **236**
Concrete
    corncobs, 160–161, **160–161**
    street, world's oldest, 171, **171**
Confederate soldier statue, 238, **238**
Congress Green Cemetery, 107, **107**
Crawford Hall haunting, 216
Crites House. *See* Octagon House
Crop circles, 78, **78, 79**
Cross, Debbie, 86
Crowe, Dr., 60–63
Crybaby structures
    bridges, 48–49, **49,** 184–185, 184–191, 186, **186, 187, 188, 189, 190–191**
    Lane, 190
    Overpass, 190
Crystal ball, world's largest, 154, **154**
Cuckoo clock, world's largest, 148–149, **148**

D

Dahmer, Jeffrey, 114–115, **114, 115**
Davies, David, 94, 96
Dead Man's Curve, 202
Dean's Hollow Bridge, 192
Delta Kappa Epsilon house ghost, 218
Demon Tree, 17
Devil's Heartbeat Bridge, 192
Devil's Leap, 47
Diamond, Richard and Alwida, 172
Dickens, Charles, 75
Dillinger, John, 104, 133, 167, **167**
Dillon, Thomas Lee, 108–110
Drive-in theaters, abandoned, 271–274, **271, 272, 273, 274**

E

Eagle River, Wisconsin, pancakes from space, 74
Eberson, John, 219
Edison, Thomas Alva, 115–116
Egypt Road Crybaby Bridge, 186, **186, 187**
Elephant, muffler, 163, **163**
Elizabeth's Grave, 245–246, **245, 246**
Elmore Rider, 196–197
Erie Street Cemetery, 230, **230**
Eugene, 106

F

Fabled people and places, 44–63
Felines, mysterious, 82–85, **83, 84**
Findlay Ghost Town, 176–177, **176, 177**
Five Points ghosts, 201
Floyd, Charles Arthur "Pretty Boy," 104, **104, 105**

Flying Heads, 97
Foggymoore, 47
Ford, Clyde E., 77
Ford, Gerald, 256
Ford, Henry, 116
Fort, Charles, 34, 64, 65, 70
Fort Ancient, 41–42, **41, 42**
Fort Ancient culture, 35
Fothergill, Charles, 43
Fox, Louiza Catharine, 250–251, **250**
Franklin Castle, 56, **56, 57,** 58–59, **58**
Fred the Janitor, 219–220
Freed, Fred, 71
Frey, Russell, 17, 48
Frogman, **92,** 93
Frogtown Flower Farm, 141
Frostop root beer mug, 151, **151**
Fry, Richard, 110
Fudge Road Bridge, 191

G

Galitza, Edward and Louis, 176
Garfield, James A., 232
Gates of Hell, 18–19, **18, 19**
German Socialist Party, Franklin Castle and, 58
Ghosts, phantoms, 205–227.
    See also Cemeteries
    bicyclist, 175
    Confederate soldiers, 238
    Dead Man's Curve, 202
    Egypt Valley, 250–251
    Esther Hales, 198–199
    felines, 82–83
    Five Points, 201
    kangaroos, 86

Ness, Eliot, 232
Noose, ghostly, 192

O

Octagon House (Crites House),
    269, **269**
Octagon mound, 36–37, **36**
Ohio State Reformatory (Mansfield
    Reformatory), **194,** 195, **260,**
    261–262, **261, 262**
Ohio State University, 212–214, **212,**
    213
Ohio University
    Athens State Hospital grounds,
        264, 266
    ghosts, 215–216
Oldenburg, Claes, 147
Old Kenyon ghosts, 217
Old Xenia Road, 224, **225**
One and Only Presidential Museum in
    the World, 117–119, **117, 118**
Orphanage of Light and Hope.
    See Gore Orphanage
Orton Hall ghost, 213
Otterbein Cemetery, 247, **247**
Our Lady of Guadalupe, 156, **156**
Outhouse, brick, 175
Oxford Motorcycle Ghost, 20–21

P

Packard, Frank, 231, 270
Packo, Tony, 170
Pahys, Nick Jr., 116–119, **118**
Pancakes from space, 74
Panthers, mysterious, 82–83, **83,** 84,
    85
Patrick, James, 86

Patterson Tower. *See* Witches Tower
Paxton, Jamie, 108–109, 110
Peet, Reverend Stephen, 42
Peninsula Python, 87, **87**
People Love People Church, 137–139,
    137, 138
Personalized properties, 120–143
Phantoms. *See* Ghosts
Phillips, Carrie, 242
Pierpont, Harry, 167
Pierson, Stuart, ghost of, 218
Plug sculpture, 147, **147**
Pomerene Hall ghost, 212
Prospect Place (Trinway Mansion),
    208–209, 209
Putnam, Frederic Ward, 34

R

Rasor, Wilbur and Nettie, 180–181
Reese, John D., 70
Reformatory Road, **194,** 195
Reincarnation, Edison and, 116
Renner, Ivan and Noel, 143, **143**
Reynolds, Jeremiah, 107
Richetti, Adam, 104, **105**
Rickenbacker, Eddie, 231, **231**
Ridges Asylum (Athens Asylum for the
    Insane; Athens Mental Health
    Center), 263–264, **263, 265,** 266,
    266
Riegler, Donna, 89
Ritter, Percy and Anna Gay, 55
Roadside distractions, 144–181
Roads less traveled, 182–203
Rockefeller, John D., 232, **232**
Rocking chair, giant, 149, **149**
Rogue's Hollow, 17, 48–49, **49**

Romano family, 58–59
Roseville Prison, 267, **267**
Ross C. Purdy Museum of Ceramics,
    154
Rubber stamp sculpture, **146,** 147
Ruppert, James, 111, 113

S

Salem Cemetery, **250,** 251
Sam and Eulalia Frantz Park, 160–161,
    160–161
Samuel Spitler House, 180–181, **180,**
    181
Santa, giant, 155, **155**
Satan's Hollow, 16
Schaffner, Ron, 86, 88–89, 93
Schilling, Margaret, ghost of, 264, 266
Scott, Voltaire, 162
Screaming Bridge, 193
Sea monster, 94, **95,** 96
Seneca Hotel, 270, **270**
Serpent Mound, **30, 32–33,** 33–35,
    34, 35
Servants of Mary Center of Peace,
    156
Shaffer Speech Building, 218
Shockey, Ray, 93
Show Boat Drive-in, 272–273, **273**
Simonton, Joe, 74
Skyline Drive-in, 272, **272**
Snakes, 87, **87**
Sniper, 108–110
Sockalexis, Louis "Chief," 230
Solid Rock Church, 158, **158–159**
South Bay Bessie (Lake Erie Monster),
    94, **95,** 96
Spitler House, 180–181, **181**

Spontaneous human combustion (SHC), 75

Spring Grove Cemetery, 237, **237**

Sprunger, Reverend John, 13, 14

Squire's Castle, 206–207, **206, 207**

Staley Road, 200–201, **200–201**

State Old Insane and Penal Cemetery, 236

Statues. *See also* Monuments
    Boy with the Boot, 162, **162**
    Brice Baughman's, 136, **136**
    Confederate soldier, 238, **238**
    George Bartholomew, 171, **171**

Stewart's Folly. *See* Golf-ball house

Stonewall Cemetery, 252–253, **252–253**

Streets
    oldest concrete, 171, **171**
    world's shortest, 174, **174**

Stringfield, Leonard H., 72–73

Sturgeon, 94, 96

Subway, abandoned, 276–277, **276, 277**

Suicide girl ghost, 220

Super-Sargasso Sea, 64

Swallowed objects collection, 166, **166**

Swan, Anna (Giantess of Nova Scotia), 101–102, **101**

Swift Mansion, 13–14, **13**

Swormstedt, Todd, 169

Symmes, John Cleves, 107

T

Talbot, Ashleigh, 75

Temple of Tolerance, 131–133, **132, 133**

Thunderwater, Chief, 230

Thurber, James, 231, **231**

Tiedemann family, 56–59

Tombstones. *See* Cemeteries; Graves; Monuments

Top O' the World, 50–52, **50, 51, 52–53**

"Touchdown" Jesus statue, 158, **158–159**

Traffic light, world's oldest, 171, **171**

Trinway Mansion. *See* Prospect Place

Trolls, 91, **91**

Tunnels, haunted, 25–29, **25, 26, 27, 28, 29**, 226, **226**

Twistee Treat ice-cream parlor, 150, **150**

U–Z

UFOs and aliens, 65–74

Underground Railroad, 185, 209

Unexplained phenomena, 64–79

Van Bruggen, Coosje, 147

Wagner, Reverend Albert, 137–139, **137**

Wagner, Hans "Honus," 70, **70**

Walker Funeral Home, 210–211, **210**

Washington, George, 117

Water tower, pumpkin, 162, **162**

Weaver Cave, 16

Well-Dressed Man ghost, 220

West State Street Cemetery, 237, **237**

Wilber, Nicholas and Harriet Kellogg, 14

Wilson, Jeffrey, 78

Wilson, Nathaniel, 252–253

Wilson Hall ghost, 216

Windsor Madonna, 156, **156**

Wise, Phoebe, ghost of, 195

Witches
    graves, 244, **244**
    Witches Tower (Patterson Tower), 22–24, **22, 23, 24**
    woods, 227

Wolfe Cemetery, 244

Wood County Historical Museum, 103

Woodland Cemetery, 234, **234, 235**

Woods, haunted, 224, 227

Wright, Orville and Wilbur, grave of, **235**

Wright-Patterson Air Force Base, 72–73, **72–73**, 74

Zoratti, Silvio, garden of, **128**, 129–130, **130**

Weird Ohio

By
James A. Willis, Andrew Henderson, and Loren Coleman

Executive Editors
Mark Sceurman and Mark Moran

Contributing authors: Debra Jane Seltzer, Larry Harris, and Ryan Doan

ACKNOWLEDGMENTS

JAMES A. WILLIS
would like to thank the following people:

Mark and Mark at *Weird N.J.*, for giving me the opportunity of a lifetime; Troy Taylor, my "invisible friend"; Stephanie, without whose help and unending support none of this would have been possible; Susan and Sara, for showing me that from ghosts can come wonderful friendships; Rick, for carrying me out of the Gates of Hell; all of the members of the Ghosts of Ohio organization, especially Adele, Darrin, Janine, Sherry, Jeff, Eric, Julie, and Lisa; everyone who has ever opened up their home or business to the Ghosts of Ohio; my father, Arthur Willis, for giving me the gift of storytelling; Patsy, Donna, and Cathy, for helping me survive a really weird family; Britches, Strats, and Khashoggi, for teaching me the meaning of unconditional love; my best friend, Geoff, who has been telling me for thirty years that I'd write a book one day; and finally, thank you to everyone out there who believed in me, no matter how weird things got.

DEDICATION

This book is dedicated to the memory of Rosalie B. Willis, who waited
as long as she could for her son to finally write a book.

Publisher:	Barbara J. Morgan
Assoc. Managing Editor:	Emily Seese
Editor:	Marjorie Palmer
Production:	Della R. Mancuso
	Mancuso Associates, Inc.
	North Salem, N.Y.

ANDREW HENDERSON
would like to thank:

Mary Henderson, Mandi Barker, Chris Mershon,
Brooke Mershon, Ryan O'Neill, Melanie Denyer,
Heidi Hughes, Kate Sette, Michael Sette,
Corinne Labita, David Caperton, Greg Beswick,
Vicky Lapka, Greg Gossett, Eric Rose,
Josh Penning, Kristin Weider, Jenn Hague,
Kristin Wyse, Jenny Burdge, Meghan Trivette,
Tara Simpson, Sarah Ammerman,
Leo Kendzierski, Julie Weese, Jeremy Garrett,
Jeff Ruetsche, and Erik Rothlisberger.

DEDICATION
Dedicated to my father, Larry Henderson.

LOREN COLEMAN

would like to express much appreciation for the Ohio
research assistance I received from all the eyewitnesses
I interviewed in Ohio from the 1960s to the present and
thank them for the deep insights they have given me
into this very weird state.

PICTURE CREDITS

All photos by the authors or public domain except as listed below:

SHOW US YOUR WEIRD!

Do you know of a weird site found somewhere in the United States, or can you tell us about a strange experience you've had? If so, we'd like to hear about it! We believe that every town has at least one great tale to tell, and we're listening. It could be a cursed road, haunted abandoned site, odd local character, or bizarre historic event. In most cases these tales are told only in the towns in which they originated. But why keep them to yourself when you could share them with all of America? So come on and fill us in on all the weirdness that's lurking in your backyard!

You can e-mail us at: Editor@WeirdUS.com,
or write to us at:
Weird U.S., P.O. Box 1346, Bloomfield, NJ 07003.

www.weirdus.com